Spiritually Desperat

BY

Dr. Rachelle Y. Benson

ISBN-13: 978-1482728644

TAYLOR MADE PUBLISHER
951-500-7636

Table of Content

Dedication...3

Acknowledgments..4

Introduction..5

Chapter 1: Desperate For Balance...6

    God's Master Plan..6

    God's Order Of Prioritization...7

    Areas Of A Woman's Ministry: Proverbs 31 Woman...7

    Desperate Enough To Seek Good Counsel...9

    Desperate Housewife Survey..11

Chapter 2: The Ministry Of Your Family..12

    What Does The Bible Say About Family?..44

    Characteristics Of A Godly Home...45

    Spiritual House Cleaning...47

    Hezekiah's Cleaning Service..49

    Compulsive Hoarding...53

Chapter 3: The Ministry Of Living Single...57

    Dealing With The Challenge Of Life As A Single Parent..57

    Balancing Tips For Single Mom..58

Chapter 4: The Ministry Of Your Marriage..60

    Difference Between Men And Women...60

    Characteristics Of A Godly Marriage...62

    Your Husband..65

    The Power Of A Mood Setter...69

    How To Love Your Wife..70

Chapter 5: The Ministry Of Your Children...75

    What About My House?...76

    Spending Time With Your Children..77

    Parenting Skills..79

    Stressful Families Cause Child Health Issues..81

    Communicating With Your Children..83

Chapter 6: Your Ministry Within Your Church..**102**

Church Over-programming...102

Chapter 7: The Ministry Of Your Job..**105**

Balancing Your Workload On Your Job..105

Working With Difficult People..107

Daily Devotion 110

Chapter 8: The Ministry Of YOU!..**111**

Taking Care Of You: Christian Codependence 112

Dealing With Anxiety...113

Dealing With Depression..115

Dealing With Past Trauma: Inner Healing...117

Dealing With Grief 127

Crisis Management..132

Forgiveness: No More Grudges...135

Seven Keys To Forgiveness 136

Resentment: An Unhealthy Way To Live..138

Spiritual Warfare: How To Forgive Others.......................................144

Benefits Of A Healthy Diet..146

Eating Disorders: Stress...147

Self-Esteem Issues...157

Christ Esteem...163

The Power Of Staying Positive..166

Chapter 9: Time Management..**169**

Managing Goals..169

Managing Your Home..171

Organize Your Life And De-clutter...174

Managing Procrastination..178

Conclusion:..**182**

Bibliography:..**184**

Dedication

I would like to dedicate this book to my Mother, Delores M. Hall, who was able to find balance in her life by ministering to the saints of God, her natural children, her husband, and to herself. My mother has taught me the true meaning of a virtuous woman. Her grace and meekness inspires me daily.

Acknowledgements

To God be the Glory! I would like to acknowledge the individuals in my life who have supported and encouraged me to follow my dreams. To my wonderful husband, Pastor William A. Benson Ph.D., who is truly the love of my life. I thank God that I am married to my best friend and life partner. To my dedicated and loving mother and father, Bishop Joseph R. Hall, Ph.D., and Pastor Delores M. Hall. To my identical twin sister, Rachel L. Harris, for whom I enjoy sharing my life with. Thank you for being my sunshine in the mist of every storm. To my Beautiful daughters, Shavonne and Grace, and my son Willie; through you my legacy will never be forgotten.

To all my spiritual sons and daughters at Total Deliverance Worship Center in Southern California. My spiritual children have inspired me and challenged me to be the spiritual mother that God is calling for in these last and evil days. I love you with all my heart!

My deepest gratitude to all my friends who have stood by me throughout my life. I will forever appreciate your encouraging support.

I would like to acknowledge the institute that launched this educational project; the California University of Theology. To the Chancellor, Bishop Robert T. Douglas Sr. Ph.D., and my Dean, Dr. Paulette Douglas, I say thank you and appreciate all your time and effort in inspiring your students to strive for excellence.

Introduction

As women of God we often struggle to find a balance between home, our business profession, and our spiritual commitment to the church. In our quest to find balance we become "Spiritually Desperate Housewives"; needing to make critical decisions in our life to accomplish harmony and peace of mind. Without the pursuance of balance many children are neglected, marriages torn apart, church families left broken, and souls left yearning. Desperate women must take desperate measures in prioritizing their individual life and coping with challenges strategically. If we choose not to pursue balance within our hectic schedules, it can produce a negative effect in many areas of our life. This book will take you on a journey to explore different areas of your life ministry and ultimately assist you with understanding that life is your ministry, and finding balance will be your mission.

Jeremiah 29:11 "For I know the thoughts that I think toward you, saith the LORD, thoughts of peace, and not of evil, to give you an expected end."

God's plan in your life is for you to have peace and spiritual fulfillment. After reading this book you will receive the tools necessary to deal with the stresses of life. This book will focus on prioritizing your day-to-day life, strategic planning, time management, family counseling, stress management, health and wellness. You will also take an in-depth look at what ministry really means in the different areas of your life; such as: your family, your marriage, your children, your work place, your church, and yourself. As you learn more about your role as a Proverbs 31, "virtuous woman" in Christ, you will be given examples of mighty women and men in the bible that knew how to lay their petition before the Lord.

Chapter #1

Desperate For Balance

Before we can begin this journey to find balance in our day-to-day life, we must first take a closer look at what balance means to a woman of God. Life is a balancing act, we are consistently arranging, adjusting, and prioritizing the different areas of our life to achieve symmetry. Symmetry affords us to become well proportioned as a whole. Although many may claim to have acquired balance; most will never reach the full potential of a harmonious, peaceful life until they make Christ the center point of their world. Without Christ as the center of your life you will live in a sense of what the Bible calls "false balance". Proverbs 11:1 states:

"A false balance is abomination to the Lord: but a just weight is his delight."
(King James Bible - Proverbs 11:1)

If you fake balance God is not pleased because other parts of your life will be neglected and not prioritized. If you are spending all your time at church and never with your family, God is not pleased. If you are spending all your time with your children and never with your spouse, God is not pleased. If you spend all your time at work and never go to church, God is not pleased. Convincing yourself that you have everything in proportion might make you feel good, but you can't fool God. Proverbs 16:11 says:

"A just weight and balance are the Lord's: all the weights of the bag are his work. (King James Bible – Proverbs 16:11)

We must come to the understanding that God created all the weights that we are trying to balance within our life. God is the one who gave you your spouse, your children, your job, your church family, your body, and he is expecting to get the glory in all of these areas. Christ must be the center point of all these weights, just like the center of a balance bar; everything around it is being weighed and continuously adjusted, but the center is stable and unchanging.

God's master Plan

The Bible says in Proverbs 3:6

"In all thy ways acknowledge him, and she shall direct thy paths."
(King James Version bible—Proverbs 3:6)

There are two points I want you to grasp concerning this key scripture: the first point is that God requires that we put him as the key guidance of our life by acknowledging him in all our ways. The second point is that "paths" is plural. Here we must realize that God has many "paths" that we must walk in our life and he plans on guiding us through them all, but only if we acknowledge him. Each area of our life encompasses Ministry. If we neglect one area, our Ministry is neglected. So therefore we must strive for balance because our Ministry depends on it.

As women of God we are called to the Ministry in multiple areas of our life. These Ministries consist of: the Ministry of your family, the Ministry of your marriage, for some the Ministry of living single, the Ministry of your children, the Ministry within your church, and the Ministry of you.

God's Order Of Prioritization

A major part of developing balance in your life is to understand God's prioritization. The first thing we must realize is that God has an order of prioritization that he expects us to live by. If you mix this order up, you will create disorder. God's order requires that he is the head of every household. We can never put ourselves above God. Unfortunately many Christians often become confused and disoriented when distinguishing these areas. God's order: first God, then the family, the church, and everything else. Without the proper prioritization many families face dilemmas that introduce chaos and confusion in their life. We all know that God is not the author of confusion, but of peace. (King James Bible – I Corinthians 14:33)

Areas Of A Woman's Ministry: Proverbs 31 Woman

We want to encourage women to serve God in every aspect of their lives.

1. **Faith** - A Virtuous Woman serves God with all of her heart, mind, and soul. She seeks His will for her life and follows His ways. (King James Bible -Proverbs 31: 26, Proverbs 31: 29 – 31, Matthew 22: 37, John 14: 15, Psalm 119: 15)

2. **Marriage** – A Virtuous Woman respects her husband. She does him good all the days of her life. She is trustworthy and a helpmeet. (King James Bible -Proverbs 31: 11- 12, Proverbs 31: 23, Proverbs 31: 28, 1 Peter 3, Ephesians 5, Genesis 2: 18)

3. **Mothering** - A Virtuous Woman teaches her children the ways of her Father in heaven. She nurtures her children with the love of Christ, disciplines them with care and wisdom, and trains them in the way they should go. (King James Bible - Proverbs 31: 28, Proverbs 31: 26, Proverbs 22: 6, Deuteronomy 6, Luke 18: 16)

4. **Health** – A Virtuous Woman cares for her body. She prepares healthy food for her family. (King James Bible - Proverbs 31: 14 – 15, Proverbs 31: 17, 1 Corinthians 6: 19, Genesis 1: 29, Daniel 1, Leviticus 11)

5. **Service** - A Virtuous Woman serves her husband, her family, her friends, and her neighbors with a gentle and loving spirit. She is charitable. (King James Bible - Proverbs 31: 12, Proverbs 31: 15, Proverbs 31: 20, 1 Corinthians 13: 13)

6. **Finances** - A Virtuous Woman acknowledges her husband in her finances and spends money wisely. She is careful to purchase quality items which her family needs. (King James Bible - Proverbs 31: 14, Proverbs 31: 16, Proverbs 31: 18, 1 Timothy 6: 10, Ephesians 5: 23, Deuteronomy 14: 22, Numbers 18: 26)

7. **Industry** – A Virtuous Woman works willingly with her hands. She sings praises to God and does not grumble while completing her tasks. (King James Bible - Proverbs 31: 13, Proverbs 31: 16, Proverbs 31: 24, Proverbs 31: 31, Philippians 2: 14)

8. **Homemaking** – A Virtuous Woman cares about her home. She creates an inviting atmosphere of warmth and love for her family and guests. She uses hospitality to minister to those around her. (King James Bible - Proverbs 31: 15, Proverbs 31: 20 – 22, Proverbs 31: 27, Titus 2: 5, 1 Peter 4: 9, Hebrews 13: 2)

9. **Time** - A Virtuous Woman uses her time wisely. She works diligently to complete her daily tasks. She does not spend time dwelling on those things that do not please the Lord. (King James Bible - Proverbs 31: 13, Proverbs 31: 19, Proverbs 31: 27, Ecclesiastes 3, Proverbs 16: 9, Philippians 4:8)

10. **Beauty** – A Virtuous Woman is a woman of worth and beauty. She has the inner beauty that only comes from Christ. She uses her creativity and sense of style to create beauty in her life and the lives of her loved ones. (King James Bible - Proverbs 31: 10, Proverbs 31: 21 – 22, Proverbs 31: 24 -25, Isaiah 61: 10, 1 Timothy 2: 9, 1 Peter 3: 1 – 6). (King James Bible)

Desperate Enough To Seek Good Counsel

How desperate are you to find balance in the areas of your life? Are you desperate enough to begin to cry out to God and allow him to lead you to wise counsel? Who you receive counsel from can either be a blessing or cause things to get worst.

Psalm 1:1 "Blessed is the man that walketh not in the counsel of the ungodly, nor standeth in the way of sinners, nor sitteth in the seat of the scornful." (King James Bible – Psalm 1:1).

Wise counsel has the ability to sustain you and keep you from going down the wrong paths. Wise counsel should be supported by biblical soundness.

These guidelines can help you make wise decisions in choosing a biblical counselor. A counselor should be someone who:

- Loves people, perseveres through tough times, and is confident that Jesus is able.

- Believes that God's Word is true and is designed to provide sufficient counsel for all of life's issues. (King James Bible - 2 Pet. 1:2-4; Heb. 4:12; 2 Tim. 3:16-17)

- Gives clear evidence of a vital personal relationship with Jesus Christ.

- Is your pastor (or trusted Christian friend) willing to provide wise, biblical, loving, and faithful counsel?

Steps you should take:

1. **Pray**. Ask God for wisdom as you seek a Christian counselor. God promises to give you wisdom if you ask for it in faith (King James Bible - James 1:5-8). As you step out in faith, he will direct your steps to the right counselor. (King James Bible - Proverbs 16:3 and Philippians 4:6-9.)

2. **Seek counsel from your church**. There is wisdom in a multitude of counselors (King James Bible - Prov. 11:14; 15:22; and 24:6). If you belong to a church, seek counsel from your pastor (King James Bible - Heb. 13:17) and other church leaders, as well as wise, trustworthy Christian friends. Will they help you? Can they recommend someone who can? If you do not belong to a church, seek the counsel of godly, Bible-believing Christians. They may be able to recommend godly pastors who can help shepherd you.

3. **Seek outside counsel, if necessary**. In some cases, wise, biblical counsel might not be found in the leadership of a church. Or you may not belong to a church, so you may need to find biblical counsel outside the church context.

Questions to Ask:

The questions below will help you get a clearer picture of what a counselor believes and how he or she conducts the counseling sessions. If possible, ask the prospective counselor these questions on the phone before any appointment. Otherwise, discuss them during your first meeting. Write down the counselor's answers and explain that you would like to consider them before continuing with counseling. Then talk to your pastor, elder, or wise Christian friend about the counselor's answers in light of God's Word.

Ask your prospective counselor:

1. How would you describe your approach to counseling? How do you understand people's problems? How do you help them grow and change through counseling? Please describe the process.

2. What books or other resources do you recommend on a regular basis? What books have most influenced your approach to counseling?

3. Are you a Christian? How does your faith affect your view and practice of counseling?

4. Do you bring Christian truth into your counseling practice? How? What role does Scripture play?

5. Do you pray with those you counsel?

6. Do you attend church? If so, where? How long have you been a member?

7. What is your educational and professional background? What role does it play?

8. Are you married? Do you have children? Have you ever been divorced? How does your marriage and family situation affect how you counsel people?

Counseling is an interactive process. It is established and maintained on the basis of trust. Open and honest dialogue between a counselor and a counselee is the most important component of building trust. If you cannot establish this foundation early on, so that you are confident that the counselor will be wise, biblical, loving, and faithful in your interaction, you may need to look elsewhere. If you find a wise counselor who uses God's Word to help you grow in your Christian walk, your marriage and your family, Scripture says you will be blessed!

Desperate Housewife Survey

God desires us to find balance in our life, yet he expects us not to neglect any of the areas of our Ministry. When a woman cannot find balance she becomes desperate and desperate women must take desperate measures in proclaiming peace in her life.

I have conducted a survey of 300 women who all attend church and have children. Here are the results:

- 92% of these women said that they felt overwhelmed with life's demands and often neglected certain areas of their life.

- 98% said they could use more strategies in assisting them with understanding and mainly finding balance in their life.

- When asked what their Ministries were, 85% of these women said that their Ministries lied within the church walls. Only 15% felt their Ministry lied outside the church walls.

- 75% of these women said that if asked, their husbands would say that they were neglected by their wife because of all the duties and responsibilities they inquire.

- 45% of these women were raised in church. Out of these women raised in church, 80% felt that their parents neglected them for the sake of the Ministry.

It becomes more obvious to me that if women do not take the time to find balance, and understand all the areas of their Ministry, it will play a vital role in the life of their entire family. As I said from the beginning, without the pursuance of balance, many children are neglected, marriages torn apart, church families left broken, and souls left yearning.

Chapter #2:

The Ministry Of Your Family

Proverbs 31:10 ask us "Who can find a virtuous woman? The term "virtuous" is from a noun meaning strength, efficiency, ability. Here it refers to strength of character, that is, moral strength and firmness.

The "Proverbs 31 Woman" shines as a bright beacon in this wonderful Old Testament book of precepts and warnings. Today as we see women of all ages following dubious role models, we are refreshed to find a timeless example of virtue, responsibility and good sense. Here, in this lovely picture of womanhood, is a woman who embodies the qualities which every believing woman should strive for in her personal life and appearance, in her family life, and in her daily duties.

The woman described in Proverbs 31 is so exemplary and so virtuous, and so diligent to perform all her duties that women today, who have a heart to please God, may find it difficult or even discouraging to try to follow her example. They might think, "How could I ever measure up to such a godly woman?

Let not your heart be troubled. In 1 Peter 2:21 believers are told to follow Christ's example and follow His steps, and yet who could ever measure up to the quality of life and virtue displayed by the sinless Jesus Christ? We all fall far short. We have not attained to His level of perfection, and yet we "follow after" and "press toward the mark" (King James Bible - Phil. 3:12-14). God has given us a pattern, a mark to shoot for, and though we may come short, yet God's standard is before our eyes. Though we may fall short, we never want to lower God's standard. We must always strive towards godly perfection.

There are other stellar examples of godly persons in the Scriptures, whose lives often put us to shame; yet it is our joyful privilege to imitate them and follow their example. Think of men such as Joseph and Daniel and Paul (as a converted man). Most Bible characters had their flaws, and certainly these men did as well, and yet nothing negative is said about these three in the Bible. They are wonderful role models for believers. In and of ourselves we will surely fail in our quest for godly living. We will come to the end of ourselves and recognize our own bankruptcy. With Paul we will cry out,

"I know that in me (that is, in my flesh) dwelleth no good thing; for to will is present with me; but how to perform that which is good I find not" (King James Bible—Rom. 7:18).

God, by His grace and by the power of His Spirit can enable us to live lives that are pleasing to the One who died and rose again for us. May we reckon ourselves to be dead indeed unto sin (King James Bible -Rom. 6:11) that the life our Lord might be manifested in and through us (KJ Bible - 2 Cor. 4:10-11). We cannot, but God can! The God who indwells us can enable us. When we do fail to measure up to the kind of person God wants us to be, we can still rejoice that we have an Advocate with the Father (a Helper in court!), Christ Jesus the Righteous One (KJ Bible - 1 John 2:1-2). He pleads on our behalf; His work on Calvary's cross has already satisfied all of God's just demands. We can confess our sins and enjoy God's wonderful forgiveness and fellowship (KJ Bible - 1 John 1:9). Let's take a closer look at this Proverbs 31 woman.

Proverbs 31:10-31

The last part of Proverbs 31, beginning with verse 10, consists of 22 verses. Each verse begins with a different letter of the Hebrew alphabet (in proper order). The same alphabetical pattern is found in some of the Psalms and may have been used as an aid in memorizing Scripture. The most well-known alphabetical Psalm is Psalm 119 where there are 22 alphabetical sections of eight verses each. In the Hebrew text of Proverbs 31, each verse is also clearly divided into two parts (for example, in verse 10, Part 1: Who can find a virtuous woman? Part 2: For her price is far above rubies). This same two-part format is found in all of these verses. The only exception might be verse 15 which seems to be divided into three parts.

In Exodus 18:21 we find the expression used of men. Moses was to find "able men" (lit.-- "men of strength") such as fear God, men of truth, hating covetousness. In light of this verse we can say that a virtuous man is one who fears God, loves truth and hates sin. Moses was to look for and find such men, and the implication is that such men were not easy to find. The expression is also used in 1 Kings 1:42 ("valiant man" or "man of strength") and 1 Kings 1:52 ("worthy man" or "man of strength"). In this latter passage (v. 52) we learn that the opposite of a virtuous man is a man in whom wickedness is found. Thus a virtuous man is a man of great moral strength, in whom wickedness is not found. He is a godly, God-fearing man. So also, the virtuous woman is a God-fearing woman--compare Proverbs 31:10 with 31:30.

The Old Testament uses this expression of a virtuous woman in two other places. In Ruth 3:11 it is used of Ruth. Everyone in the city knew that she was a virtuous woman! When a woman has strength of character (fears God, loves truth, hates sin), then others will take note and recognize this. It will be very obvious because it is so unusual. People are usually so morally weak and so anemic in character, that when a man or woman of strength shows up it is quite evident to all. The other place the term is used is in Proverbs 12:4 where we learn that a virtuous woman (lit--a woman of strength) does not make her husband ashamed.

For her price is far above rubies.

She is far more valuable and worth far more than rubies. The Hebrew term for "rubies" may not refer to rubies, but may refer to pink pearls or red coral. A pink pearl which was found in a mollusk in the Red Sea was considered of great value to the ancients. It is difficult to know exactly which stone or pearl this Hebrew word referred to, but its usage in the Old Testament tells us two things for sure: 1) It was very valuable (see Proverbs 20:15 and Job 28:18); 2) It was reddish in color (Lamentations 4:7--"ruddy").

Who can find a virtuous woman (a woman of strength)? She is like a rare gem. Precious stones are precious and costly because they are so rare. If you could go out along the roadside and collect hundreds of rubies anytime you wanted to, then they would not be worth much. It is the rare, hard to find gems that are worth so much. Also, for some reason God made most common stones unattractive; yet He made most rare stones very beautiful and brilliant and lustrous. The virtuous woman is a beautiful woman, not necessarily outwardly, but certainly inwardly (see Prov. 31:30). She is not only a rare gem but a beautiful gem.

A godly woman is rare and very hard to find. The same thing could be said about the godly man. Number one on the endangered species list is the Homo sapiens pious*: "Help, LORD; for the godly man ceaseth; for the faithful fail from among the children of men" (King James Bible - Psalm 12:1). There are hardly any such creatures around, and the few that do exist will eventually die out! May God in His infinite grace and mercy be pleased to raise up godly men and women in these difficult and trying days. Note: Pious is the Latin word for "godly."

If a young man is looking for a godly woman, how can he find her? First he should trust God to find her for him. Second, he must realize that a virtuous woman is not going to want just any man. She is going to want to find a virtuous man (a man of strength, a man valiant for the truth, a godly servant of Christ). So if you want to have any chance of finding such a gem, you must be a gem yourself. Exercise yourself unto godliness. In other words, don't desire a good woman unless you are willing to be a good man. Learn the fear of the Lord. Dare to be different. Dare to go against the flow of the world, and to be transformed by the renewing of your mind (King James Bible - Rom. 12:2). Be the kind of a man that would attract the interest of the godly woman! So in this opening verse we have learned that the godly woman is very hard to find. She is more valuable than a rare gem. She has an inner beauty, a strength of character and a moral firmness that is lacking in the vast majority of women, even believing women.

"The heart of her husband doth safely trust in her." (King James Bible — Proverbs 31:11)

Sadly, this cannot be said of most husbands today. They cannot trust their wives (and often their wives cannot trust them). Being able to fully trust your marriage partner is one of the fundamental foundations of a strong God-honoring marriage. Martin Luther said of his wife,

"The greatest gift of God is a pious amiable spouse, who fears God,
loves his house, and with whom one can live in perfect confidence"
Quote taken from Charles Bridges.

The term "husband" is the common word for husband in the Old Testament. It also means "lord" or "owner." (It is also the word that is used of the false god "Baal.") There are two reasons why the heart of the husband can trust his virtuous wife. The first reason is found in the second part of verse 11 ("so that he shall have no need of spoil") and the second reason is found in verse 12 ("she shall do him good and not evil"). See the discussion that follows.

So that he shall have no need of spoil

"No need" is the very same expression found in Psalm 23:1, "I shall not want." It means to be in need, to be lacking. Both here and in Psalm 23:1 it is used with the negative: to not be in need; to not be lacking. If the LORD is my Shepherd, then I shall not be in need because He will supply all my need. If I have a godly wife, I shall not be in need of spoil.

The word "spoil" means "plunder, booty, spoil." It is often used of booty obtained following a battle as the victorious soldiers would take anything valuable from their defeated foes and thus would gain riches from battle. Here in Proverbs 31:11 the word carries the secondary meaning of "gain." It is certainly not suggesting that if his wife were not virtuous that he would need to go to battle, slay the enemy and take of their spoil! "He shall have no need of gain" because his wife is a tremendous benefit to the family, even financially. She is not a financial liability (as the verses following will amply illustrate). She manages the home so well and she is so industrious and productive that her efforts result in great gain and even profit.

Sadly today some wives are so slothful and careless that they cause the family to suffer great financial loss. They go on shopping sprees or incur immense credit card debt or waste countless hours each week engaged in unproductive activities (television, etc.). How can her husband safely trust in her? After she has finished destroying the family budget, he has great need of gain considering all that she has lost! Of course, the problem of wasteful spending and unproductive activities is not limited to women only. Men are at fault as well.

Proverbs 31:12 - She will do him good, and not evil

Her husband can safely trust in her because he does not need to worry about her being a financial liability (v. 11) and because he knows that she will do him only good, and not evil.

"Whoso findeth a wife findeth a good thing, and obtaineth favor from the LORD" (KJ - Prov. 18:22).

Of course, the man must find the right kind of wife. Job's wife was a curse who only added to his trials (KJ - Job 2:9-10). Some men find "a crown to their head" while others find "rottenness to their bones" (KJ - Prov. 12:4). One of the reasons Proverbs 31:10-31 was written, no doubt, was to help guide men in finding the right kind of wife. Some see Proverbs 31:10-31 as a continuation of what King Lemuel's mother taught him (King James Bible - Proverbs 31:1-9), concluding with this description of an ideal wife for her royal son.] The key to finding the right woman, is to look to the Lord in prayer and steadfast trust, so that God Himself might be the One who finds her. God knows who my life partner should be.

The verb "will do" is of interest. It is not the common Hebrew verb for "do." It means to deal out, to deal fully, to deal bountifully. At times it even approaches the meaning of "to reward, to pay back." Let's illustrate how it is used. In 1 Samuel 24:17 David had just spared Saul's life even though he easily could have killed his persecutor. Saul's response: "Thou art more righteous than I; for thou hast rewarded me good, whereas I have rewarded thee evil." Saul deserved evil but David dealt with him in a good way. Saul dished out evil to David but David dished out good to Saul who actually deserved evil. In Genesis 50:15,17 the term is used of Joseph's guilty brothers who remembered what they had done to Joseph:

"Joseph...will certainly requite us all the evil which we did unto him....So shall ye say unto Joseph, Forgive, I pray thee now, the trespass of thy brethren, and their sin; for they did unto thee evil." They dealt out and dished out evil to Joseph but he did not pay them back in the same way. Joseph saw God's good and sovereign hand in it all (King James - Gen. 50:20).

This verb is also used of the LORD who deals bountifully with his servants. See Psalm 13:6; 116:7; 119:17; 142:7.

The virtuous woman deals out to her husband that which is good. She dishes out to him and serves him that which is good and not evil. She wants only God's highest and best for him. Her life and her deeds are a constant benefit and blessing to her husband.

All the days of her life

In doing good to her husband she is consistent. She doesn't serve him that which is good one day and that which is evil the next day. Her husband can count on her to do him good and to be a blessing to him. He can count on her to do this today, five days from now, one year from now, ten years from now, and all the days of her life. She is not up and down, hot and cold. Her godliness is marked with consistency.

Proverbs 31:13 - She seeketh wool and flax

Wool, of course, is the wavy or curly undercoat of a sheep which can be woven into a warm garment or fabric. Even today we wear wool sweaters or mittens to protect us from the cold. Flax was a fibrous plant used in spinning. The fibers can be drawn out and twisted into yarn or threat for the manufacture of linen. The most famous flax was grown under ideal conditions in Egypt. There was no better linen than the "fine linen of Egypt." This is one reason why the seventh plague was so terrible. This judgment involved hail stones mixed with fire. The hail stones "smote every herb of the field" (King James - Exodus 9:25), totally destroying, among other things, the flax crop. From flax can be made a variety of materials including coarse canvas, rugged sails for ships and even thin, delicate scarves.

The godly woman "seeks" wool and flax, these two basic materials to use in making clothes and garments. The term "seek" could mean that she "selects" (NIV Bible) the best quality of wool and flax or it could mean that she "seeks with care" or "cares for" the wool and flax. The word has this latter meaning in Deuteronomy 11:12,"A land which the LORD thy God careth for (seeks!)." She carefully collects and gathers and cares for the wool and flax that she will use in making clothes for her household and perhaps for others as well.

And worketh willingly with her hands

The word "willingly" is from the word meaning "delight, pleasure." She takes great delight in her work. Rather than being a laborious and boring chore, it is pleasant and enjoyable. Toil need not be tedious. It can be a tremendous source of pleasure and satisfaction.

In our modern, computerized, electronic, entertainment-saturated society we have lost the art of working with our hands. Most women don't delight in making clothes with their hands. Instead they delight in shopping for clothes at the mall and thus adversely affecting the family budget. Instead of learning from their mothers how to sew, knit, crochet, mend and mend, many children are too busy watching television or playing computer games. Unfortunately most mothers do not even know how to do these things and could not teach their children even if they wanted to. I used to watch my mother spend countless hours knitting and crocheting and sewing, but these things are becoming a lost art.

Mothers and wives who are not seamstresses may be able to exchange skills they do have for the skills of those who sew. There are times when it may be more economical, in both time and money, to wisely shop for bargains than to purchase patterns, material, zippers, etc. The wise woman uses her time and individual resources in the best way she can. The godly woman takes great pleasure in working with her hands and providing clothing for her family.

Proverbs 31:14 - She is like the merchants' ships; She bringeth her food from afar.

In verse 13 she is seeking to provide clothing for her family and in verse 14 she is seeking to provide food for her family. The Bible teaches us that with food and raiment we can be content (King James Bible 1 Tim. 6:8) and the virtuous women plays a key role, as God's instrument, in providing both.

Notice the simile. The virtuous woman is compared to the merchants' ships. Merchants are traders who buy or sell commodities for profit, and merchants' ships are filled with items from far countries. So the godly woman brings in food from afar (from distant places). The word "food" is the common Hebrew word for "bread" but it is also used of food in general.

Does this mean that she travels to far off countries to procure international delicacies for her family? Very unlikely. It probably means that she brought in foods from distant lands by trading for them. She took some of the wondrous garments or clothes that she made with her hands (v.13) and was able to bring them to some merchant men and trade them for food items which had come from afar, even from distant lands.

Today the wife usually says to her husband, "Dear, I need some money because I'm going to town to do our weekly grocery shopping." The virtuous woman said, "Dear, I'm going to town but I don't need any money because I'm taking some of the fine linen which I have made and will trade it in for some items of food which you will really enjoy." How can he complain about that?

It also seems that she recognized that it would be good for her family to give them great variety in their diet, including international dishes, and not to constantly give them the same foods all the time. Variety is the spice of life.

Proverbs 31:15 - She riseth also while it is yet night

She is up before the sun, showing that idleness and laziness have no place with her (compare verse 27). The sluggard (KJ - Prov. 6:6-11) should not only go to the ant, but should also go to the virtuous woman to learn a lesson on diligence. There are great benefits to rising up early. It is a quiet time free from the noise and distractions of the day. It is an ideal time to spend with the Lord in quiet meditation and prayer, starting the day with Him.

We also see this principle in the manna which God provided for the children of Israel in the wilderness. Manna had to be gathered anew every morning (King James - Exodus 16:14-22), just as fresh food for our souls is needed each day.

We have the example of our blessed Lord:
"And in the morning, rising up a great while before day, he went out, and departed into a solitary place, and there prayed (KJ - Mark 1:35).
The Psalmist was in the habit of morning prayer: "In the morning shall my prayer come before thee" (King James Bible - Psalm 88:13).

Rising up early also allows us to get a good start on the day. If a person sleeps in late, by the time he really gets going it may seem that half the day is gone and he time to accomplished very little. Sprinters know that the most important part of the race is how they start the race (how they get off the starting blocks). The key is beginning well. May God help us to start our days well, beginning the day with God and getting a good early start on the tasks and duties that demand our attention and diligence. Needless to say, a mother may have to sleep in after being up during the night with a sick child. the virtuous woman is diligent, yet flexible and realistic.

She giveth meat (food) to her household, and a portion to her maidens.

One of the reasons she rises up so early is to provide food for her household. When the father and children get up they are greeted with a hearty, home-cooked breakfast! Nutritionists consider breakfast the most important meal of the day, nourishing the body that has not had any food for many hours (the "breaking of the fast," that is, "breakfast") and providing energy for the toil of the day. The virtuous woman makes sure that her family gets off to a good nutritional start. This term "food" (translated by some as "game") is also used in Psalm 111:5 of God's gracious provision of food for those who fear Him.

Young women today, in many cases, hardly know how to prepare meals. Many families eat out frequently or order food that can be brought into the home. How many families take time to sit down at a meal together around the table? Often families don't eat together, don't pray together, don't read together, and as a result don't stay together.

Her maidens are her female servants. This virtuous woman was blessed with a large household that included female maids or servants. She did not live in poverty. We are reminded that under the Old Testament economy, the Israelites who honored and feared the Lord were promised not only spiritual blessings but also material blessings, and certainly the woman described in Proverbs 31 had both.

One might think that this virtuous woman could command her female servants and tell them to rise up early and prepare the breakfast meal and have it ready for her entire family. But we are told that she gives a portion of food to her maidens. Not only does this speak of her kindness to those working under her, but it also indicates that she demanded of others only what she herself was willing to do. Workers and servants will greatly respect a superior who is willing to "get his hands dirty" and do some of the very tasks which he might require of them. The term "portion" is used in that wonderful passage found in Job 23:12.

"Neither have I gone back from the commandment of His lips; I have
esteemed the words of His mouth more than my portion of food"
(King James – Job 23:12).

Proverbs 31:16 - She considereth a field, and buyeth it.

The word "considereth" is from a verb which often is used to describe the wicked who devise evil or are actively plotting evil. Here are some examples:

"The wicked plotteth against the just, and gnasheth upon him with
his teeth" (KJ – Psalm 37:12). "While they took counsel together
against me, they devised to take away my life" (KJ - Psalm 31:13).

"And now nothing will be restrained from them, which they have imagined to do" (KJ - Gen. 11:6).

In this last passage the people of Babel considered in their minds all kinds of evil, and their evil plots would have come to fruition had not God confused their tongues and scattered them.

In Psalm 17:3 this same verb is used of determining a course of action: "I am purposed that my mouth shall not transgress" (King James - Psalm 17:3). When wicked men devise evil they often will put a lot of thought and planning into it.

The godly woman considers a field (a plot of land in open country). She doesn't do this rashly or on a sudden impulse, but she has given very careful thought to the matter. She has a plan for her family and she carefully thinks about what she needs. She decides that a prosperous vineyard would be beneficial to all, and thus she decides upon a field that would be suitable.

"She buys it." Literally, she takes it. She acquires the field, probably by purchasing it. The fact that she buys a field indicates that the godly woman was involved in financial decisions relating to the family and involved in financial transactions. From what we know about this godly woman, she did not act independently of her husband. We know that the heart of her husband did safely trust in her (v. 11), which would not be the case if his wife were running around purchasing all kinds of things without his knowledge! The godly wife, under the headship of her husband, can play a significant role in managing family finances. Some wives are very good at keeping a checkbook and managing the family budget, and it would be to the advantage of the family for the husband to delegate this responsibility to her.

How many women buy all kinds of things on the spur of the moment without giving the matter careful thought and deliberation? As she races out to the shopping mall with her friends, can her husband safely trust in her? We also might ask, can the wife trust her husband when he goes shopping?

With the fruit of her hands she planteth a vineyard.

The purpose of the field was to provide a place for a vineyard so that the family and others could enjoy the fruit of the vine. The fruit of her hands signifies the result of her labor. To cultivate a field and to maintain a vineyard requires much labor. The vineyard was the fruit of her loving toil.

"Am I willing to work the field?" Many things that we purchase require a good bit of maintenance, and if we are unwilling to provide the labor that is needed for the maintenance, then the purchase is probably unwise. Think of people who rashly procure a pet, not considering all the time and effort that is required to properly take care of the animal. When the godly woman planned for the purchase of the field, she also calculated the amount of toil that would be needed to maintain the vineyard.

The "fruit of her hands" could also be understood in another way, as "the fruit of her earnings." That is, with the fruit of her hands (see verse 13) she was able to earn enough money to purchase and plant a vineyard. Perhaps she employed her servants (maidens, v. 15) to work the field or to help her work the field.

Proverbs 31:17 - She girdeth her loins with strength, and strengtheneth her arms.

Inner strength and a tenacious trust in God translates into outer strength and physical vitality and vigor. The "loins" are regarded as the seat of strength (see 1 Kings 12:10; Nahum 2:1). The term refers to the abdominal or hip region of the body (the mid-section), the region of strength and procreative power.

"To gird" means to encircle or bind with a flexible band or girdle (belt). In Bible times both men and women wore outer robes or tunics. If the tunic was ungirded it would interfere with a person's ability to walk freely. The Bible often makes symbolic use of the girdle. Jesus said, "Let your loins be girded about" (King James Bible - Luke 12:35). In other words, "Be as men who have a long race to run; gather up the folds of your flowing robes, and fasten them with your girdle; that nothing may keep you back or impede your steps." In Bible language, "to be girded" means "to be ready for action." "For thou hast girded me with strength unto the battle" (KJ - Psalm 18:39).

The virtuous woman has a reservoir of inner strength which is able to energize her and enable her to accomplish physical tasks which require a great amount of physical strength. She is not weakened by sloth or laziness but she is a wonderful example of diligence and industry. George Lawson describes her in this way:

As rust gathers on metals that are seldom used, so sluggishness of disposition contracts a rust on the powers of the body and mind; and idle persons by degrees realize those excuses for their conduct which were at first mere shams. The virtuous woman is of a very different temper. She declines not any part of her duty through aversion to toil; and by exerting her strength with a cheerful mind she improves it. Her labors give her health and vigor, and alacrity for new labors; so that she can with great ease and tranquility go through those duties which appear impossibilities to other women.

Proverbs 31:18 - She perceiveth that her merchandise is good.

The word "perceiveth" is the Hebrew word that means "taste." Literally, she tastes that her gain is good. The same word is found in Psalm 34:9, "O taste and see that the LORD is good: blessed is the man that trusteth in him." God's goodness must be tasted; it must be personally experienced. Only those who have truly trusted Him have tasted of His goodness and experienced God for themselves.

The word "merchandise" means profit, traffic, gain received from traffic or trade. The word is found twice in Proverbs 3:14, "Happy is the man that findeth wisdom, and the man that getteth understanding. For the merchandise of it is better than the merchandise of silver, and the gain thereof than fine gold" (verses 13-14). The godly woman purchased a field, planted a vineyard, and gave herself to this ambitious endeavor with great strength (verses 16-17). In verse 18 she is experiencing the rewards of her labor. She finds how profitable her industry is as she experiences the sale of its product. She sees that her trading is profitable. She is reaping what she sowed by her diligent industry, and she is finding it to be a good harvest. She is seeing the results of the labors of her hands. She learns that success results from her labors and she reaps the fruits of hard work.

Her merchandise is known to be good, and brings a ready market and a good price; and her knowledge of this is a sufficient reward of itself for her toils; for when the lazy are perpetually uneasy by their reflections on their own conduct, the consciousness of having done her duty, and the prospect of the advantages arising from it, are a constant source of satisfation and cheerfulness to the virtuous woman
(George Lawson, Commentary on Proverbs, p. 564).

Her candle (lamp) goeth not out by night.

Homes in Bible times were illuminated at night by olive oil lamps. The virtuous woman's lamp did not go out at night, that is, it was not quenched or extinguished (see 1 Sam. 3:3). What was she doing at night? Probably the activity mentioned in verse 19 (hand spinning). Here was a woman who worked day and night with amazing diligence and fortitude. We might say she "burned the midnight oil." If you were to pass by her house late at night you would see that her light would still be on. We wonder when this woman ever slept because in these verses she is working late at night and in verse 15 she rises while it is yet night. The fact that she rises indicates that she did get some sleep. We have the expression, "early to bed, early to rise," but she seems to have been in the habit of "late to bed, early to rise."

Some women are up late at night pursuing questionable activities (using inferior lamp light), but then they sleep through half the day (missing out on superior sunlight). But the godly woman is diligent both day and night, and is able to get the necessary sleep, without overindulging in sleep. The poverty mentioned in Proverbs 6:9-11 will not be her portion.

Believers need to evaluate their nighttime activities to make sure that they are pleasing to the Lord and profitable for eternity. During the day we normally have our duties and our schedule; things we need to do and places we need to be. Our time is usually well accounted for during the day. But after sunset is usually the part of the day when we have "free time," and it is important to recognize that this time belongs to the Lord. May we be about our Father's business! Then, when we finally lie down on our beds, our sleep will be sweet.

Proverbs 31:19 - She layeth her hands to the spindle, and her hands hold the distaff.

She knew how to use her hands with skill in providing clothing for her family and perhaps others. This verse describes a very ancient method of spinning used in the days before the spinning wheel even existed. The distaff was a staff used for holding the flax, tow or wool which would be spun into thread by means of the spindle. The spindle would turn and twist the fibers into threads.

The spindle was a round stick with tapered ends used to form and twist the yarn in hand spinning. The spindle and the distaff are the most ancient of all instruments used in the craft of spinning. About eight to ten inches long, spindles were used to guide the thread as it was fashioned into cloth. The weaver sometimes turned the spindle by rolling it across her thigh.

The wool or flax was wound on the distaff, which was stuck upright in the ground or held under the arm. The spindle, which had a circular rim to steady it when revolving, was attached to the thread being drawn out from the distaff. By rotating the spindle, the spinner twisted the thread. An example of hand spinning is found in the ancient book of Exodus: "And all the women that were wise hearted did spin with their hands, and brought that which they had spun, both of blue, and of purple, and of scarlet, and of fine linen. And all the women whose heart stirred them up in wisdom spun goats' hair" (King James Bible - Exodus 35:25-26).

If a woman's hands are idle and if she is not engaged in worthwhile, constructive pursuits, then watch out! "Idle hands are the devil's tools" and "If the devil can catch a man (or woman) idle, he'll set him (or her) to work."

Proverbs 31:20 - stretcheth out her hand to the poor; yea, she reacheth forth her hands to the needy.

Compare an earlier verse in the same Proverb: "Plead the cause of the poor and needy" (verse 9). Verse 20 is an example of parallelism that is found so often in Hebrew poetry. In these two phrases parallel ideas are set forth, with the second phrase saying basically the same thing as the first phrase, with only minor variations. Both phrases emphasize the fact that the virtuous woman has compassion toward the poor and needy and she shows her compassion with concrete deeds of mercy. She loves the poor, not in word or in tongue only, but also in deed and in truth (King James Bible - 1 John 3:16-18).

The word "poor" means "afflicted, humble." It is used of those who are physically and materially poor as in Proverbs 31:20, and it is also used of believers who recognize their spiritual poverty and bankruptcy ("I am poor and needy"--see Psalm 40:17; 70:5; 109:22; 34:6). No one can make progress in his spiritual life until he realizes how desperately needy he really is, and recognizes that only the Lord can supply that which is needed.

God's people are to have a heart of compassion for those who are physically and materially poor and needy. In the law, God told the Israelites that the gleanings from their vineyards and fields should be left for the poor of the land (King James Bible - Lev. 19:10; 23:22). The godly woman of Proverbs 31 faithfully obeyed the following command:

"For the poor shall never cease out of the land: therefore I command thee, saying, Thou shalt open thine hand wide unto thy brother, to thy poor, and to thy needy, in thy land." (King James Bible - Deut. 15:11).

Early in Proverbs 31, believers are encouraged to plead the cause of the poor (verse 9). In Proverbs 14:21 a benediction is pronounced upon those who show compassion to the poor and help them: "He that despiseth his neighbour sinneth: but he that hath mercy on the poor, happy is he."

In studying this Hebrew word which is translated "poor" in Proverbs 31:20, I was surprised to find it used of our blessed Lord Himself during the days of His humiliation:

"Rejoice greatly, O daughter of Zion; shout, O daughter of Jerusalem: behold, thy King cometh unto thee: he is just, and having salvation; lowly, and riding upon an ass, and upon a colt the foal of an ass" (King James Bible - Zechariah 9:9).

The word "lowly" is the same Hebrew word as "poor" in Proverbs 31:20. We are reminded of our Lord's amazing condescension.

"For ye know the grace of our Lord Jesus Christ, that, though he was rich, yet for your sakes he became poor, that ye through his poverty might be rich" (King James Bible - 2 Cor. 8:9).

The word "needy" at the end of verse 20 means "one who is in need, in want; one who is lacking." When a person lacks basic material necessities such as food and clothing, then he is considered poor, and hence the word is a synonym for poor.

The word "needy" is used to describe the spiritual condition of God's people. Every believer needs to recognize his spiritual bankruptcy: "I am poor and needy." See Psalm 40:17; 70:5; 86:1; 109:22. What we need, only God can supply. When He supplies that which we lack, then we are rich indeed.

There are people who routinely go around to churches looking for handouts and financial gifts. Supporting this kind of behavior will not really help the person to be responsible for the long term. After he profits from you he is off to the next church. We don't want to support irresponsibility.

In Bible times, the poor and blind and lame depended upon merciful almsgiving in order to survive. Things are somewhat different in our American society where (whether rightly or wrongly) there are all kinds of government programs to assist the poor and needy, and wise stewardship should take this into account. Our government is going to spend a great deal of money supporting the poor and needy (and we contribute to this through our taxes), but our government is not going to spend any money on God-honoring missionary efforts. Also we should always remember that meeting a person's physical and material needs does not solve his greatest problem. If we give a person food, clothing and good housing for his entire life, and then he dies and eventually goes to the lake of fire, what have we really done for this man? How much better to support Christ-centered mission agencies which have workers who are concerned about the material needs of the poor, but who are even more concerned about their spiritual and eternal needs.

Proverbs 31:21 She is not afraid of the snow for her houshold; For all her household are clothed with scarlet.

The virtuous woman, always concerned about the welfare of her family, is not afraid of the snow. Snow is here a symbol of the cold that accompanies it. She is not afraid of the cold because she has made preparations ahead of time to dress her family in warm clothing. "Household" may also include servants.

Her household was "clothed with scarlet." The scarlet color (compare Isaiah 1:18 and Joshua 2:18 where the same word is used), of itself, did nothing to warm them. "The scarlet clothing is of wool, which as such preserves warmth, and, as high-coloured, appears at the same time dignified (King James Bible - 2 Sam. 1:24)" (Keil & Delitzsch, see under Proverbs 31:21). Thus they were protected by the wool and the scarlet provided ornamentation. "Scarlet" is "obtained from the Tola, a cochineal-like insect, which, being crushed, produces a fine deep red, or rich crimson dye, much admired by the Orientals. It is the 'worm' of Psalm 22:6, to which our Lord likens Himself, He who was bruised and slain that all His redeemed might be clothed in splendor for eternity" (Ironside, Proverbs/Song of Solomon, pages 477-488).

One lesson here is that believers and the children of godly parents do not need to be dressed in dull clothing. Drabness and dullness of apparel do not add to one's spirituality. There seems to be an allowance for clothing that is colorful and attractive. At the same time dress should be modest and should not unnecessarily draw attention to self or to one's body.

Proverbs 31:22 - She maketh herself coverings of tapestry; her clothing is silk and purple.

"She makes coverings for herself" (NASB). Apparently these were coverings which she made for her bed (see ESV). The only other place in the Old Testament where this Hebrew word "coverings" is found is in Proverbs 7:16 where it is clearly referring to coverings for a bed: "I have decked my bed with coverings of tapestry." The virtuous woman took time to decorate and adorn her bedroom with beautiful bedspreads and coverings.

Her clothing is attractive and beautiful, of the finest material. "Silk" refers not to silk as we know it today, but to the "fine linen of Egypt" which has already been discussed (see under verse 13). The modern translations render it "fine linen."

"The purple was manufactured by the Phoenicians from a marine mollusk (shellfish). The shell was broken in order to give access to a small gland which was removed and crushed. The crushed gland gives a milky fluid that becomes red or purple on exposure to the air. Piles of these broken shells still remain on the coast at Sidon and Tyre" (The International Standard Bible Encyclopedia, Vol. IV, p. 2509). Purple was prized by the ancients and exported far and wide. "Great labor was required to extract the purple dye, and thus only royalty and the wealthy could afford the resulting richly colored garments" (Unger's Bible Dictionary, p. 904). A total of 250,000 mollusks was required to make one ounce of the dye, which helps us to understand how valuable this dye was (*Nelson's New Illustrated Bible Dictionary*, p. 288). Purple cloth was used in the furnishings of the tabernacle (KJ - Exodus 25:4), in Solomon's temple (KJ - 2 Chron. 2:14; 3:14) and in the high priest's dress (KJ - Exodus 25:4; 26:21). It was a royal garment worn by kings (KJ—Judges 8:26). It was a symbol of luxury and wealth, worn by the rich man of Luke

16:19 and by the luxurious harlot woman of Revelation 18:16. In mark 15:17,20 our Saviour was mockingly dressed in purple when a kingly robe was put around Him. Lydia was a seller of purple (King James Bible—Acts 16:14).

What is the meaning of this verse? The virtuous woman did not dress in a shabby manner. She was industrious and enterprising, and she was able to purchase the finest materials, and with her own hands make the finest of garments. She did not consider it a mark of spirituality to go around looking impoverished, dilapidated, and threadbare. Rather, as was often true under the former dispensation, material prosperity was a sign of God's blessing, and was not to be despised. She wore expensive clothing, royal clothing, to match her regal and godly character. Her outward garments of beauty and splendor matched her inner beauty. "The virtuous wife is robed in what bespeaks her true character and dignity" (Ironside). She was not vain or arrogant and she well understood that external beauty fades (as we will see in verse 30). She was not snobbish in the way she dressed. She understood that the most important clothing was the adorning of the inner man: "strength and honor are her clothing."

It is important to remember that the wearing of costly garments did not come at the expense of her family or the poor, nor did it interfere with any of her God-given duties:

If the virtuous woman has coverings of tapestry for her house, she makes them herself; if she is clothed with silk (or fine linen, as it may be rendered) and purple, she earns it by her labors and good management. She does not starve her charity by her finery, nor spend upon her dress that which might support a poor family, and she does not reckon herself superior to the duties of a wife, nor exempted by wearing silk and purple from using her spindle and distaff. From all this it appears that the inspired writer allows the use of costly array to none but those who can afford it in a full consistency with the duties which they owe to their families, to the poor, and to all men.

The temple in the Old Testament was quite elaborate and beautifully adorned, and this adornment included fine linen and purple. As believers, our bodies are the temple of God (King James Bible - 1 Cor. 6:19-20). Should not our "temple" express something of the Lord?

But let it be the hidden man of the heart, in that which is not corruptible, even the ornament of a meek and quiet spirit, which is in the sight of God of great price" (King James Bible— 1 Pet. 3:4). "That they may adorn the doctrine of God, our Savior, in all things" (King James Bible - Tit. 2:10).

Dressing well, both inwardly and outwardly, is a virtue, not a vice.

The Godly Woman and Costly Array

The godly woman of Proverbs 31 was dressed in costly array. In 1 Timothy 2:9 Christian woman are instructed not to adorn themselves in costly array. How do we explain this apparent contradiction? Is it wrong for a believing woman today to go out and buy an expensive dress? Should she instead only shop at thrift stores where she can spend a minimal amount on necessary attire?

In the Old Testament, great wealth and godliness were not incompatible. Abraham had tremendous wealth, as did David and Solomon, and they were not condemned for possessing riches. They were condemned for setting their heart on their riches (KJ - Psalm 62:10). Wealthy believers in the New Testament era, though not extinct, are harder to find. It is not easy to amass wealth while being persecuted by a Christ-hating world. Those who are rich are not condemned for their riches, but are told not to trust in them (KJ - 1 Tim. 6:17) and to be generous in the distribution of them (KJ - 1 Tim. 6:18).

Homer Kent explains that the passage is 1 Timothy 2:9 does not forbid the wearing of expensive clothes: It should be clear that Paul is not forbidding the wearing of any gold or pearls or expensive garments, any more than Peter in a similar passage was forbidding the wearing of clothes (KJ - 1 Pet. 3:3-4). But those things are not to be the means whereby the Christian woman makes herself attractive to other Christians. Good taste should always prevail and display for vanity's sake is out of place (The Pastoral Epistles, pages 111-112).

Paul is not insisting on drab dress. Even this may be worn with vanity; the very drabness may be made a display. Each according to her station in life: the queen not being the same as her lady-in-waiting, the latter not the same as her noble mistress. Each with due propriety as modesty and propriety will indicate to her both when attending divine services and when appearing in public elsewhere (The Interpretation of St. Paul's Epistles to the Colossians, to the Thessalonians, to Timothy, to Titus and to Philemon, p. 560).

There were certain women in Paul's day who would flaunt their wealth and draw attention to themselves by wearing expensive clothes. The expensive dresses worn by wealthy women could cost up to 7,000 denarii. Pliny the Elder, a first-century Roman historian, described a dress of Lollia Paulina, wife of the Emperor Caligula, which was worth several hundred thousand dollars by today's standards (*Natural History* 9:58). Dresses of the common women could cost as much as 500-800 denarii. The average daily wage of a common laborer was one denarius. (An average laborer would need to work two years to be able to purchase such a dress!)

Albert Barnes offers a well-reasoned, balanced conclusion: It is not supposed that all use of gold or pearls as articles of dress is here forbidden; but the idea is that the Christian female is not to seek these as the adorning which she desires, or is not to imitate the world in these personal decorations. It may be a difficult question to settle how much ornament is allowable, and when the true line is passed. There is one general rule which is applicable to all, and which might regulate all. It is that the true line is passed when more is thought of this external adorning, than of the ornament of the heart. Any external decoration which occupies the mind more than the virtues of the heart, and which engrosses the time and attention more, we may be certain is wrong. The apparel should be such as not to attract attention, such as shall leave the impression that the heart is not fixed on it. (Barnes' Notes on 1 Timothy 2:9)

Proverbs 31:23- Her husband is known in the gates, When he sitteth among the elders of the land.

It is remarkable that in a passage devoted to a godly and virtuous woman we find this verse which says nothing about the woman, but only describes her husband as a prominent leader of the land. It was at the city's gates that public business was transacted and cases were decided (the "gates" served as the city's courtroom). What then do we learn about the virtuous woman from this verse?

A well-known proverb says, "Behind every good man is a good woman." A godly wife contributes greatly to the success and prosperity of her husband.

"A virtuous woman is a crown to her husband, but she that maketh ashamed is as rottenness to his bones" (King James Bible - Prov. 12:4).

Where would the man mentioned in Proverbs 31:23 be without his godly, industrious, loving, faithful wife? The value of a godly wife is illustrated from the life of Daniel Webster. The following is from *High Call High Privilege* by Gail MacDonald (pages 99-100):

A wife can be a tremendous influence for good or for ill; nevertheless the husband is responsible before God to live rightly regardless of the spiritual and moral state of his spouse. If a man fails spiritually, it is first and foremost his fault. He must not blame anyone but himself. His wife may be a negative influence, but he is responsible to follow God, not her. Think of the example of Job. His wife said, "Curse God and die!" but in spite of her negative influence, Job remained faithful to the Lord. "Behind every good man is a good woman" is not always true. "Behind every good man **is** a great God!"

Proverbs 31:24 - She maketh fine linen and selleth it, and delivereth girdles unto the merchant.

This capable, industrious woman was very enterprising and she operated an amazing home business. She wove fine linen garments, a process which has already been discussed (see under verse 13). Linen garments are mentioned in Judges 14:12-13. Thirty sheets or thirty linen garments were to be the payment to Samson if the Philistines could not figure out his riddle. Linen garments are also mentioned as having been worn by the sinful daughters of Zion in Isaiah 3:23.

She also manufactured girdles or belts (richly adorned belts?) or sashes (ESV) which had value on the trade market. This word "belt" is used in 2 Samuel 20:8 to describe Joab's belt which held a sword. The term "girdle" as used in the Bible refers to an article of dress encircling the body, usually at the waist.

She may have enlisted some of her children to help her in this business. She delivered these goods to the merchants or traders. These were Phoenician traders, according to the meaning of the Hebrew word. Phoenicians were known for their trade and commerce and their skill seafaring people. Phoenicia's two major ports were Tyre and Sidon.

The virtuous woman provided a source of income for her family through her business.

"When other women impoverish their husbands by buying, she enriches her husband by selling those valuable commodities for which there is a constant demand" (George Lawson, *Commentary on Proverbs,* page 567).

"It is only modern pride and laziness which has introduced the idea that it is inconsistent with the dignity of a fine lady to make profit of her own manufactures. This virtuous woman, although her husband sits among the elders, does not think it a discredit, but an honor to herself, to make fine linen and girdles for sale; and the wise will praise her on account of it" (George Lawson, p.576).

Proverbs 31:25—Strength and honor are her clothing

Her wardrobe is remarkable. These items of clothing are not available at any marketplace or shopping mall. The LORD Himself provides these garments to the believing heart that is looking to Him. Such clothes adorn the inner man which is renewed day by day (2 Cor. 4:16).

Those ladies who wear gold and jewels dazzle the eyes and draw the regard of ordinary understandings; but how much brighter are the ornaments of a meek spirit, of strength and honor, which are the constant dress of the woman of virtue! Those who wear costly array rejoice for the present, because they think themselves the object of all men's admiration; but they are often preparing future sorrow for themselves by their extravagance, and their neglect of those accomplishments which would gain them respect in old age (George Lawson, *Commentary on Proverbs,* p. 568). Concerning her garment of strength, see the discussion under Proverbs 31:17. The virtuous woman knew that the LORD was the strength of her life (KJ—Psalm 27:1).

The word "honor" means splendor, majesty, honor. In Psalm 8:5 it is used of the honor and majesty conferred by the LORD upon Adam and Eve:

"...and hast crowned him with glory and honor." In Psalm 21:5 it is used of the God-given majesty David had as king: "honor and majesty has thou laid upon him." (King James—Psalm 8:5)

We learn that honor and majesty are before Him (KJ—Psalm 96:6), and that the LORD is clothed with honor and majesty (KJ—Psalm 104:1). This was certainly true of our Lord Jesus Christ in His-pre-incarnate state. We catch a glimpse of Christ in His majesty in Isaiah 6:1-3 (see John 12:41 in context where the glorious king of Isaiah 6 is identified as Christ). This splendid King of the Universe stepped out of His ivory palaces and descended to this world of woe. He laid aside His majestic garments, as it were, and humbled Himself by taking upon Himself our humanity (KJ - John 1:14). In Isaiah 53:2 we have a description of God's suffering Servant, the Messiah Himself: "when we shall see Him, there is no beauty that we should desire Him." The word "beauty" is the same word as "honor" (majesty, splendor) which is found in Proverbs 31:25. The Lord laid aside His glorious splendor so that He could die as the perfect Substitute for sinners (Isaiah 53), thus making it possible for the believer to be clothed with garments of majesty and splendor; we who were once dressed only with filthy, bloody rags (Isaiah 64:6, "filthy rags" - bloody cloths).

And she shall rejoice (laugh) in time to come

The word "rejoice" (KJV) is the Hebrew word meaning "laugh." It is used in Ecclesiastes 3:4--"A time to weep, and a time to laugh." In Psalm 37:12-13 we learn that "the LORD shall laugh at him (the wicked); for He seeth that his day (of judgment) is coming." The virtuous woman will laugh at "time to come" (coming time), a clear reference to the days ahead, the future. She will laugh at the future.

In reliance on her ample stores, and still more her inward strength and skill, she laughs at the future as respects the evil that it may perchance bring. This "laughing at the future" is of course not to be understood as expressive of a presumptuous self-confidence (see Proverbs 27:1), but only of a consciousness of having all appropriate and possible preparation and competence for the future (Lange's Commentary under Proverbs 31:25).

It is the privilege of every believer in Christ to confidently laugh at the future. We have been guaranteed a bright, eternal future, if we live right. (KJ - John 6:37-40; 10:27-30). We have the sure promise of God that the future ("things to come") cannot separate us from the love of God (KJ - Rom. 8:38). In fact, in 1 Corinthians 3:22 we learn that we possess the future! It is ours! The future belongs to us. God has marked out a glorious future for every child of God, that we should be conformed to the image of Christ (KJ - Rom. 8:29). This is what predestination is all about. Never does the New Testament teach that a person is predestinated to hell. The term "predestination" is used to teach us that God has marked out a glorious future for every believer.

Unsaved people dread the future and they have good cause to do so. They have nothing to look forward to but eternal punishment and an eternity without Christ (KJ - Matthew 25:41,46). Their future promises that, unless they repent, they will perish (KJ - Luke 13:3,5). Unless they repent they will someday hear these frightening words, "I never knew you; depart from Me, ye that work iniquity (lawlessness)" (Matthew 7:23 and compare Matthew 25:41). But the saved person can thankfully laugh at the future, knowing that someday he will hear God's invitation to enter eternal bliss (see Matthew 25:34).

How confident we can be! We do not know what the future holds, but we know who holds the future. We know that everything that happens to us in the future is for God's glory and for our good (KJ - Romans 8:28). We are fully persuaded that the God who began a good work in us will complete that good work in the future (KJ - Philippians 1:6).

Proverbs 31:26 - She openeth her mouth with wisdom, and in her tongue is the law of kindness.

This is the only verse in this passage which speaks of the godly woman's tongue and the words of her mouth.

Our Lord taught that "out of the abundance of the heart the mouth speaks" (King James Bible - Matthew 12:34).

What comes out of the mouth is an indication of what is in the heart. Our speech reveals our heart. Out of a wise heart come wise words. Out of a kind heart come kind words. Out of a loving heart come loving words. Be careful when you speak because your heart is showing. The word "kindness" is the commonly used Hebrew word hesed. It occurs about 200 times in the Old Testament. It is found in the following familiar passages.

The general import of this word seems to be, the full flow of natural affection, corresponding to storgé in Greek. The Hebrew word for "stork," so remarkable for affection to her young, is derived from this word. The corresponding word in Arabic is used of the flowing of the mother's milk to the breasts, so nearly connected with affection for her offspring; hence has been derived, probably, the phrase, "full of the milk of human kindness.

The law of kindness (hesed) is in her tongue. The term "law" (torah) refers to instruction. The term is used in Isaiah 2:3 of the teaching ministry of the Messiah during the millennial kingdom: "...for out of Zion shall go forth the law (instruction), and the word of the LORD from Jerusalem." "The teaching of kindness is on her tongue" (ESV).

The instruction of the virtuous woman will be characterized by kindness and steadfast love. It will be kindly, faithful, loving and gracious instruction. We assume that the primary beneficiaries of her loving instruction are her children and perhaps her household servants. "My son, hear the instruction of thy father, and forsake not the law [instruction] of thy mother" (Proverbs 1:8; see also Proverbs 6:20, 23).

The godly mother is a teacher. In love she wants God's highest and best for her children. Women have a valuable and essential teaching ministry according to Titus 2:3-5.

The words which come from the lips of the true wife are as a law giving guidance and instruction to those that hear them, but the law is not proclaimed in its sterner aspects, but as one in which "mercy tempers justice," and love, the fulfilling of the law, is seen to be the source from which it springs. (F. C. Cook, Barnes' Notes--Proverbs, p. 84)

She is not trifling, but thoughtful and sensible in her words. As idleness is the source of talkativeness (KJ - 1 Tim. 5:13), so industry is its antidote. Jamieson, Fausset and Brown, Commentary--Proverbs, p. 513

As a sandy hill is to the feet of the aged, so is a wife full of words to a quiet man; but the virtuous woman plagues neither her husband nor any other man with her talk. She does not lock up her lips in a sullen silence, but when she speaks it is a pleasure to hear her, for she opens her mouth with wisdom. Besides her other labors already mentioned, she rises in the morning, and finds time to read the Bible, and other instructive books; she meditates and reflects, and receives instruction from what she hears, and prays to the Father of lights; and so she improves daily in knowledge and prudence; and when she opens her mouth, she says nothing but what is well worthy of being heard....Kindness is painted on her countenance, and flows from her tongue; for it possesses the throne of her heart, and gives law to all her words and actions. (George Lawson, Commentary on Proverbs, pages 568-569)

But the godly matron has not only the law of love in her heart, but wisdom in her mouth, and in her tongue the law of kindness. The same love that binds her heart, governs her tongue, not with the caprice, but with the law, of kindness--a law, which she received from wisdom, and which gives the mould to her whole spirit, so that she says nothing that is foolish, nothing that is ill-natured. (Charles Bridges, *Proverbs*, pages 625-626).

Proverbs 31:27 - She looketh well to the ways [doings] of her household

She "looketh well" or keeps watch. The verb means to look out or about, to spy, to keep watch. It is used in a bad sense in Psalm 37:32, "a wicked man spieth upon the righteous." It is used of a watchman in 2 Kings 9:17 and Ezekiel 3:17; 33:7. A watchman looks for enemies and for anything that may endanger the city. The godly woman is alertly watching over her household, looking for any danger that may hurt the family: evil companions, vile entertainment, dangers from the internet.

As a spy seeks to gather information about the enemy, so the godly woman seeks to find out what is going on with her children. Some parents do not keep any watch. They don't know what their children do or where they go or what they watch on television or what music they listen to. Parents need to be very much aware of what is really taking place, so that they can best help their children, discipline them, restrict them as needed, and channel them into wholesome and profitable activities. Parents should be "looking well to their moral habits, their religious instruction, and attendance on the means of grace; giving them time for secret prayer, and reading the Word of God, bringing them to the daily ordinance of family worship; inculcating the careful observance of the Lord's Day; anxiously watching over their manners, habits, and connections...Who can have the claim to *a virtuous woman,* who does not feel this weight of family responsibility?" (Charles Bridges, *Proverbs*, p. 625)

And eateth not the bread of idleness

Idleness is not on her diet. She avoids the carbohydrates of idleness, and does not indulge herself in slothfulness. The word "idleness" means sluggishness, laziness. This word is used in Proverbs 6:6,9; 10:26; 19:15; 24:30. Anyone who reads the description of the godly woman in Proverbs 31 knows very well that she is anything but lazy! One wonders how she has enough hours in the day to do all that she does! Her hours are characterized by diligent industry and laborious involvement in wholesome activities.

"She worketh willingly with her hands."
"She riseth also while it is yet night."
"She layeth her hand to the spindle."
"She maketh fine linen and selleth it," etc. She is the opposite of a sluggard!

Proverbs 31:28 - Her children rise up and call her blessed; her husband also, and he praiseth her.

She is praised by her own family members. Those who know her the best praise her the most. She invested herself in her loved ones, and she is recognized and rewarded by the same.

I know a godly couple who years ago were facing the challenges of raising their six children, all in their teen years. When the wife came to her husband for encouragement and advice, he remembered Proverbs 31:28 and commented to his wife, "Dear, as hard as things are now, just remember that someday your children will rise up and call you blessed." His beloved wife wryly responded, "Yes, but right now they are just rising up!"

Her husband and children will "call her blessed" or pronounce her happy. This Hebrew term "blessed" was used by Leah when she pronounced herself blessed: "Happy am I, for the daughters will call me blessed" (KJ - Genesis 30:13). The son born of Zilpah was named "Asher" which is from this same Hebrew term, and means "happy, blessed" (KJ - Genesis 30:13).

Godliness and happiness go together. The godly woman is the happy woman, and she is blessed. The virtuous woman seeks first the kingdom of God, and all these things (including happiness) are added unto her (King James Bible - Matthew 6:33). Happiness is a byproduct of honoring the Lord and putting Him first. It is not an end in itself. Those who seek happiness and who make that their goal, never find it. Those who seek the Lord find in Him their true happiness. He satisfies the heart that is devoted to Him.

God's formula for happiness is found in the following verses, all of which contain this same Hebrew word "blessed" or "happy":

Charles Bridges describes the happiness of the godly woman as follows:

For what greater earthly happiness could she know, than her children's reverence and her husband's blessing? We may picture to ourselves her condition—crowned with years; her children grown up; perhaps themselves surrounded with families, and endeavoring to train them, as themselves had been trained. Their mother is constantly before their eyes. Her tender guidance, her wise counsels, her loving discipline, her holy example, are vividly kept in remembrance. They cease not to call her blessed, and to bless the Lord for her, as his invaluable gift. No less does her husband praise her. His attachment to her was grounded, not on the deceitful and vain charms of beauty, but on the fear of the Lord. She is therefore in his eyes to the end, the stay of his declining years, the soother of his cares, the counselor of his perplexities, the comforter of his sorrows, the sunshine of his earthly joys. (Proverbs, pages 626-627).

Proverbs 31:29 - Many daughters have done virtuously, but thou excellest them all.

This verse is different from all the others in this section. All of the other verses speak about the virtuous woman in the third person. For example, verses 12-22 all begin with the word "she." She will do him good.... She seeketh wool.... She is like the merchants' ships.... She riseth also... etc. But in verse 29 the second person pronoun is used for the first time: "But thou (you) excellest them all." It is more personal, familiar and intimate. Apparently it is her husband himself who is speaking these words.

At the end of verse 28, we were told that her husband praises her. In verse 29 we have the husband's praise in his own words: "Many daughters have done virtuously, but thou excellest them all."

The Hebrew term for "daughters" literally means daughters, but here it is used more generally of women (as in Genesis 30:13). The word "virtuously" is the same word as found in verse 10--"Who can find a virtuous woman?" The term "virtuous" is from a noun meaning strength, efficiency, ability. Here it refers to strength of character, moral strength and firmness. See the fuller discussion under Proverbs 31:10. This husband knew his wife was not the only godly, virtuous woman on the planet. He knew that there were other God-fearing women of moral strength and of virtuous character. Such women were rare (verse 10) but they were not extinct. How we should thank God for all women who live godly in Christ Jesus and who reflect the person of their Saviour in their walk and talk! May the beauty of the LORD our God be upon them all (KJ –Psalm 90:17).

The husband then directs his praise to his own wife: "but thou excellest them all." You surpass them all! You have raised yourself above them all. You are excellent and incomparable! You surpass all others. Was this man married to the most virtuous woman in all the world, or did it just seem so to him? When a man has found a priceless gem (compare verse 10), he considers his treasure better than all others. To him, she is the most precious wife anyone could ever have. From his vantage point, no other woman could rival her. "There's not another woman in the whole world like you!" "When I married you, God gave me the best gift this side of heaven!" He lavishes praise upon her, and she does not mind his exaggerations. In his mind, she excels all others.

George Lawson beautifully observes: The praises of her husband will be still more delightful to her ears than those of her children. What earthly happiness can a good wife desire, like the affection and approbation of the guide of her youth? and this a virtuous woman can scarcely fail of possessing, for what heart has so much marble in it as to be able to resist those virtues which every hour appear in his other self? He cannot refrain from bestowing praise on one whom he finds the sweetener of all his cares, his faithful adviser in perplexities, his comforter in every distress, the instrument of a great part of his earthly felicity; his best friend, his unceasing joy, and his brightest crown. No wonder if the experience of such goodness and happiness makes him eloquent in her praise, and draws commendations from his tongue, that must be understood in a restricted sense to make them true. He prefers her to every other wife who ever lived upon earth; and he is sincere in doing it, for she ravishes his heart by the beauties of her mind and conversation. Piety will dispose a man to think meanly of himself, in comparison with other men, but highly of his wife, when he compares her with other women.

Proverbs 31:30 - Favor is deceitful, and beauty is vain

The word "favor" is the Hebrew word for "grace." In this verse the word "grace" is speaking of a woman's outward appearance and form. It is paralleled with the word "beauty," and both words carry the same idea. Webster, in his original 1828 dictionary, has numerous definitions for grace, one of which is "beauty, whatever adorns and recommends to favor." Gesenius defines the Hebrew word to mean "gracefulness, beauty."

In Proverbs 17:8 the word "grace" is used to describe a stone. It is a beautiful or precious stone, pleasant and agreeable to the eyes. Precious stones are usually brightly colored and beautiful in outward appearance. So also, a woman of grace is one who is pleasant and agreeable to the eyes, a beautiful woman.

In Proverbs 6:25 a strong warning is given concerning a wicked harlot: "Lust not after her beauty in thine heart, neither let her take thee with her eyelids." The beauty of this woman is only skin deep. It's like "a beautiful garment on a body covered with loathsome sores" (George Lawson, *Commentary on Proverbs,* p. 86). Under the surface is great ugliness as a jewel of gold in a swine's snout, so is a fair [beautiful] woman who is without discretion" (King James Bible - Prov. 11:22).

The beautiful gold piece of jewelry does not go well with the beast that wears it, whose nose delights in shoveling mud. Beauty that covers vileness is not true beauty. In verse 30 we are told two things about outward gracefulness and external beauty: 1) Favor is deceitful; 2) Beauty is vain.

External beauty is deceitful. The Hebrew term refers to that which deceives and disappoints. What you see is not really what you get. It seems that you are looking at a very beautiful person, a very special person, but the surface appearance belies the inner person. The woman's outer charm covers up her inner deformity. It would be like a nut with a fine looking shell, but when you crack it open you find that the nut inside is rotten and undesirable. Beautiful actresses and supermodels are often known for their broken marriages, substance abuse, personal problems, etc. indicating that under the external shell there lives a sinful and very troubled person who needs God's transforming grace.

External beauty is vain. "Vain" describes that which is evanescent (tending to vanish like vapour). It is used of that which soon vanishes away, like vapour, breath, or a bubble. The term "vain" is used of the vanity of idols. t is used in Psalm 39:5,11, "man at his best state is altogether vanity." It is the key word in the book of Ecclesiastes and is used to describe the meaninglessness and emptiness of life under the sun apart from God ("vanity is used 31 times in Ecclesiastes"). External beauty is not long lasting. It is here today and gone tomorrow. There is great emphasis in our day on external beauty. Makeup is used in such abundance that Jezebel would feel right at home in our society (2 Kings 9:30). All kinds of supplements and health products are offered to try to help people look young and attractive, and to slow down nature's natural deterioration. Surgical procedures are offered which can change and improve a person's outward appearance. Diet programs and exercise programs garner millions of dollars from people who want to look beautiful and feel good. Television shows are devoted to showing how a plain or unattractive person can be transformed and made over into an outwardly attractive person by means of makeup, hair styling, weight loss, exercise, surgery, etc. There is no end to the attempts of mankind to beautify the body and to try to preserve the external.

Real beauty in the sight of God is not the product of cosmetics but the outshining of the indwelling Christ. A lady was once asked the secret of her beautiful complexion. She said, "I use truth for my lips; for my voice, prayer; for my eyes, pity; for my hands, charity; for my figure, uprightness; and for my heart, LOVE." These heavenly cosmetics are worthy of trial, and are supplied free to every applicant at the Throne of Grace.

External improvement and transformation projects can only last so long. A beautiful woman may win a beauty contest, but she is not going to win one thirty years later! Beautiful actresses grow old and in spite of all they do to preserve their youth, they lose the battle with time and their beauty deteriorates. External beauty can be marred and scarred by injury, serious burns, diseases, etc., and this can happen even to those who are young. Time will always win, and all humanity will ultimately decline, and end up as dust (King James Bible - Gen. 3:19; Eccl. 3:20; Psalm 39:4-5; 103:14; 104:29).

But a woman who feareth the LORD, she shall be praised.

Inner beauty comes from a right relationship with the Lord. True beauty is impossible apart from the fear of the Lord. When the Lord is enthroned within, His glory will shine without.

"And let the beauty of the LORD our God be upon us: and establish thou the work of our hands upon us; yea, the work of our hands establish thou it" (King James Bible - Psalm 90:7).

Peter speaks of that inner beauty that ought to grace the life and conduct of every believing woman: The fear of the Lord is essential in the cultivation of inner beauty. If the fear of the Lord is absent, then it is impossible to radiate the beauty of the LORD.

Fear can be a bad thing; fear can also be a good and healthy response. If I meet a bear in the woods, I should have a healthy respect for the animal, knowing something of its power and potential ferocity. This is a healthy fear that could save my life. We are to fear and respect God in the right way, knowing that He is a loving, caring Heavenly Father who bids us to cast all of our care upon Him and come boldly to His throne of grace to obtain mercy and find grace to help in time of need. Fallen Adam feared God in the wrong way and hid from Him (King James Bible - Gen. 3:10). The right kind of fear of God causes us to draw near to Him.

The one who fears God believes that God is great and deserves his utmost respect and reverence. He is afraid to do anything that would displease such an awesome God. In Genesis 22 Abraham was faced with the seemingly unreasonable command of sacrificing his beloved son Isaac. In verse 12 God gave this testimony of Abraham: "for now I know that thou fearest God." Abraham feared God; that is, he believed that God was so great that to disobey Him was unthinkable!

Often, instead of fearing *God we fear men!* The fear of man is a great snare (King James Bible - Prov. 29:25). We begin thinking like this:

"What will they think of me?" "What will they say?" "Will they get angry?" "Will they be pleased?" "Maybe they will see me!" "I'm afraid of what they might do to me!" "Will they be upset or offended?" "Will they still be friendly towards me?" "What will they want me to say?" "What will they want me to do?" "Where will they want me to go?" "I'm afraid they will not be happy with me!" "I don't think they will approve of this!" "They might frown on my actions!" "I hope they will really appreciate what I'm about to do!"

This then is the fear of men. What is the fear of God? To answer this question, simply read the above sentences again and substitute the word "God" for the word "they." This is the fear of God.

Proverbs 31:31- Give her of the fruit of her hands; and let her own works praise her in the gates.

A godly and virtuous woman will be rewarded. What she gives out she will get back. It is the boomerang effect: she hurls out many a good deed, and they are all going to come back to her. In devotion to her God and in love for her household, she is willing to expend herself ("to spend and be spent"). As she steadfastly labors and abounds in the work of the Lord, she knows that her labor will not be in vain (King James Bible - 1 Cor. 15:58). God is a very generous Rewarder of those who diligently seek Him (King James Bible - Heb. 11:6), "knowing that whatever good thing any man doeth, the same shall he receive of the Lord" (King James Bible - Eph. 6:8). The Lord who knows all our works will faithfully reward all that is done in His Name and for His glory. It pays to live in a right manner. It pays to fear the Lord.

The "fruit of her hands" indicates the result of her labor. In this passage we have seen that her hands have been very busy for good (verses 16, 19, 20). As Frances Havergal wrote, "Take my hands and let them move at the impulse of Thy love."

What is the significance of the phrase "in the gates"? In ancient cities, the space inside the gate was a public meeting place, where all manner of business was conducted (like our city hall). Her own works, her own deeds will praise her in the gates. That is, she will be publicly recognized for her good works and accomplishments. The idea of the verse is simply this: Give her the praises which she so richly merits.

"Say to the righteous, that it shall be well with them; for they shall eat the fruit of their doings" (King James Bible - Isaiah 3:10).

So today may Christian women adorn the doctrine of God our Saviour by their good works (compare Titus 2:10). God's special people should be "zealous of good works (fervently seeking to please God in all we do)" (King James Bible - Tit. 2:14). May our light shine before men, that they may see our good works, and glorify our Father who is in heaven (King James Bible - Matt. 5:16).

A comparison of Ruth and the Proverbs 31 Woman:

Comparison of Ruth & the Proverbs 31 Woman		
Devoted to her family	Ruth 1:15-18	Proverbs 31:10, 11, 12, 23
Delighted in her work	Ruth 2:2	Proverbs 31:13
Diligent in her labor	Ruth 2:7,17,23	Proverbs 31:14, 15, 16, 17, 18, 19, 20, 21, 24, 27
Dedicated to godly speech	Ruth 2:10,13	Proverbs 31:26
Dependent on God	Ruth 2:12	Proverbs 31:25, 30
Dressed with care	Ruth 3:3	Proverbs 31:22, 25
Discreet with men	Ruth 3:6–13	Proverbs 31:11, 12, 23
Delivered blessings	Ruth 4:14,15	Proverbs 31:28, 29

Middletown Bible Church (2008) The Virtuous Woman . Retrieved April 2012 .
Middletownbiblechurch.org.

A contrast of a **Voluptuous Woman** and what the bible calls a **Virtuous Woman:**

A CONTRAST

THE VOLUPTUOUS WOMAN	THE VIRTUOUS WOMAN
Described in the first nine chapters of Proverbs	Described in Proverbs chapter 31
SHE IS LEWD (Proverbs 6:24; 2:17).	SHE IS LOYAL (Proverbs 31:11).
SHE IS A HOME BREAKER (Proverbs 7).	SHE IS A HOMEMAKER (Proverbs 31).
SHE IS EASY TO FIND (Proverbs 7:10-12).	SHE IS HARD TO FIND (a rare gem) (Proverbs 31:10).
SHE IS CHEAP (Proverbs 30:20)	SHE IS PRECIOUS (Proverbs 31:10).
SHE HAS OUTER BEAUTY Surface attraction (Proverbs 6:25).	SHE HAS INNER BEAUTY Heart attraction (Proverbs 31:30; 1 Peter 3:4).
SHE WORKS WITH HER MOUTH (lively lips but no life) (Proverbs 21:9,19; 25:24 etc.).	SHE WORKS WITH HER HANDS (a lovely life producing loving deeds) (Proverbs 31, many verses).
SHE IS RELIGIOUS (Proverbs 7:14).	SHE IS RIGHT WITH GOD (Proverbs 31:30).
SHE IS OUTSIDE THE HOME (Proverbs 7:11-12).	SHE ABIDES IN THE HOME (Proverbs 31:27).
SHE DOES HER HUSBAND NOTHING BUT HARM (Proverbs 2:17).	SHE DOES HER HUSBAND GOOD (Proverbs 31:12).
SHE IS ON THE LOOSE AT NIGHT (Proverbs 7:9,18).	SHE IS RESTING AT NIGHT SO SHE CAN AWAKE EARLY (Proverbs 31:15).
SHE KILLS HER VICTIMS (Proverbs 7:23).	SHE BLESSES HER FAMILY (Proverbs 31:28).
SHE LIVES BY LUST (Proverbs 7:10).	SHE LIVES BY LOVE (Proverbs 31:20).

Middletown Bible Church. (2008) The Virtuous Woman. Retrieved April 2012 from middletownbiblechurch.org.

What Does The Bible Say About Family?

The American family is falling apart. Consider the following statistics. In 1950, about one out of every 20 children born in this country was born to an unmarried woman, and there were very few abortions. By 1990, more than one out of every 4 children was born to an unmarried woman and hundreds of thousands more were aborted. Approximately half of all marriages that take place this year in the U.S. will end in divorce. Imagine what this looks like today.

Experts have told us that if we decrease the number of children per family, increase the education of parents, and spend more on government programs to improve child welfare, we will have higher "quality" children and improve the well-being of those children. But as Barbara Dafoe Whitehead points out in an article entitled "Dan Quayle Was Right" in the April, 1993 issue of the Atlantic Monthly, we have done all these things and what have been the results? Child poverty has increased substantially faster than poverty among adults. Juvenile crime has seen a similar rapid increase. School performance has declined. The teen suicide rate has tripled, and other measures of less severe emotional problems have escalated dramatically. Whitehead blames many of these problems on the demise of the two-parent family, writing:

If we fail to come to terms with the relationship between family structure and declining child well-being, then it will be increasingly difficult to improve children's life prospects, no matter how many new programs the federal government funds. Nor will we be able to make progress in bettering school performance or reducing crime or improving the quality of the nation's future work force, all domestic problems closely connected to family breakup.

What is wrong with families today? The Biblical answer is clear: We have believed society's lies and ignored Biblical truth. What are some of these lies? Here are three:

Society's lie #1: Men and woman are essentially the same. The Bible tells us that, while equal before God, we are different in important ways.

Society's lie #2: We need to stand up for our own rights and demand that our own needs are met, even if that means breaking a solemn marriage vow, deserting our children, or rebelling against our parents.

As Whitehead reports: "Fewer than half of all adult Americans today regard the idea of sacrifice for others as a positive moral virtue." What does the Bible tell us? "He who seeks to gain his own life will lose it" and "it is more blessed to give than to receive."

Society's lie #3: Children are a burden, or, at best, an ornament, or, perhaps, an experience. It's useful to have one in order to go through the experience, but take care that you don't spoil your life prospects by having too many.

The Bible says: "Children are an inheritance from the Lord; the fruit of
the womb a reward from him. Like arrows in the hands of a warrior
are children born in one's youth. Blessed is the man whose quiver
is full of them." (King James Bible - Psalm 127)

Children are God's; we "inherit" them from him, to bring up and hold in trust. They are gifts, rewards; our lives are filled by being poured out for them.

Characteristics Of A Godly Home

What is the relationship between parents and children in a family founded on Biblical principles? We know that children are an inheritance from the Lord, not burdens, ornaments, possessions, or experiences for the parents. What does Paul tell us in this passage? Chapter 6 of Ephesians:

"Children, obey your parents in the Lord for this is right. Honor your
father and mother which is the first commandment with a promise,
that it may go well with you and that you may enjoy long life on
the earth. Fathers, do not exasperate your children; instead, bring
them up in the training and instruction of the Lord." (King James
Bible – Ephesians 6:1-4)

As with the husband and wife, Paul instructs each of us to do that which is most difficult. These commands are not easy, they are not natural. Naturally, children will rebel and dishonor their parents. Naturally, fathers will become overbearing, expecting too much and frustrating their children. But God calls us to something different. Children are given two injunctions: to obey and to honor their parents. Obedience is doing what one is told, willing submission to the authority relationship imposed by God. But children are to obey their parents for the good of the family, to build their own character, even when the parent is wrong, as he surely will be at times. Honoring parents is somewhat different. Honoring implies respect, building up one's parents, not putting them down to your peers, not taking family differences of opinion outside the home. Parents are given three injunctions here: to instruct, to train or discipline, and not to exasperate. Instruction is the responsibility of the parents, something our society seems to have forgotten. We cannot depend on schools alone to educate our children academically; we cannot depend on Sunday School alone to instruct our kids in the Word of God. In Deuteronomy chapter 6, God says through Moses:

"These commandments I give you this day are to be upon your hearts,
and you shall teach them diligently to your children" at all times.
(Deuteronomy 6)

Parents have the responsibility to instruct their children in God's word by example and direct teaching. Let us make sure we live up to that responsibility.

Secondly, parents are to train, or discipline their children. Once again, our attitude needs to be one of servant leadership. Discipline must be for the good of the child, not because our feelings were hurt or because we had a bad day at the office. We must discipline our children, even when it is a chore and inconvenient, and, believe me, administering correct discipline can be a chore for the parent. The child must be assured of our love, and must realize that that very love will not let us tolerate defiant disobedience on the part of the child. This can be a first step towards the child gaining an understanding of the love, justice, and grace of God. Finally, our actions and attitudes must never exasperate our children, or anger them unnecessarily. We must not frustrate them or make them give up hope by expecting them not to behave like children, or expecting them to act beyond their years. Our instruction and discipline should be building them up, not tearing them down. One key to this is ensuring that we have our children's interest truly at heart, and not follow the world in doing what is right for ME.

The world tells us: "Look out for yourself." The American family is in such a mess in large measure because of this attitude. How can we deal with this huge problem, "the American family?" If these problems are to be solved, it will not be through government programs or institutional reform. The only solution to the problem is for American families to change, one by one, your family, my family; the solution is for each of us to know Christ, for Him to change our hearts, so that we may be able to follow the Biblical injunction to think of others more highly than ourselves, to place the needs of our family members above our own. Ask yourself these questions:

- Do I know Christ?
- Have I acknowledged Him in my life?
- Have I asked Him to give me the power to reflect his love to my family?

Jesus tells us, "Apart from me, you can do nothing" (King James Bible - John 15). We certainly cannot follow his command without his strength within us. If you do not know him, ask him into your heart now, today. Feel free to discuss this with me, or one of the elders. If you do know Jesus as Lord, ask yourself:

1. Am I respecting and submitting to my husband?
2. Am I giving myself up for my wife?
3. Am I obeying and honoring my parents?
4. Do I consider others' welfare above my own?
5. What can I do today to serve my family?
6. In what areas do I need my spouse's forgiveness?

7. In what areas do I need my child's or parent's forgiveness? Seek it today.

8. May God give us the grace and strength to serve him by serving our families.

Spiritual House Cleaning

Are you in need of a SPIRITUAL HOUSECLEANING? Paul apparently thought so. He wrote, "Therefore, having these promises, beloved, let us cleanse ourselves from all defilement of flesh and spirit, perfecting holiness in the fear of God." 2 Corinthians 7:1 (NASB). Notice several very important things that Paul mentions as he writes to the church at Corinth concerning the spiritual cleansing that was needed.

1. He writes with affection ("beloved").

2. He employs the plural ("us", "ourselves").

3. He puts the burden of cleansing upon ourselves…not on God!

4. He challenges the church and himself to perform a complete cleansing ("all defilement of flesh and spirit").

5. The Apostle goes on to encourage everyone to "perfect holiness" in the fear of God. The call is not to "tidy up" our lives, but to cleanse our lives. Let us start by cleaning our intellectual attic. (That way you will have to clean the main "living area" only once!). Proverbs 23:7 reads, "As a man thinks within himself, so he is." (HCSB). Solomon encourages us to "get our head on straight." Sanitize your "mindset" of all bitterness, wrath, pride, arrogance, haughtiness, envy, jealousy, prejudice and an unforgiving spirit. Read Ephesians 4:31 and Galatians 5:19-21 for scriptural support. The writer of Hebrews adds another intellectual blunder we need to clean out of our thinking.

> "Do not be carried away by all kinds of strange teachings." Hebrews
> 13:9 (NIV). We are wise, indeed, if we "speak the things which are
> proper for sound doctrine." Titus 2:1.

In today's world, we must be careful what we coddle in our minds. John writes, "Beloved, do not believe every spirit, but test the spirits, whether they are of God; because many false prophets have gone out into the world." (King James - I John 4:1).

How do we test the spirits? Test them by the Word of God. We all need to be like the believers in the church at Berea for they "searched the Scriptures daily to find out whether these things were so." Acts 17:11. Paul tells us to focus on the truth, writing, "If then you were raised with Christ, seek those things which are above, where Christ is, sitting at the right hand of God. Set your mind on things above, not on things on the earth." Colossians 3:1-2

Let us proceed to the "LIVING AREA" of your daily life. Some "closets" in our spiritual life that may need to be cleaned. Bad habits need to be removed, profane speech needs cleaned up, some TV shows might need turned off, and some books that need to be trashed. It is imperative to clean out your life. Spiritually cleaning your home or office is a must.

PEACE IN THE HOME

Your house must be cleaned from articles, occult jewelry, occult books, etc., for you to enjoy complete freedom. Spiritual house cleaning should be done by anointing with olive oil in the name of Jesus. Jesus taught us that we have the power to bind demonic spirits. Binding and commanding all powers of darkness to leave is shown in (King James Bible - Matt. 18:18).When driving evils spirits out, anoint the doorways, windows, discard all statues and images of animals. Many unknowingly invite demonic attack by dabbling in jewelry with occult symbolism and power.

In the cause of objects dedicated to demons (idols, artifacts, etc.), the best course of action is to destroy them. Moreover, one should check secondhand cars, homes, and apartments also. This precaution is mainly due to the former owners may have had a Ouija board, occult paraphernalia, or were involved in serious bondage to sin. In these cases there is every reason to suspect that evil spirits may be lingering behind. These spirits can and will cause trouble to the new owners. Additionally, keep in mind that any prayers offered to anyone or anything, other gods, than Jesus Christ, constitutes prayers and/or worship to demons. Very often these are answered in the form of curses, for demons can and do respond to those who request of them. Also, if you are aware of demonic prayers against your family, break the curses placed against you in the name of Jesus.

We always suggest that two believers go on a mission such as this with The Bible in hand. The following should be destroyed:

- Look for sun gods, idols, incense

- Buddha, hand-carved object from Africa or the Orient, Ouija Boards

- anything connected with astrology; horoscopes, and fortune telling, and so on

- Books or objects associated with witchcraft, good luck charms, or the cult religious (Metaphysics, Christian Science, Jehovah's Witnesses, etc.)

- Hard rock and some rap music all fall in the category of things which have been often loaded with evil spiritual power.

Verbally denounce Satan and his power, and all of his demon hosts and claim authority as a believer-priest because of the name of Jesus Christ and the authority of His shed blood. (There is more power in the spoken word.) Some Scripture which has proven useful in this includes: (King James Bible Rev. 12:11; 22:3; Gol. 2:14-15; Gal. 3:13; Deut. 21:23, 32:5; Num. 23-8, II Sam. 7:29).Read these scriptures out loud in the house. In some cases the door lintel and window sills have been anointed by touching them with olive oil. Other things such as statues have been so anointed in Jesus Name and many times the demonic power is checked or destroyed. Any specific areas of demonic activity or influence of which you are aware should be denounced by name, (*King James Bible—Prov. 3:33*).

Hezekiah's Cleaning Service

It happens about once or twice a year. People wash walls, strip floors, clean windows, wipe cupboards, defrost the refrigerator/freezer, wash curtains, dry-clean drapes, steam-clean the carpets, sanitize the bathroom, paint the bedroom, clear out the garage, clean out the attic, reorganize the closets, take junk to the dump, pile bags of papers and boxes of unwanted items by the road for the garbage man to haul away. Maybe you did that not long ago, or maybe you are planning to do it soon. It's called house cleaning. It's a big job and a dirty job. But once it's done, it feels so good. You feel like you accomplished something. And the house smells fresh and clean again. You can park the car in the garage again. You enjoy sitting in the family room again. That awful smell whenever you open the kitchen cupboards is gone. And you can open the refrigerator door without embarrassment or fear, knowing that the green stuff growing inside has been neutralized.

Well, this passage in 2 Chronicles 29 is about cleaning house. And not just any old house. It's about cleaning the Lord's house, the temple in Jerusalem. It took place around 715 BC in the first year of King Hezekiah's reign.

Hezekiah was one of the few God fearing kings of Judah. Most of the twelve kings before him did what was evil in the sight of the Lord. They brought ruin, shame and apostasy to Judah. Hezekiah's father was one of those godless kings. During Ahaz's 20 year reign, Judah declined in every way; morally, spiritually, politically and socially. Ahaz broke covenant with God; he desecrated the temple with idols and false worship; the people became decadent under his rule; justice failed, and Judah became a puppet state for Tiglath Pilesar III, king of Assyria. When Hezekiah took the throne, it was high time to clean house.

And Hezekiah did. The words of our text express the sincerity, determination and dedication with which the king began to reform the country. He said: "Listen to me, Levites! Consecrate yourselves now and consecrate the temple of the Lord, the God of your fathers. Remove all defilement from the sanctuary. Our fathers were unfaithful; they did evil in the eyes of the Lord our God and forsook Him. They turned their faces away from the Lord's dwelling place and turned their backs on him . . . now I intend to make a covenant with the Lord, the God of Israel, so that his fierce anger will turn away from us." Hezekiah took three significant actions that I would like us to take note of three steps in cleaning the Lord's house. He began by opening the doors of the temple. We read in verse three, "In the first month of the first year of his reign, he opened the doors of the temple of the Lord and repaired them." That's the very first thing Hezekiah did. It is significant. The doors of the temple had been closed and barred during the reign of Ahaz. Ahaz had introduced foreign gods into Judah and encouraged the people to worship them. He erected images of Baal throughout the land and introduced the worship of Asherah in the high places. To encourage worship of the Assyrian gods, he stopped the temple sacrifices, put out the temple lamps, damaged several of the temple's sacred vessels and closed the doors. And when he did, praise to God was silenced. No more singing. His grace was no longeren. The fear of God faded. Worship ceased.

So Hezekiah opened the doors. Before establishing social and moral reforms, before restoring political power, before he did anything else he opened the doors to the temple and restored the worship of the God.

The next thing Hezekiah did was remove the filth from the temple. We read that in verses 16-17: "The priests went into the sanctuary of the Lord to purify it. They brought out to the courtyard of the Lord's temple everything unclean that they found in the temple of the Lord. The Levites took it and carried it out to the Kidron valley. They began the consecration on the first day of the first month, finishing on the sixteenth day of the first month." Under Ahaz the temple had fallen into disuse. Dirt, filth and stench accumulated. The gold no longer shone. The incense no longer filled the surrounding chambers with a sweet odor. Nothing was maintained. What was once a sanctuary filled with the glory of God's presence, was now nothing but a dirty, dusty, moldy, smelly shell filled with clutter and filth. God was no longer present there.

Hezekiah removed the filth. He employed 14 Levites and a number of priests and other workers. We don't know how many exactly, but it was an impressive crew. They went into the Holy of Holies to clean out the cobwebs and sweep out the dust. The heavy tapestry was no doubt cleaned and washed. The huge curtain covering the inner sanctuary was restored to its original beauty. The vessels were polished and the lamps trimmed and lit. They restored damaged sacred vessels and polished them to their original shine. They gathered up idols which had accumulated in the temple over the years. The altar was placed in its original position. The show bread was put back. It took them 16 days to clean and purify the temple. And when they were finished, the temple once again glittered. Its original splendor and beauty was restored.

Finally Hezekiah burned the garbage. We read that the priests carried the junk out of the temple and brought it to the Kidron valley. The Kidron valley was a burial sight just outside the city of Jerusalem, between its eastern walls and the Mount of Olives, but it had become a popular place where abominable things such as idols and cult objects were burned. Asa used the site to burn a lot of unclean stuff, so did Josiah, 100 years after Hezekiah. Jeremiah had prophesied that this place, the Kidron valley, would be holy to the Lord. Perhaps that prophecy was fulfilled when Jesus took his disciples through the valley over the brook Kidron, towards the garden of Gethsemane to pray shortly before his arrest and crucifixion. That is where Hezekiah burned the filth which had accumulated in the temple after years of defilement and disuse.

Hezekiah did not store the idols and cult objects left in the temple. He didn't use the garbage taken out of the temple in any way and didn't even recycle it. He got rid of it, burned it once and for all. His father Ahaz had desecrated the temple by placing idols and pagan altars in it, and by allowing filth and dirt to accumulate within the temple. But Hezekiah consecrated the temple by burning it all. He disposed of it, and that was an act of consecration. When it was done, the service of the temple could resume. Worship of God could continue.

Hezekiah did much more than clean house. He also cleansed the land. The high places and images, the Asherah poles and altars to pagan gods throughout Judah were destroyed. Hezekiah's reform was one of the most sweeping religious reforms in Judah's history. But it began by cleaning up the Lord's house. That's the story about Hezekiah cleaning house. It happened almost three thousand years ago, and yet it contains a lesson. There's a strong message in this story for us today.

The New Testament speaks about a temple too, not a building mad up of stone and wood — but a temple made up of believers like you and me. I Peter 2:5 says:

"Like living stones be yourselves built into a spiritual house." (I Peter 2:5)

And Ephesians 2:19–21 says believers are a structure built upon the foundation of the apostles and prophets, Christ Jesus being the cornerstone in whom the whole structure is joined together and grows into a holy temple in the Lord. The Old Testament temple no longer exists. It was but a shadow of the reality that has come in Christ. It only prefigured what we now see, the temple of all believers. The temple in Jerusalem foreshadowed God dwelling in and among his people. It has served its purpose and is obsolete.

Believers as a corporate body make up God's temple today. Believers individually are temples of the Holy Spirit. I Corinthians 3:16 says: "Do you not know that you are God's temple and that God's Spirit dwells in you?" And I Corinthians 6:19 says:

"Do you not know that your body is a temple of the Holy Spirit within you which you have from God?" We are God's temple now. You, an individual believer, are God's temple. (I Corinthians 6:19)

And so the question that 2 Chronicles 29 asks each of us today is, "What about that temple? What about you? Do you need to clean house? Does that temple, you, need some cleansing and purifying and consecrating?

Remember the first thing Hezekiah did? He opened the doors of the temple. Are the doors of your heart open to God? Many Christians have closed the doors of their hearts, and the worship of God is no longer that important to them. They have been attracted to other ideas, other ways of thinking about God. They have become interested in things other than the worship of God, lured away by worldly pleasures. They spend their time enjoying other activities, following other paths, setting other priorities. They have closed the temple doors; closed the doors of their heart and locked God out.

Perhaps some of you have done that. Just like the temple in Jerusalem, you have allowed the light of God's Spirit to go out. The incense of prayer no longer rises up to God in your life. You need to renew your love of God. You need to restore your relationship with him. Open the door of your heart and let God in again. That's where you need to begin.

The second thing Hezekiah did was carry the filth out of the temple. Many Christians allow garbage to accumulate in their lives. They fill their hearts and minds with impure thoughts and stack their shelves with unholy books or magazines. They load their VCR's and DVD players with unclean videos. They keep godless friends and frequent profane places. The lives of some Christians are dirty and cluttered with sins they enjoy too much. They don't shine any more. They don't radiate God's glory any more. Perhaps some of you are like that. Your thinking is clouded. Your understanding of God has become confused. Your commitment to him has become weak. As God's temple you don't sparkle anymore, because you haven't removed the filth from your life. You need cleansing. You need to let the purity and holiness of God shine in you again. You need to restore his splendor in your soul. Carry out the filth. Remove the dirt. Let God shine in you and through you again.

The last thing Hezekiah did was burn the garbage, remember? He disposed of it. I meet so many Christians who tell me they want to change, but they don't. They say they want to clean up their lives, but they commit the same sins. They hang on to the garbage and don't get rid of it. They may stop for awhile, but then they go back to the familiar places, read the same magazines, repeat the same lies, enjoy the same offensive images, tell the same unedifying jokes. They want to change, but they don't burn the garbage. Perhaps some of you are like that. You want to change but you don't. But if you want to be a temple of the Lord, you have to get rid of the garbage that defiles the temple once and for all. You can't just move it around. You can't store it somewhere for future reference. You can't recycle it into something more acceptable. You have to get rid of it. It's hard, but it is possible. If you really want to, God will help you. He'll even start the fire to burn it once and for all.

Brothers and sisters, there comes a point in all of our lives, when we need to clean house. Whatever it is that prevents us from shining as temples radiant with God's Spirit, we need to get rid of it. Whether it's a book, a thought, a boyfriend, a girlfriend, a habit, a bar, a fantasy, a desire, whatever it is, get rid of it. Whatever minimizes our devotion to God, whatever hinders our faith, whatever pulls us away from Christ, whatever defiles the temple, get rid of it. That stuff doesn't belong in your life. You are God's temple. God's Spirit dwells in you. You be careful what you do with his temple. "Sanctify yourselves and sanctify the house of the Lord", Hezekiah said, "and carry out the filth from this holy place." Destroy the garbage before it destroys you.

I have had to clean house many times in my life. Maybe this is your time to clean house. If it is, what better time than right now to do so. Open the doors of your heart. Carry the filth out of your life. And get rid of it once and for all. If and when you do, God's praise will echo in your heart again. God's glory will sparkle in and through your spirit. And God's presence will return to your soul. Isn't that what you want, child of God? I do.

Let us pray:

- Lord Jesus I long to be a perfect whole.
- I want Thee forever to live in my soul.
- Break down every idol, cast out every foe.
- Now wash me, and I will be whiter than snow.
- I plead the Blood of Jesus in my house!

Compulsive Hoarding

Compulsive hoarding is a common and potentially disabling problem, characterized by the accumulation of excessive clutter, to the point that parts of one's home can no longer be used for their intended purpose. Compulsive hoarding, which may affect up to 2 million people in the United States, is often found in patients with other diseases, including dementia, Alzheimer's, schizophrenia and anorexia. It's most often seen in patients with obsessive-compulsive disorder (OCD). Researchers aren't certain whether compulsive hoarding is a subtype of OCD or a separate disorder.

Is hoarding a kind of obsessive-compulsive disorder?

Right now, compulsive hoarding is considered by many researchers to be a type of obsessive-compulsive disorder. However, for some people, compulsive hoarding may also be related to:

- Impulse control disorders (such as impulsive buying or stealing)
- Depression
- Social anxiety
- Bipolar disorder
- Certain personality traits

How common is compulsive hoarding? What are its features?

- We don't know exactly. Some researchers have guessed that about half of one percent of the population suffers from compulsive hoarding, but the actual number may be much higher.

- People usually start hoarding during childhood or early adolescence, although the problem usually does not become severe until the person is an adult.

- Compulsive hoarding may run in families.

- Many people with compulsive hoarding do not recognize how bad the problem really is; often it is a family member who is most bothered by the clutter.

What causes compulsive hoarding?

Compulsive hoarding is thought to result from problems in one or more of these areas:

- **Information processing.** People with compulsive hoarding often have problems such as: Difficulty categorizing their possessions (for example, deciding what is valuable and what is not). Difficulty making decisions about what to do with possessions. Trouble remembering where things are (and so they often want to keep everything in sight so they don't forget).

- **Beliefs about possessions.** People with compulsive hoarding often: Feel a strong sense of emotional attachment toward their possessions (for example, an object might be felt to be very special, or a part of them). Feel a need to stay in control of their possessions (and so they don't want anyone touching or moving their possessions). Worry about forgetting things (and use their possessions as visual reminders).

- **Emotional distress about discarding.** People with compulsive hoarding often: Feel very anxious or upset when they have to make a decision about discarding things. Feel distressed when they see something they want and think they can't feel better until they ac-quire that object. Control their uncomfortable feelings by avoiding making the decision or putting it off until later.

Treatment for Compulsive Hoarding

There is no "cure" for compulsive hoarding, meaning there is no treatment that will make the problem go away completely and never come back at all. However, some treatments may help people to manage the symptoms more effectively.

Medications

Research studies using antidepressant medications (that increase the level of serotonin activity in the brain) show that some people with compulsive hoarding respond well to these medications, however, many do not. People with compulsive hoarding do not appear to respond as well to medications as do people with other kinds of obsessive-compulsive symptoms.

Cognitive-behavioral therapy

Cognitive-behavioral therapy is a form of counseling that goes beyond "just talking". In this form of treatment, the therapist often visits the person's home and helps them learn how to make decisions and think clearly about their possessions. There have not been as many studies of this kind of treatment, therefore it's hard to say with certainty how effective it is for hoarding. However, the available evidence suggests that cognitive-behavioral therapy is effective for many people with compulsive hoarding, perhaps more so than medications.

When a Loved One Hoards

In our hoarding clinic and research program, one of the most common inquiries we get is: "My (mother, father, sibling, friend, spouse, etc.) has a terrible hoarding problem. But he/she doesn't seem to recognize that it's a problem and isn't interested in doing anything about it. How can I make him/her see that this is a problem and get the help he/she so badly needs?"

The short answer: In most cases, you can't. That is, assuming that your loved one is an adult who is legally competent to manage his/her own affairs (meaning he/she has not been declared incompetent by a judge and appointed a legal guardian), and the clutter is not immediately life-threatening, he/she has the right to hoard, even though the hoarding might have terrible consequences for his/her quality of life.

The long answer: Even though in most cases you can't make the person do anything, you can alter your approach to minimize the likelihood of getting a defensive or "stubborn" reaction. Often, it's tempting to start arguing with the person, trying to persuade them to see things the way you do. This kind of direct confrontation rarely works.

We find that the best way to help people increase their motivation to work on the problem is to start with three key assumptions:

- Ambivalence is normal.

- People have a right to make their own choices.

- Nothing will happen until the person is ready to change.

Here are some general principles to guide your conversations:

Show empathy. Showing empathy doesn't necessarily mean that you agree with everything the person says. But it does mean you are willing to listen and to try to see things from the other person's perspective.

Don't Argue. There is simply no point in arguing about hoarding. The harder you argue, the more the person is likely to argue back. The only solution is to get out of the argument.

Respect Autonomy. Remember, most of you are dealing with an adult who has freedom of choice about his or her own possessions. Try to engage your loved one in a discussion (rather than an argument) about the home and his or her behavior. Ask your loved one what he or she wants to do, rather than just telling him or her what you want: "What do you think you would like to do about the clutter in the home?"; "How do you suggest we proceed?"

Help the person recognize that his/her actions are inconsistent with his/her greater goals or values. Ask the person about his or her goals and values: "What's really important to you in life?"; "How would you like your life to be five years from now?"; "What are your hopes and goals in life?" Discuss whether or not the person's acquiring, or difficulty organizing, or getting rid of things fit with those goals and values. This is most effective if you ask, rather than tell: "How does the condition of your home fit with your desire to be a good grandmother?"; "You've told me that friendships are very important to you, how well can you pursue that goal, given the way things are right now?"

If you have been accustomed to arguing, threatening, and blaming, your new approaches will surprise your loved one and it may take a little time before the person begins to trust you. Try these methods in several conversations and notice whether the balance seems to be tilting in the right direction. If so, be patient and keep up the good work.

Compulsive Hoarding and 6 Tips to Help

Hoarding belongs to a syndrome which also includes:

- Indecisiveness

- Perfectionism

- Procrastination

- Avoidance behaviors

- Difficulty organizing tasks

Interesting stats: hoarding obsessions and compulsions are present in approximately 30 percent of OCD cases. However, as a group, OCD-affected individuals with hoarding symptoms have a more severe illness, a greater prevalence of anxiety disorders, and a greater prevalence of personality disorders than people with OCD who don't have hoarding symptoms. Hoarders are often less responsive to treatment than non-hoarding OCD patients.

Six anti-clutter strategies for compulsive hoarders:

1. **Make immediate decisions about mail and newspapers.** Go through mail and newspapers on the day you receive them and throw away unwanted materials immediately. Don't leave anything to be decided on later.

2. **Think twice about what you allow into your home.** Wait a couple of days after seeing a new item before you buy it. And when you do purchase something new, discard another item you own to make room for it.

3. **Set aside 15 minutes a day to declutter.** Start small—with a table, perhaps, or a chair—rather than tackling the entire, overwhelming house at once. If you start to feel anxious, take a break and do some deep-breathing or relaxation exercises.

4. **Dispose of anything you have not used in a year.** That means old clothes, broken items, and craft projects you'll never finish. Remind yourself that many items are easily replaceable if you need them later.

5. **Follow the "Make a Decision" rule.** Only Handle It Once. If you pick something up, make a decision then and there about it, and either put it where it belongs or discard it. Don't fall into the trap of moving things from one pile to another, again and again.

6. **Ask for help if you can't do it on your own.** If you feel these strategies are impossible to carry out and you cannot cope with the problem on your own, seek out a mental health professional.

7. **Pray and Ask God.** Pray and ask God to help you to remove that stronghold.

Chapter #3:

The Ministry Of Living Single

Finding balance as a single parent is not easy. Anyone who is single with children knows just how hectic things can get. In addition to being exceptionally busy, you will find that things seem to be going in a million directions at once. To be the best single parent possible while salvaging your own sanity, it is essential that you find a way to balance life.

For starters, when people offer to help, accept it. Sometimes, we have so much pride that we simply feel we cannot ask for or accept help. The bottom line is that to balance life as a single parent, you need to let friends and family help. For instance, if you have a family member that offers to take your kids for an afternoon so you can get some things done, let them. If a friend offers to come over to fix dinner, let her.

In addition, I recommend that you take full advantage of your local resources. In this case, you will find several outlets where you live that can make life easier and more enjoyable. You might consider finding a mommy's day out organization whereby the kids are enrolled in various activities so you can have a day to yourself. In addition, many communities have groups that involve both mom and the children for some much-needed fun. Remember, especially after a divorce, you need to have quality time with the kids when things are not running at 100 miles per hour.

Finally, make sure you have real time for you. Unfortunately, most single moms always put the kids first, which is admirable but also not reasonable. You should never feel guilty about having a manicure or pedicure, going to the gym, taking time out for lunch with a friend, and even dating. Unless your stress level is reduced, things in the home will be chaotic. Instead, you can still provide well for your children but you also need to provide well for you but without the guilt.

Dealing With The Challenge Of Life As A Single Parent

Single parents suffer enormous challenges full of stresses. If remedial steps are not taken to balance their lives, the situation will only continue to worsen with no way to get out. They play multifaceted roles of father, mother, provider, driver, cook and the list goes no. Their work hours can be from dusk to dawn without a break. They juggle from home to work detouring to the day care centers to drop and pick the children before and after work. What should they do to balance their lives?

Start with a good support system consisting of family, friends, neighbors, parents of friends of the children, church, hospital or clinic etc. The immediate family sticks together thick and thin. Usually protocol is not needed to ask them to take care of the children or to run errands or to seek for help in the day to day life.

Research and find the nearby hospital or clinic that is willing to take care of sick children who may not have a serious problem. Though this service may be at a cost at least there is peace of mind to be able to go to work when your child is ill, knowing the child is in good care. Look out for jobs that give the flexibility to work around the Single Parent's schedule. Some employers may even be willing to permit work from home.

Children too will have their own schedule. It may not be possible for the Single Parent to attend all the events of their children if they have other children who are too small to attend. Have a network of other single parents so that they may be prepared to watch the children in order to go for at least some of the events if not for all. As the children grow their activities may also be extended to after school hours. Transportation will pose a problem unless support of other parents are sought to car pool and take turns. Parents should communicate to the children the transport arrangements. A white board detailing the weekly program indicating the relative information may be a good idea. That way there will be no confusion. Parents and children should be aware of each other's daily program and have the easy access telephone numbers to each other.

Single parents must find ways to have fun with their children without having to spend too much money. It is important that children do not miss out on their childhood activities and spend quality family time. Absence of one parent should not be a deterrent to these factors.

Last but not least, the parent too must find time for herself to do things she likes without the children. A time away from them will give added strength and energy. These are some of the ways for single parents to balance their hectic lives.

Balancing Tips For Single Moms

As a single mom, many women have to balance active children and the home. When I was single, I had one full time job and one part-time job. While that probably sounds like it should have driven me crazy trying to keep up, I actually did a pretty decent job of balancing work and my family's home life just by using the following tips.

Get organized. Using a calendar located in a visible place for everyone helps plan meals and keeps track of activities. I bought a cheap desk calendar and plan out meals usually two weeks at a time so that I can buy the biggest share of my groceries every two weeks. Planning meals like this not only helps us know what we are having for dinner every night but helps me budget my groceries because I only buy what I need. I will jot down my children's activities so they both know what they have going on each day.

Leave work issues at work. You should never bring problems at work home with you. I have learned over the years that it doesn't do any good to bring home your worries from work. If you must bring it home, make it a point to talk about it for a brief period of time and then let it go. My main goal when I'm at home is to focus on my children and my time at home. I spend so little time at home that I want to focus on it when I am there. As a role model for my children, I want to be a positive person in their lives and focus what is best for them.

Get help. Enlist the help of your children as a means of getting household chores done. No matter how old they are they can help do something so there is more play time for all of those in the house. As my children have gotten older, I have started assigning them more chores. They are just as capable of doing some of the things around the house as I am, and if they help me get things done, then we will have more time to do things together as a family.

Find ways to relax. Figure out a hobby or something that helps you relieve stress when the going gets too tough. When the stress gets to be too bad for me to handle, I do some writing, journaling or sometimes even some scrapbooking; I cuddle up with a good book in bed to help me sleep. If I just really want to vent, I would either call a good friend or my mom. After a busy week, you and your children may like to relax with a movie night and/or a game night.

Keep the faith. Stay encouraged and focused. As Christians, we understand that Romans 8:28 tells us that all things work together for our good. I like to remind myself everyday that nothing can stop the favor of the Lord!

Chapter #4:

Ministry Of Your Marriage

Your marriage is important to God. He is expecting both spouses to minister to each other. Marriage was created to help you to stay in God's will. If marriage is done successfully, it will actually help you to stay saved and keep your natural needs satisfied and your spiritual needs supported. Although in Christ, God does not see male or female, but in the home, God has required that there is an order and individual roles. Because men and women don't always relate their emotions and thoughts in the same manner, it becomes challenging to operate within these roles at times. Let's take a closer look at understanding the differences between men and women.

Difference Between Men And Women

Genesis chapter 1, beginning in verse 26:

Then God said, let us make man in our image, in our likeness, and let them rule over the birds of the air, over the livestock, over all the earth, and over all the creatures that move along the ground. So God created man in his own image; in the image of God he created him; male and female he created them. (King James Bible - Genesis 1:26-27)

This passage implies that two aspects of God's image found in humans are that we are created to rule, and that we are created to be in relationship. Thus, in some sense our sexuality is a reflection of the image of God. Now turn to chapter 2, in which we will read verses 7, 15, 18, and 21-25:

The Lord God formed the man from the dust of the ground and breathed into his nostrils the breath of life, and the man became a living being. . . 15 the Lord God took the man and put them in the Garden of Eden to serve* it and watch* over* it. . .18 The Lord God said, 'It is not good for the man to be alone. I will make a helper suitable for him.'. . 21 So the Lord God caused God caused the man to fall into a deep sleep; and while he was sleeping, he took one of the man's ribs and closed up the place with flesh. Then the LORD God made a woman from the rib he had taken out of the man, and he brought her to the man. The man said, WOW*, this is now bone of my bones and flesh of my flesh; she shall be called woman for she was taken out of the man. For this reason a man will leave his father and his mother and hold* fast* to his wife, and they will become one flesh. The man and his wife were both naked, and they felt no shame.

This is all we know about man and woman in God's perfect creation. The very next verse describes the temptation that leads to the fall. So what can we discern from these verses?

First of all, note the relationship between Adam and Eve. The man & woman were in a perfectly intimate relationship. There was no hiding, there were no barriers between them. The man is to "hold fast" to his wife. This Hebrew word, traditionally translated "cleave", is not a sexual term in this context. In several places in the Old Testament the same word is used commanding the Israelites to "hold fast" to God. It signifies the unity of man and wife, the degree of commitment and bonding between them. The next phrase, becoming one flesh, is clearly sexual, but also how much more!

Second, what does this passage tell us of the differences between man and woman in the perfect created order? There is no definitive theology here, but there are several intriguing hints. I would like to propose that this passage suggests that MAN IS PRIMARILY FUNCTIONAL IN ORIENTATION while WOMAN IS PRIMARILY RELATIONAL IN ORIENTATION. What do I mean by "functional" and "relational?" Man is functional because he receives his greatest satisfaction from performing a task or accomplishing a deed. Woman is relational because she receives her greatest satisfaction from building up of relationships. There are at least three hints or clues that suggest this conclusion:

HINT 1: What material is used to create the man and the woman? Man is made of an inanimate substance -- dust -- while woman is made from part of another person.

HINT 2: What tasks are they assigned? For what purpose was each of them created? In verse 15, man is put in the garden to "work" or "serve" it; to "take care of" or "watch over" it. It is interesting to note that man was created to "serve" and "guard" the creation. This word translated "work" in the New International Version that I have rendered "serve" is the same word that God uses when he speaks through Moses to Pharaoh saying "Let my people go that they may serve me in the desert." Man's relationship to creation is not domineering, but one of tending, serving, and guarding.

Well, what is the task of the woman? She is created, in verse 18, as a "helper suitable" for the man. The word translated "helper" is a military term; "ally" is a possible translation. But in the Old Testament the word usually refers to God, frequently coupled with "shield", "My help and my shield." Psalm 121 includes these well-known verses that shed some light on the meaning of the word: "I will lift up mine eyes unto the hills. From whence cometh my help? My help cometh from the Lord who made heaven and earth." Thus, this word does not imply any difference in importance, or any type of hierarchy between man and woman. The difference is in focus. Man's focus tends to be on the created order; woman's focus tends to be on serving people.

HINT 3: For hint number three we need to turn to chapter 3 and the results of the fall. As we read, note that the results for each are frustration & pain in their primary area of focus: relationships for the woman, working creation for the man. We read beginning in verse 16:

> To the woman he said, "I will greatly increase your pains in childbearing; with pain you will give birth to children. Your desire will be for your husband, and he will rule over you." To Adam he said, "Because you listened to your wife and ate from the tree about which I commanded you, 'You must not eat of it,' cursed is the ground because of you; thru painful toil you will eat of it all the days of your life. It will produce thorns and thistles for you and you will eat the plants of the field. By the sweat of your brow you will eat the food until you return to the ground, since from it you were taken. For dust you are, and to dust you will return." (King James Bible - Genesis 3:16-19)

Let's consider the woman first. As a result of her sin, she will experience frustration and difficulty in her family relationships, both with her children and with her husband. The phrase "your desire will be for your husband" is talking not about sexual desire but about the desire to dominate and control. Note that the same phraseology is used by God in speaking to Cain in chapter 4 verse 7: "Sin is crouching at the door; it desires to have you, but you must master it." This interpretation is supported by the next phrase "yet he will rule over you." The woman will experience frustration in her marriage, in which she will desire to dominate and control her husband, but in the end he will dominate and rule over her. Now, have we seen the word "rule" used with regard to the man and the woman prior to this? No. Man's rule over woman is a result of the fall, part of the frustration that woman experiences after that event. This is not a command to man "you shall rule." As we shall see later, this is not a prescription for a Biblical marriage.

Well, what about the results of the fall for man? His frustration, his toil, is with respect to the created order, the ground. Thus, if this functional/relational difference between man and woman is correct, God points out to each of them that their sin will hurt them in the very area they care about the most. This is the essence of sin; we hurt and destroy what we love and want most.

Let me emphasize that these functional/relational differences between men and women are differences on a continuum; relationships and function are both important to all of us. Each of us is at a different point on the continuum; the differences between men and women are true in general, not necessarily for every two individuals. I encourage you to reflect on your own experience, and see if this perspective makes sense in understanding yourself and members of the opposite sex. Most of all, I encourage you to search the Scriptures to see if these things are true, to dig more deeply into this and other passages in order to figure out what God tells us about differences between men and women.

Characteristics Of A Godly Marriage

What is the relationship between husband and wife in a marriage founded on Biblical principle? Let's look at Ephesians, chapter 5, verse 18. We will mainly be looking at the section beginning in verse 21, but notice that Paul gives us the command to "Be filled with the Spirit" in verse 18. In the Greek, the next 3 verses are a continuation of this sentence as Paul tells us four ways we exhibit this filling of the Spirit: speaking to one another, singing & making music in our hearts, giving thanks in everything, and then, in verse 21, "submitting to one another out of reverence for Christ." Note that each of us is to submit to other believers; this is part of being filled with the Spirit, part of becoming Christ-like. Submission is not a topic for wives only; it is an appropriate attitude for every Christian as it is so clearly exhibited in Christ himself.

Paul now explains how this idea of mutual submission works itself out in the home, first with regard to wives and husbands, then with regard to parents and children. As we read this section, note how, if you accept the functional relational differences between men and women, Paul's command to the wife is to do what is hardest for her; Paul's command to the husband is to do what is hardest for him. Let's read beginning in verse 22:

> Wives, submit to your husbands as to the Lord. For the husband is the head of the wife as Christ is the head of the church, his body, of which he is the Savior. Now as the church submits to Christ, so also wives should submit to their husbands in everything. Husbands, love your wives just as Christ loved the church and gave himself up for her to make her holy, cleansing her by the washing with water through the word, and to present her TO HIMSELF as a radiant church, without stain or wrinkle or any other blemish, but holy and blameless. In this same way, husbands ought to love their wives as their own bodies. He who loves his wife loves himself. After all, no one ever hated his own body, but he feeds and cares for it, just as Christ does the church -- for we are members of his body. "For this reason a man will leave his father and mother and be united to his wife, and the two will become one flesh." This is a profound mystery -- but I am talking about Christ and the church. However, each one of you also must love his wife as he loves himself, and the wife must respect her husband. (King James Bible - Ephesians 5:22-33)

Paul commands the wife to submit to and respect her husband. He tells the husband to love his wife. Why doesn't he instruct the wife to love her husband? Because, for a woman, loving her husband is relatively easy. But as we saw in Genesis 3, "her desire shall be for her husband," she desires to dominate and control her husband. So submitting to and respecting the husband are frequently a woman's hardest tasks.

Well, what about this word, "submission?" What does it really mean? The Greek word is a military term, and a military analogy may help us to understand it better. Imagine a case in which a nation is fighting a war, and two army corps have been fighting in separate locations, under two generals of the same rank. The commander-in-chief instructs the two army corps to come together to do battle with the enemy at a particular location. In such a situation, the commander-in-chief must name one of the two as commanding general of the engagement. The other must submit to the leadership of the commanding general. Now, the commanding general, if he is wise, will seek the counsel of his subordinate. He will listen to his subordinate's advice, especially to that general's assessment of the qualities and capabilities of the units under his command. Ideally the two generals will agree on an overall plan for the engagement. But if they do not, in the end the commanding general must assume responsibility and decide on the course of action to be taken. The subordinate general must submit, even if he is convinced that the chosen course of action is a mistake. Why should he submit? Not because the commanding general is smarter, wiser, or more senior than he, although he may be; not because the commanding general's plan is superior to his, although it may be; but he submits because the commander-in-chief, with the good of the country in mind, has placed him under the command of his fellow general. What happens if the subordinate general disobeys orders, and tries to carry out his own plan? The two corps will act in an uncoordinated fashion, and then the enemy is likely to defeat the two parts of the army one by one, leading to disaster for the country.

This is the true meaning of "submission." There is no implied difference in worth or ability, just as the two generals may have been of the same rank and skill. Instead, submission implies that one person voluntarily agrees to follow the leadership of another for the good of everyone concerned. This point becomes obvious when we consider how the word is used elsewhere in the New Testament. Christians are told to submit to the government, at a time when they were living under despotic rulers like Nero. Jesus submits to the Father; indeed, Jesus is said to have been in submission to his earthly parents. Clearly, Jesus was not inferior to his parents. Christians of that era were clearly more righteous than those governing them. Nevertheless, the Bible tells us that submission was the proper attitude in each case. Thus, submission for the wife means that she willingly acknowledges the headship of her husband over her, and has confidence in God that He has set this authority over her for her own good.

Turning now to husbands, tell me if this is what Paul says: "Rule over your wives with an iron fist; make her obey your every whim." Is this what Paul says? Not at all. Instead, Paul tells husbands to love their wives, How? "As Christ loved the church!" How did Christ love the church? He gave himself up for her, he died for her, he poured himself out for her. And what was the result of this sacrifice on his part? He presented "TO HIMSELF a radiant church without stain or blemish." And this happens to us also. One of the central paradoxical truths of Christianity is that those who seek to please themselves in the end are the most miserable, and those who seek to serve others in the end are the most blessed. Husbands who serve their wives selflessly, who build up their wives spiritually, will usually end up with a beautiful, fulfilling marriage that will more than meet their every need.

Now, where did Paul put all the words about "headship" and "submission?" Did he tell husbands "make sure that your wives acknowledge your headship and submit to you?" Did he tell wives "nag your husband whenever he is not acting selflessly towards you?" Not at all. Each partner is to check him or her self. Further, as we pointed out when looking at Genesis, note that there is no mention of the husband "ruling" over the wife anywhere in this passage. In many ways these injunctions to the marriage partners are parallel. The emphasis is different because of the differences between men and women outlined above, but essentially the two partners are to have the same attitude towards each other. Neither partner is to try to ensure that his or her needs are met, or to stand up for his or her rights. Neither partner should be badmouthing or telling demeaning stories about the spouse when out with friends. Each should be looking out for the other's welfare, looking for ways to serve the spouse, building each other up, seeking advice from each other, not dominating or trying to dominate.

One more point that is frequently misunderstood: the passage does NOT say: Wives IF YOUR HUSBAND LOVES YOU AS CHRIST LOVED THE CHURCH, then submit to him. Nor does it say: Husbands, IF YOUR WIFE SUBMITS TO YOUR HEADSHIP, then love her. These actions on our part are to be unconditional. Other Scriptures make this point obvious. 1 Timothy discusses the case of a believing wife and an unbelieving husband, saying that her submission could lead to her husband becoming a believer. The first chapters of Hosea tell the opposite story, that of a faithful husband and a wife who has become a prostitute. God has Hosea actually go and buy back his wife at the slave market when she has sunk as low as she can go -- thus exhibiting the same type of love that God shows to us. So our love for our husbands or wives is to be unconditional.

Now, what does this mean for a dysfunctional marriage? Clearly it does not imply that a woman should continue to take physical abuse from her husband. Nor does it imply that a spouse must continue to live with a partner who is continually engaged in sexual relationships outside the marriage. As James Dobson says, "Love must be tough;" sometimes love requires that we take severe action. At times this may require physical separation until such time as a correct marriage relationship can be resumed. But the point of the passage is that all such decisions are made not because of the welfare of the individual alone, but considering the welfare of the marriage partner even more highly than one's own.

Your Husband

Your husband is your Ministry. He needs your time, your labor, and your body. As women God has made us uniquely strong.

> *Kelly is a 32 year old Godly woman with three children. She is married to a 36 year old Minister named Sam. Both Kelly and Sam have jobs, hold positions in church, and are parents to young children. Kelly's weekly schedule consist of taking the kids to school, helping them with homework, cooking dinner, cleaning the house, going to work, choir rehearsal, bible study, missionary meeting, and she takes at least one days out of the month to get her hair, nails, and toes done. Where does she find time to spend with her husband? His needs are important and he is also a part of her Ministry.*

Kelly cannot just say I don't have time to address my husband's needs. As a Godly woman, she must communicate with her husband concerning the areas of need to assist her with time management. Kelly may ask Sam to assist with taking the children to school. She may consider cooking less throughout the week or having Sam assist in some way. Kelly should also consider not being on so many auxiliaries in the church while her children are still young and in need of her attention. Working together can make it possible for goals to be accomplished. If Sam is not interested in contributing in some way to assist Kelly with her overwhelming task, then they must seek wise counsel or the marriage will become strained and could possibly be in jeopardy. Neither Sam nor Kelly will be fulfilled if the husband and wife do not find a way to meet each other's needs by Ministering to each other; both spiritually, affectionately and sexually.

We live in a very difficult time where it actually takes two incomes to survive and properly care for a family with children. We know God is a provider, but wisdom affords us to understand we live in a different day. Because of this reality, most wives work as well as their husbands. Husbands need to step-up and share responsibilities when it comes to household chores, but this does not take away from your roles as husband and wife. Most husbands like to rest after working an eight hour job and relax by taking a shower, eating and enjoying some down time. Wives would like to enjoy this same luxury, but often find themselves working a second job when they get home; cooking dinner, doing laundry, helping with homework, cleaning the house, preparing children for school the next day, as well as sexually gratifying their husbands. Wives need help!!! Many wives decide to neglect some of these areas because they are overworked and underappreciated. If husbands will step-up and challenge themselves to be more helpful in these areas, a team is formed and life becomes more comprehensive and workable. It takes not only two financially, but two people working together as a team in the home (Chores) as well. Instead of getting frustrated, wives should sit down with their husbands and communicate their frustrations in a loving way and give their husbands clear instructions on how they can support and help the family unit. Most men don't take hints, so it's best to be clear and honest with them. Sometimes you don't get help, because you don't ask, in a loving way.

The Bible tells us that "There is a time for everything under heaven." Ask God to help you to see how you can take the time to connect with each other in meaningful ways. "Couples need to make the most of little opportunities, even if it's only 10 to 20 minutes here or there. If couples wait for the semiannual vacation trip to connect, they will drift apart, two weeks a year is not enough together time. To keep their marriage healthy, couples need to connect every day (even if it's just finding 'pockets of time where we can' together). Even "pockets of time" that you take together, a cup of coffee here, a walk together there, even going out for a quick ice cream cone or a soda where you intentionally make the time to connect together can help.

Have you noticed how you drift away from your spouse when you don't make time to talk and interact on purpose, not just out of necessity? Have you noticed how you drift away from God when you forget to pray and are so busy you don't make time to meet with Him? Just as we need to be intentional in our relationship with God to mature spiritually, we have to do the same in our marriages to grow closer to our spouse.

So, in order to bridge the gap between you, here are 10 tips for making time together. It tells you what to do when you do find the time:

How to Spend More Time Together

In order to discuss how to spend time together, you must first agree that you need to spend tine together. I know that sounds overly simplistic, but this is where so many couples falter. To keep from failing before you get out of the gate, you must commit to spending time together no matter what. Just as a house does not clean itself and a checkbook doesn't automatically balance, nor does a marriage remain passionate and a husband and a wife stay connected if they do not give and make the time to be together.

If that is the marriage you want, then before you read any further, I implore you and your spouse to hold hands, look each other in the eye, and say, "Babe, let's walk together every morning; let's commit to making time to be together." Write it down; date it. Now, let's make it happen.

<u>Training Tips</u>

One of the vital things you must do after deciding to spend time together is commit to protecting that time from all invaders and marauders, which include the phone, work, household chores, and yes, the children. As you are training yourselves to spend time together, you must train the kids, as well. The "Three B Rule" When the parents are having some "connecting time," the kids can only interrupt, if someone is *bleeding*, someone is *broken*, or something is *burning*. Beyond that, they must wait to talk to the parents.

For those of you without children, the task of making time can still be difficult. Since the wedding is over, you may be more inclined to take the marriage for granted while focusing on careers, a house, or hobbies. The earlier you start training to spend regular time together, the easier and more effective you will be when future stealers of your couple time arrive. Now, you've decided to make time to be together and to protect it from all intrusion; what's next?

10 TIPS for making time together:

1. **Mark your calendar with a specific time.** You must set this up just like a business or dentist appointment. If you just say, "Let's spend some time together tonight," those great time-thwarters such as the stacks of mail, laundry, and dishes will rob you.

2. **Make one day a week your calendar time.** This is a time when you plan your together times for the week. It can be simply ten to fifteen minutes to arrange calendars, but it is where you *write down* when you will connect during the coming week. Sunday nights work well.

3. **Plan different types of time.** There needs to be time simply talking about our days, time for conflict resolution, and *fun only* times (dates, cuddles, walks) that we protect from any type of conflict.

4. **Implement a set of rules.** Turn off cell phones, and TVs. If your kids are old enough, talk to them about what Mom and Dad are going to do. It will teach them much for their own future marriages as well as give them security in yours.

5. **Find a specific place.** In the winter, my husband and I like sitting in front of the fireplace; in the summer, it's on the porch (both times while the kids clean the kitchen). Bedrooms can be a good place to talk but I encourage you to not let the bedroom become a place of conflict resolution; it should be a place of intimate connecting. The symbolism is important.

6. **Establish goals.** Answer, "Why do we want to spend time together?" From that, you realize that you really do want the same thing, a fun, emotionally intimate marriage.

7. **Protect, protect, protect.** Too many clients leave my office vowing to spend time together, only to return several days later without having done it once. They let other things invade. Instead of training to run, they ate Twinkies.

8. **Drop defensiveness.** Research has shown that couples in conflict are more prone to interpret their mate's comments and actions in a negative way, even when their mate meant them as neutral or even positive. Believe the best about your partner; remember, you both want the same thing, a good marriage.

9. **Be realistic.** Saying you will spend time together seven days a week will frustrate you and eventually cause you to give up. There should be a brief "How are you?" connection every day, but as far as carving out twenty to thirty minutes to share your heart, three to four days per week is more realistic.

10. **Don't give up.** Keep working to make it happen. A marathoner has to get over the soreness and get into a routine, but once established, it is easier to keep the training going. I'm convinced that the single biggest contributor to the breakdown in relationships today is the fact that couples aren't spending enough time together. They aren't making their relationships a number one priority. The relationship gets put on the back burner. Everything else seems more important - careers, children, hobbies, community involvement, and personal pursuits. And when relationships aren't attended to as they should be, trouble sets in. People who don't prioritize their relationships tell me that they often end up fighting during the little time they do have together. They argue about day to day issues; unpaid bills, unclean houses, unruly children. And it's no wonder. It's difficult to do what needs to be done to keep life moving in a productive direction, let alone try to coordinate your efforts with your partner's when you're under a time crunch. But the truth is, arguing about "who's doing what around the house," is really just a symptom of deeper problems - isolation, loneliness and resentment. You argue about the mundane issues when your emotional needs aren't being met. The coke can left in the living room becomes a symbol of a lack of caring for you. And here's the Catch-22. If you and your spouse are arguing a lot, you don't feel like spending time together. In fact, you want to spend as little time as possible with him or her. Unfortunately, avoidance only makes matters worse. More distance, more tension, less cooperation, more conflict, and so on.

Some couples who don't prioritize their relationships don't argue when they're together. They simply have little to do with each other. They resign themselves to the distance and experience bouts of resentment from time to time. Leading parallel but separate lives, they start to fall out of love with each other or become strangers. "I just don't love him anymore," she says. Or, "We've just grown apart," says he. Distance in relationships is love's silent killer.

But there's good news in all of this. Time together can be the great healer. Even if it's awkward at first, when two people commit to investing energy and time in their love life, only good things can come from it. When people put their relationships first, they feel appreciated and important. They feel loved. Spending time with your partner tells him or her in no uncertain terms, "You matter to me." Time together gives people opportunities to collect new memories, do activities they enjoy, and laugh at each other's jokes, to renew their love.

You don't have to spend enormous amounts of time together to breed closeness and connection. Regular, brief get-togethers work too. Sometimes people think that nothing short of a total revamping of their lives would be necessary to find time together, but it simply isn't so. Small changes in your schedule can make a huge difference. And, whatever you do, don't leave "rendezvousing" up to chance. You need to plan and schedule dates together.

Relationships are a serious business. Here are some more do's and don'ts:

- If you have kids, do leave them at home. You and your spouse need time alone. The best thing you can do for your kids is make your marriage work.

- Don't waste time trying to figure out whose fault it is that you haven't been spending time together. It really doesn't matter.

- Don't let angry feelings get in the way of making plans with your partner. Research shows that the fastest way to change how you feel is by taking action. Doing something enjoyable together will make you and your partner feel more loving. As a result, you may even be able to resolve heated topics more easily in the future.

- Don't think you have to go to a tropical island to make time together meaningful. You don't have to spend a lot of money to show your love for your partner. Go for a walk around the block. Read a novel together. Set aside ten minutes each day to talk. Ride a bike. Be creative.

- Finally, always keep in mind that there's little that's more important in life than loving people and having them love you back. Give the gift of your time. It will be well worth your while.

Your husband needs his wife to be a virtuous woman. Proverbs 31:11-12 "The heart of her husband doth safely trust in her, so that he shall have no need of spoil. She will do him good and not evil all the days of her life." Proverbs 12:4 "A virtuous woman is a crown to her husband: but she that maketh ashamed is as rottenness in his bones." (King James Bible – Proverbs)

The Power Of A Mood Setter

As women we have the power to set the mood in our house. I have often noticed that no matter how frazzled or grumpy my husband might be when he walks through the door, all I have to say is "I have been thinking of you all day long, come here and give me a big kiss." Wow, his mood changes from night to day. Sometimes as women, we don't realize the power we have to show love, nurture, and support. To our families, setting the atmosphere is essential. We all know that when the wife is not happy, the entire family is not happy. Part of our Ministry is to set the mood within our homes. I challenge you to speak only positive words within your home and watch the results manifest right before your eyes. Your children and your husband will respond to you in a much more positive way. Also remember that you are his help mate. God made you for him; he needs you!

Some people think because the husband is the head of the wife, which means he has a right to be the boss and keep her in line. Well the Scriptures teach that the husband is the head of his wife, but there is more to be said. Let us explore this important Bible teaching. Let's ask the question, "How should a husband treat his wife?" Marriage is one of the great gifts God has given to man. I can think of nothing more precious than a husband and wife who have lived their whole lives in a covenant of love and marriage. All marriages have their problems, but I am convinced that when two people love God and love each other they will be able to live together "till death do they part." When people pursue their marriages on God's terms and keep God's laws, they find that their marriages are happy and fulfilling. Here we are focusing on how husbands should treat their wives in the marriage relationship.

The apostle Paul gives us God's description of marriage in Ephesians 5:22-33: Wives, submit to your own husbands, as to the Lord. For the husband is the head of the wife even as Christ is the head of the church, his body, and is himself its Savior. Now as the church submits to Christ, so also wives should submit in everything to their husbands. Husbands, love your wives, as Christ loved the church and gave himself up for her, that he might sanctify her, having cleansed her by the washing of water with the word, so that he might present the church to himself in splendor, without spot or wrinkle or any such thing, that she might be holy and without blemish. In the same way husbands should love their wives as their own bodies. He who loves his wife loves himself. For no one ever hated his own flesh, but nourishes and cherishes it, just as Christ does the church, because we are members of his body. "Therefore a man shall leave his father and mother and hold fast to his wife, and the two shall become one flesh." This mystery is profound, and I am saying that it refers to Christ and the church. However, let each one of you love his wife as himself, and let the wife see that she respects her husband. The Scriptures clearly teach that the husband is the head of his wife, and she is to be subject to him. In our day, when equality seems to be so important, some people think this is unfair, that God gave authority to husbands over their wives. But the idea that this authority somehow gives the man the right to abuse or dominate his wife in an unkind way is not the will of God. Any man who treats the woman he married unkindly is acting very foolishly. He is not only disobeying God, he is deceiving himself. Only an unwise person could think that abusing his wife will be a benefit to him. Wise husbands know that the better they treat their wives, the more their wives will respond with love and respect. When husbands fail to love their wives, their wives react with behavior that shows a lack of respect. When husbands sense a lack of respect from their wives, they often act in ways that are unloving. So these feelings of being disrespected and unloved tear apart the marriage. But when husbands show love and wives show respect, the marriage prospers and develops.

You can make your marriage brighter and better, husbands, if you can learn to demonstrate Christian love to your wife. IF a disrespected husband will love his wife anyway, and if a woman who feels unloved will respect her husband anyway, they can together start putting that marriage back together. A wise husbands pays attention to his wife. He is able to see the things that she and every woman need to find happiness in this life. Every woman needs to feel that her husband is close to her and cares about her. Many husbands keep their distance from their wives, and their wives feel unloved because of it. Wives need husbands who will open up enough to share his thoughts and feelings with her. She feels unwanted or unneeded when he closes up and shuts her out of his life. When he keeps his life secret from her, she feels he doesn't love her enough to trust her. Wives need to know their husbands are loyal to the marriage, that he is not looking elsewhere. She also needs to know he sees her as the most important person in his life (except for God). She needs to know that he cherishes and honors her. The most important thing a husband can do is love his wife. 1 Corinthians 13:4-8 says, "Love is patient and kind; love does not envy or boast; it is not arrogant or rude. It does not insist on its own way; it is not irritable or resentful; it does not rejoice at wrongdoing, but rejoices with the truth. Love bears all things, believes all things, hopes all things, endures all things. Love never ends." Love may start with a warm feeling, but we have to learn how to love our wives; and wives have to learn how to love their husbands. Some folks are harder to love than others, and love will require lots of patience and kindness. Love demands that we set "self" aside. I cannot love someone else if selfishness and self-centeredness is my way. Love rules out envy, arrogance and rudeness. It learns to let small things slide and not be irritated all the time. Love puts up with a lot of demands, believes and hopes the best for others, and endures. Love is the determination to put the best interests of another before our own, regardless of the cost. Jesus loved the church like that, and He asks husbands to love their wives that way. Loving your wife involves taking the time to be close to her and to listen to her. The happiest couples spend time with each other, talking and listening to each other. Husbands and wives should spend a good while each day in meaningful conversation. Turn the television off, get away from the computer, and talk face to face.

A wise husband will take the time share his life with the woman he loves. He wants to know about her and is willing to invest his life in her by listening. To fail to pay attention to your wife is to say to her that you do not care what she has to say. Such behavior is abusive not loving.

James said in James 1:19-20, "Know this, my beloved brothers: let every person be quick to hear, slow to speak, slow to anger; for the anger of man does not produce the righteousness that God requires."

Much of the anger in our homes would go away if people would take the time to listen and understand the people they love. Listen to your spouse, let her finish her sentences, don't act rashly or hastily. Try to understand her life from her point of view.

Treat her with kindness 1 Peter 3:7 says: "Likewise, husbands, live with your wives in an understanding way, showing honor to the woman as the weaker vessel, since they are heirs with you of the grace of life, so that your prayers may not be hindered."

Some husbands have the awful attitude that because they are the head of the wife, that this position of authority gives them the right to dominate or abuse their wives with their power. Any man who treats his wife like a doormat is violating the will of God. Abusive power is a marriage killer. Husbands, treat your wife kindly, tell your wife how important and valuable she is to you. Watch for the loving smile on her face when you do! The Proverbs writer said, "An excellent wife, who can find? For her worth is far above jewels. The heart of her husband trusts in her, and he will have no lack of gain." (Proverbs 31:10-11). Notice how the wise husband trusts his wife's judgments and realizes how fortunate he is to have her. It is utter foolishness for a man to expect his wife to love him and meet all his needs, while he treats her unkindly. Husbands, love your wives. Jesus taught in the Sermon on the mount.

"In everything, therefore, treat people the same way you want them to treat you, for this is the Law and the Prophets" (Matthew 7:12).

I am amazed at times how kind and good people can be to those outside the family but treat their own families with disrespect. Husbands and wives both should obey the golden rule with their spouses. If we could see ourselves as we really are and how we treat our families, we might be quite shocked. If we had a tape recording of our words or a video of our actions, we might see ourselves the way our families see us. Some folks never consider how difficult they make their family's lives. That's why, every now and then, it is good for all of us to step back and take a long look at how we have treated our families. Empathy is the ability to see things through the eyes of another and to feel what she is feeling. Sometimes we look at ourselves through other's eyes. When we do that, what will we see? Will we like what we see? Jesus also cautions husbands in the Sermon on the Mount to control their eyes and their thoughts about women other than their wives.

He said in Matthew 5:27-30: "You have heard that it was said, 'YOU SHALL NOT COMMIT ADULTERY'; but I say to you that everyone who looks at a woman with lust for her has already committed adultery with her in his heart. If your right eye makes you stumble, tear it out and throw it from you; for it is better for you to lose one of the parts of your body, than for your whole body to be thrown into hell. If your right hand makes you stumble, cut it off and throw it from you; for it is better for you to lose one of the parts of your body, than for your whole body to go into hell."

Looking at other women is for many men a terrible habit. It says to his wife that she is not the focus of his attention, that there is someone better out there. Job knew that a righteous man kept his eyes in control. He said in Job 31:1-4, "I have made a covenant with my eyes; how then could I gaze at a virgin? What would be my portion from God above and my heritage from the Almighty on high? Is not calamity for the unrighteous, and disaster for the workers of iniquity? Does not he see my ways and number all my steps?" Unfortunately, many husbands are caught up in the habit of pornography. Looking at smutty pictures and videos, they commit adultery in their hearts by turning their attention to someone other than their spouse. Husbands are not alone in this sinful behavior; many wives are now habitual viewers of pornography. When pornography fills the heart, it won't be long before adultery of the heart becomes adultery in life. More than a few homes today are being destroyed by pornography in videos, in literature, and on the internet. The word pornography itself arises from the Greek word *porneia*, a reference to fornication and prostitution. Wise husbands who love God and their wives keep their hearts, their eyes, and their lives clean. A wise husband will also be a spiritual leader in his home. One of the most spiritually important things couples can do is spend time together singing, praying, and reading the Bible. There is great value in a husband and wife privately praying together every day. Prayer allows husbands and wives to take their burdens together to God our Father. It allows them to express in each other's presence and in the presence of God their concerns and needs. When two people pray with each other, they develop a spiritual intimacy and unity that builds their relationship.

Christian marriages, where God is the center of the home, where love is the order of the day, and where patience and forgiveness are present, and where God's laws are obeyed, almost never end in divorce. When people truly live the Christian life, the way God intended, they find their marriages to be the happiest and most loving.

Husbands, do your best to make your home what God would have it to be. Have private devotions at home but also go to church and get involved in the work of the Lord. God's way is truly, truly, a way of blessing. Not every Christian man or woman is happily married. What can you do if your needs are currently not being met? First, identify and acknowledge your hurts to yourself and your spouse. Hurts cannot be healed, and needs cannot be met, if they are ignored. Most men have a hard time reading their wives minds; wives need to spell it out for their husbands. Each one needs to talk openly, honestly, and lovingly to the other about what he or she needs. Now, the emotional baggage caused by unmet needs doesn't just "go away" with time. Husbands and wives both need to acknowledge their feelings of anger, bitterness or resentment to their spouses. But once you have taken the time to reveal a fault, then forgive your spouse. Paul said in Ephesians 4:31-32, "Let all bitterness and wrath and anger and clamor and slander be put away from you, along with all malice. Be kind to one another, tenderhearted, forgiving one another, as God in Christ forgave you." The most important thing any couple can do is learn how to settle their differences. Everyone needs to learn the fine art of apologizing and forgiving. All couples have disagreements, but the ones who survive and thrive learn how to put problems behind them. They learn how to talk out a problem and solve it rather than let it fester and destroy the marriage. Peter said, "Love covers a multitude of sins" (1 Peter 4:8). God is so wonderful to forgive us; His forgiveness teaches us how to forgive even the deepest of hurts. God loved you and me enough to send Jesus to die for our sins and to cleanse us from all unrighteousness. When we place our faith in Christ as Lord and the Son of God, when we turn away from sin in repentance, when we confess the name of Jesus before others, and after we are baptized, the Lord forgives us (Acts 2:38). Why not today get your life right with God. Some need to obey the gospel, and some need to be restored to a right relationship with the Father. Don't wait another day. Get right with God today.

She Is Your QUEEN!

If you want to be treated like a KING, then treat your wife like a QUEEN. Most women are quick and ready to respond to a husband who will love them and become considerate of them. Four times in the New Testament we are told that the husband is to love his wife. Not once is there a direct commandment in the scripture for the wife to love the husband. The wife will respond to the husband's love.

The same thing that will rob you of communion with God and from loving your wife and children is SIN. Lust of sin is one of the greatest hindrances in a marriage. Ephesians 5:21 Submitting yourselves one to another means have a servant's heart toward each other. A servant is one who becomes excited about making other people successful. This attitude should be toward your wife. Some men think that women are their slave and they can do anything they want. Some treat their wives like a hired hand. Ephesians 5:22 "Wives, submit yourselves unto your husbands..." Men, you are not to use this or emphasize this; it does not apply to men. Rather 5:25 "Husbands, love your wives..." Do not become bitter towards her but instead, love her.

How did Christ Love the Church? He voluntarily limited Himself. Men are to limit themselves and let the wife express herself in her spiritual gifts. He was exceedingly patient with us. He was completely empty of self desire. Do what is appealing to your wife. Let her be first place in your life. He gave second and third chances. Peter denied the Lord three times. Am I sensitive when my wife is seeking to please me? Do I notice the little things? Verbalize it. He comforted in time of sorrow. You do not necessarily have to be saying anything, but just being there to comfort, put your arms around her, even if you don't understand her. Sometimes she feels that she least deserved comfort, but she able to weep in your arms. He anticipated needs and then supplied every need as if it were for the glory of God. He spent much time in prayer. He completely sacrificed Himself even unto death.

How does a husband demonstrate genuine love? Take leadership in the home and not hide behind your wife.

- Take your coat off for your wife when she needs a bit of warmth.
- Show concern.
- Take time to understand her problems.
- Be sensitive and not have more interest in reading the paper or looking at your cell phone.
- Have a right attitude – problems do not go away if you ignore them.
- Be an example of a believer in your home. Be grateful. No longer procrastinate.

Chapter #5:

The Ministry Of Your Children

Motherhood is a Ministry from God. A mother is positioned for a mission. God has assigned a mother to care and watch over their child in a way that is dynamic to that child's needs. Just like God trusted Mary to bare his son, mothers are instructed to carry a soul, birth that soul, and guide that soul until the age of accountability. God gives a high regard to the role of a mother. God purposely has chosen you to mother the child he has set before you. Yes, little Ray Ray and Junebug are suppose to be in your care. No matter how bad the situation is, you must ask God for help and seek guidance. It was not a coincidence that God chose you to be a mother. He knew that one day your family would be in trouble and you would have the tenacity to call on the name of Jesus!

God will hear a desperate women's cry! For instance, let's take a look at the Syrophoenician woman. (Matthew 15:21-28) Here we find out how desperate women do desperate things to get God's attention. The Syrophoenician woman's home was under attack and she was desperate for help. Is there a woman reading this book who is desperate for God to do something in their family's life? The definition for desperate is 'having extreme and intense emotions. Desperate can also be described as a reckless force. ("Desperate." American Heritage Dictionary. 3rd ed. 1997. Print.) This is why God will listen to a desperate woman's cry, because her praise is extreme and undignified, her worship is excessive, and her cry is intense. Her approach to God is so desperate it appears to look like it moves with a reckless force. The Syrophoenician woman came to Jesus out on the coast and demanded his attention.

> She cried out "Have mercy on me, O Lord, thou Son of David; my
> daughter is grievously vexed with a devil. (King James Bible -
> Matthew 15:22)

She obviously did not care about how she looked to others; it was about getting to Jesus, the only one who could help her situation. Her child was in trouble and she made up in her mind to intercede for her family. As mothers and wives, God has placed us in a position to intercede for our families in the time of need.

> Matthew 15:28 "Then Jesus answered and said unto her, O woman,
> great is thy faith: be it unto thee even as thou wilt. And her daughter
> was made whole from that very hour" (King James – Matthew 15:28)

Wow, if you are desperate enough to intercede on behalf of your family, God can make your family whole from that very hour! Thank you Jesus. Why don't you take a praise break and cry out right now!

What About My House?

We must understand that salvation begins in the home, not at the church. If we really seek unity in the church we must first have unity at home! God is concerned about our families. The devil is not just after you, but he desires to devour your entire family. If there was ever a time to call on Jesus on behalf of your family, it's now. "Lord, what about my house?" Our families need healing, deliverance, and restoration. We have to stop making excuses and take time out for the Ministry within our own homes.

In Luke 8:40-56, we find a great man named Jairus, who worked as a leader in the synagogue. Jairus was a man of prestige and honor. He was placed in charge of the services of the synagogue. But one day, out of all the families he had assisted; now his own family was facing a major crisis. As leaders and working lay-members in the church, we spend a great deal of time helping, supporting, and taking care of everyone else, but there will come a time when you will need to cry out to God on behalf of your family. Jairus becomes desperate concerning his home situation. So desperate that he goes on a mission to find this man named Jesus. Jairus heard that he was a healer; a miracle worker. When Jairus sees Jesus, he throws himself at Jesus feet and begs him to come to his house and help his twelve year old daughter who was close to death. "Lord what about my house". There might be someone reading this book right now, who may feel that your home situation is out of control, and that you are in need of healing in your house, listen when I tell you that God is just waiting for you to through yourself down at his feet and cry out to him about your need.

> II Chronicles 7:14 "If my people, which are called by my name, shall
> humble themselves, and pray, and seek my face, and turn from their
> wicked ways, then will I hear from heaven, and will forgive their sin,
> and heal their land".

God desires for us to seek his face concerning the troubles in our life. David said in Psalm 34:4 "I sought the Lord, and he heard me, and delivered me from all my fears." That means seeking the Lord has a noise to it. God wants to "hear" you seek him. If you cry out to the Lord he will come to your house and bring healing, deliverance, and restoration. I truly believe that God's plan is to heal our marriages, heal our children, and heal our broken spirits. In Luke 8, Jesus shows up at Jairus's house and he puts everyone out except for the mother, father, a few disciples. When God is healing, you can't let just everyone in your house. Bad spirits can hinder your deliverance. All Jesus had to do was tell Jairus's daughter to arise. Jesus wants our marriages to arise out of the chaos they are in, our children to arise and find order, and our life to arise and find peace.

I remember a personal situation I had to face with my daughter. She was only 9 years old when she had what I thought was an asthma attack. I took her to the hospital and the doctor said he would hook her up to a heart monitor. The doctor told me that the test results showed that my daughter had a server heart problem. They hooked her up to the EKG five times, yes five times, and it still showed a server heart issue. The doctor then scheduled me to see a heart specialist at Children's Hospital. Wow, all I could think of is that I had been in church all my life, and helped a lot of people, but now my house was in trouble. Just like Jairus, I went to the Lord and fell on my knees. I became Desperate like the syrophonecian woman. I needed Jesus and I needed Jesus now! "Lord, what about my house". I needed a miracle. My family came together and my father spoke life into my situation. My father said to me that God could make it like it never happened. I held on to his wise words and began to let God know that I trusted him. When we went back to the doctors, they tested my daughter again by hooking her up to an EKG. The doctors came into the room and began to apologize for the terrible mistake they had made when they first told me my daughter had a server heart problem. The doctors were very embarrassed, but all I could do was shout and scream out praises in the hospital. God showed up and visited my house; in his hands he brought healing, deliverance, and restoration. I know that God worked a miracle for me that day. I remember shouting all in the parking lot of the Children's Hospital in San Diego. Thank you Jesus! Please understand if God can do this for me, he can do this for your family. He is just waiting for you to ask. The Lord can make it like it never happened.

Spending Time With Your Children

Growing up in the church, my father often spent his time working down at the church and very little time at home. My brother and sister took this as a common factor required by Pastor's, but it still hurt. My mother was a desperate housewife who consistently cried out to God for help because she understood the importance of spending time with her children, her husband, the church, and her job. God gave her the wisdom to find balance, but it wasn't always easy. She often sought wise counsel with her spiritual mother and father. They advised her to stay encouraged and to keep order in every area in her life. They assured her that God would bring her balance. My father, later repented once we were older, and told us that he wished that he had spent more time with us as a family because he missed out on so many stages of our life. He had missed all of our sporting events, banquets, school celebrations, performances, and award ceremonies; all for the sake of doing what he felt was God's work. He was too busy doing work at the church than to spend time with his children and wife. I say this as a testimony to those who do not understand the importance of putting your family, not before God, but before your church work. A leader in the church is a high calling, but your family is your calling as well. Your children need you and they need your time! Children that feel neglected often grow up with emotional issues and difficulty relating to others. There is a cause and effect of not spending time with your children. Your child begins to feel and become neglected.

What is Neglect? A child has been neglected when parents or other per-sons responsible fail to provide care, protection, and nurturing necessary for the child's emotional and/or physical wellbeing to such an extent that the negative effect is apparent and social service intervention is clearly necessary. Examples: failure to provide adequate food, clothing, shelter, or medical care.

Warning Signs of Neglect
> *Hoarding of food*
> *Stealing food from other children*
> *Poor hygiene*
> *Wearing the same clothes day after day*
> *Dental problems*
> *Lack of trust*
> *Difficulty with attachments*

Ways to Spend Time with Your Children, Even When You Are Busy

Spending quality time with our children is extremely important for their development and happiness. Thousands of children around the world have been interviewed and insist that the time spent does not have to be long, but it must be "quality". We must find ways then to slow down and slip in some memorable time that will let our children know that we love and care for them. Many children will let you know in their own "subtle" ways if they feel that you are not giving them the attention that they need. Some will withdraw while others will "act out." You might see it when a child gives "lip" to a teacher, fights with another classmate or resorts back to behaviors that once got your attention like increased crying, throwing tantrums or even bed-wetting. This is a way to capture your attention, albeit often negative, so that they can enjoy "focused" time with you. Essentially the thought process is, "if I can't get her attention by doing something good, I'll get her attention by doing something bad." Nobody wants that! So how can you find time when you feel you don't have any to spend?

1. One-on-one time: Alone time with your child is best when you are doing something you both enjoy. With one family it may be the time when Dad takes the baby so Mom can spend time with the older child. This could mean going to a movie, going to the local theater to see Cinderella, or just sitting at the park on a bench and talking. The frequency of one-on-one time is up to you, but the children I interviewed said at least once a month is the minimum. If you are a single mother with more than one child you could arrange it so that each Saturday you spend quality time with one of your children and the last Saturday of the month you spend quality time as a family. Marking your dates down on a calendar is a great idea and shows your children you make this time a priority.

2. Integrate Together Time into Your Daily Schedule: Children love to help. Do you have a mailing to do? Have them put the stamps on the envelopes. Need to go shopping? Make grocery shopping "fun time" with you. Need to make dinner? Let them help you by contributing to the preparation process. While it might be messier and it may time more time in the beginning, you will see that the children will become your greatest helpers and they will look back and remember that "before dinner" was always special time with you.

3. Phantom Time: Don't have a moment to spare until about 3 a.m.? You can still let your children know that you care. Write notes and drop them into their lunch boxes. This was one of the top ten things children told me made them feel loved and cared for by their parent. Other ideas would be to record a short video for them using a camera and leaving it for them at the breakfast table. Be creative here!

4. Break time: Everyone is busy. Some parents are busier than others. Slide in a "break time" so that you and your children can spend 15 minutes or a half hour together. Set a timer if you need to so that everyone knows when "break time" starts and finishes. Give warnings to your children when 2 minutes are left so that it doesn't come as a surprise. Don't even have break time available? Wake your child up 15 minutes early so that you can spend a little extra time doing something fun in the morning. You might not think that 15 minutes is any significant time at all, but to a child, it is 15 extra minutes with you.

Spending time with your children provides them with opportunities to learn and to be heard. Most of all, it provides you and your children with time to connect. It's these connections that make your children feel loved. So leave the beds un-stripped for another few minutes and put the coffee on an automatic timer. Take those extra moments to spend with your children. When you look back, you will be thankful for the memories.

Parenting Skills

Parenting is a difficult task if not address properly. The 10 Principles of Good Parenting.

1. What you do matters. This is one of the most important principles. What you do makes a difference. Your kids are watching you. Don't just react on the spur of the moment. Ask yourself, "What do I want to accomplish, and is this likely to produce that result?"

2. You cannot be too loving. It is simply not possible to spoil a child with love. What we often think of as the product of spoiling a child is never the result of showing a child too much love. It is usually the consequence of giving a child things in place of love things like leniency, lowered expectations, or material possessions.

3. Be involved in your child's life. Being an involved parent takes time and is hard work, and it often means rethinking and rearranging your priorities. It frequently means sacrificing what you want to do for what your child needs to do. Be there mentally as well as physically. Being involved *does not* mean doing a child's homework; or reading it over or correcting it. Homework is a tool for teachers to know whether the child is learning or not. If you do the homework, you're not letting the teacher know what the child is learning.

4. Adapt your parenting to fit your child. Keep pace with your child's development. Your child is growing up. Consider how age is affecting the child's behavior. The same drive for independence that is making your three-year-old say 'no' all the time is what's motivating him to be toilet trained. The same intellectual growth spurt that is making your 13-year-old curious and inquisitive in the classroom also is making her argumentative at the dinner table.

For example: An eighth grader is easily distracted, irritable. His grades in school are suffering. He's argumentative. Should parents push him more, or should they be understanding so his self-esteem doesn't suffer? With a 13-year-old, the problem could be a number of things. He may be depressed. He could be getting too little sleep. Is he staying up too late? It could be he simply needs some help in structuring time to allow time for studying. He may have a learning problem. Pushing him to do better is not the answer. The problem needs to be diagnosed by a professional.

5. Establish and set rules. If you don't manage your child's behavior when he is young, he will have a hard time learning how to manage himself when he is older and you aren't around. Any time of the day or night, you should always be able to answer these three questions: Where is my child? Who is with my child? What is my child doing? The rules your child has learned from you are going to shape the rules he applies to himself. But you can't micromanage your child.. "Once they're in middle school, you need let the child do their own homework, make their own choices, and not intervene.

6. Foster your child's independence. Setting limits helps your child develop a sense of self-control. Encouraging independence helps her develop a sense of self-direction. To be successful in life, she's going to need both. It is normal for children to push for autonomy. Many parents mistakenly equate their child's independence with rebelliousness or disobedience. Children push for independence because it is part of human nature to want to feel in control rather than to feel controlled by someone else.

7. Be consistent. If your rules vary from day to day in an unpredictable fashion or if you enforce them only intermittently, your child's misbehavior is your fault, not his. Your most important disciplinary tool is consistency. Identify your non-negotiable. The more your authority is based on wisdom and not on power, the less your child will challenge it. Many parents have problems being consistent. When parents aren't consistent, children get confused. You have to force yourself to be more consistent.

8. Avoid harsh discipline. Parents should never hit a child, under any circumstances. Children who are spanked, hit, or slapped are more prone to fighting with other children. They are more likely to be bullies and more likely to use aggression to solve disputes with others. There is a lot of evidence that spanking causes aggression in children, which can lead to relationship problems with other kids. There are many other ways to discipline a child, including 'time out,' which work better and do not involve aggression.

9. Explain your rules and decisions. Good parents have expectations they want their child to live up to. Generally, parents over-explain to young children and under-explain to adolescents. What is obvious to you may not be evident to a 12-year-old. He doesn't have the priorities, judgment or experience that you have.

An example: A 6-year-old is very active and very smart, but blurts out answers in class, doesn't give other kids a chance, and talks too much in class. His teacher needs to address the child behavior problem. He needs to talk to the child about it. Parents might want to meet with the teacher and develop a joint strategy. That child needs to learn to give other children a chance to answer questions.

10. Treat your child with respect. The best way to get respectful treatment from your child is to treat him respectfully. You should give your child the same courtesies you would give to anyone else. Speak to him politely. Respect his opinion. Pay attention when he is speaking to you. Treat him kindly. Try to please him when you can. Children treat others the way their parents treat them. Your relationship with your child is the foundation for her relationships with others.

For example, if your child is a picky eater: Children develop food preferences. They often go through them in stages. You don't want turn mealtimes into unpleasant occasions. Just don't make the mistake of substituting unhealthy foods. If you don't keep junk food in the house, they won't eat it.

Likewise, the checkout line tantrum can be avoided. Children respond very well to structure. You can't go shopping without preparing them for it. Tell them, 'We will be there 45 minutes. Mommy needs to buy this. Show them the list. If you don't prepare them, they will get bored, tired, upset by the crowds of people. Parents forget to consider the child, to respect the child. You work on your relationships with other adults, your friendships, your marriage, dating. But what about your relationship with your child? If you have a good relationship, and you're really in tune with your child, that's what really matters. Then none of this will be an issue.

Stressful Families Cause Child Health Issues

Researchers discover children whose parents and families are under ongoing stress have more fevers and illness than other children. The new study posits children's natural killer cell function, part of the body's innate immune system, increases under chronic stress, unlike adults, whose function is decreased.

The University of Rochester study is published in the peer-reviewed journal *Archives of Pediatric and Adolescent Medicine*.

"These findings show us possible new avenues for improving children's health," said Mary Caserta, M.D., principal investigator of the study and associate professor of Pediatrics in the division of Pediatric Infectious Diseases at the University of Rochester Medical Center.

"Families under stress might think their children were sick more often when they actually weren't, but fevers are not subjective. These kids living with chronic stress in their families really were sick more often." "While an illness with a fever isn't necessarily any worse than an illness without one, it does point to an objective sign of illness, often an infection", Caserta said, Medical Doctor. This suggests an association between family stress and susceptibility to infectious diseases.

Caserta undertook the study with collaborator Peter Wyman, Ph.D., associate professor of Psychiatry at the University of Rochester. Wyman, who designed one of the stress surveys used in this study, has led other studies of urban families and their children under stress and his research has shown links between chronic parent stress and children's emotional well-being.

This new study is innovative because it links stress to objective health and biological indicators of immune function. The study is one of the few that have examined the effects of stress on children's immune function.

One of the more surprising findings of the study is that children's natural killer cell function increases under chronic stress. Previous research with mostly older adults has shown that chronic stress decreases their natural killer cell function. (Natural killer cells are part of the immune system that exists before a new germ is introduced; it is the first line of defense for the body until the immune system adapts to fight a specific bacteria or virus.) Dr. Caserta felt that it may have something to do with the fact that children's immune systems are still developing or maybe they're compensating for a defect someplace else.

The study followed 169 diverse 5 to 10 year olds for 3 years. Children and their parents were recruited from a population already participating in a study of childhood infections at the University's Golisano Children's Hospital at Strong. The study involved seven visits about six months apart. Parents were given digital thermometers and they were asked to record their children's health status every week and every time their children were ill.

Parents also completed surveys to assess their own and their family stress over the course of the study. They were asked about psychiatric symptoms, such as depression and anxiety, and they were asked about their relationship with their children, such as whether they felt detached from their child or overwhelmed by their parenting responsibilities. In addition, parents reported on external stressors such as exposure to violence and unemployment.

Building on this study, the researchers hope to determine what types of parental and family stress lead to increased illnesses and what biological processes control susceptibility to infections.

Communicating With Your Children

Communicating positively with children helps them develop confidence, feelings of self-worth, and good relationships with others. It also helps make life with young children more pleasant for children and parents.

Positive communication focuses on respect for the child and involves both speaking and listening. Communication is what we say and how we say it. Positive communication leads to nurturing relationships, cooperation, and feelings of worth. Poor communication can lead to kids who "turn off" adults, conflicts and bickering, and feelings of worthlessness. Adults sometimes have difficulty communicating positively with children when feelings are involved-either their own or the child's. There are ways for parents to improve their communication with children.

Get the child's attention before speaking

Children can only concentrate on one thing at a time. Look directly at the child and call her name. A touch on the shoulder or taking her hand will help get her attention. Give her time to look at you before you start speaking. *(Example: "Sarah." Wait until she stops playing with the doll and looks at you.)*

Communicate on the same level as the child

Communication is more effective if both people are on the same level. Adults need to stoop down to the child's level or sit beside her. Making eye contact with the child lets her know that she has your attention and is much less intimidating to the child.

Speak as if you mean it

Make important requests firmly. Use a firm tone of voice without sounding angry or pleading. Tell the child what you want her to do and why. Give clear, consistent instructions. Remember your body language. It should show that you are serious and expect the child to comply. Say "Please," "Thank you," and "You're welcome" to the child. Modeling appropriate behavior is one of the best ways to get desired behavior from a child. Children also deserve the common courtesies that we, as adults, expect. Children are more likely to carry out desired behaviors when we add these courtesies. Nagging a child to say "please" or "thank you" sets a bad example. They are more likely to use courtesies if they are not constantly reminded.

Make requests simple

Too many requests are confusing for a young child to remember. Make sure that your requests are short, clear and consistent. Laughing at a behavior one time and reacting angrily another sends the child a contradictory message.

Use more positive direction than negative

Positive communication with children uses more "Do's" than "Don'ts." In other words, tell the child what to do rather than what not to do. Children respond much quicker to positive demands than negative ones. Allow children to make choices when possible. They are more likely to show appropriate behavior when they have some control over their actions.

Talk with-not at-children

Adults should communicate with children with the respect and consideration they give their friends. Sometimes, adults spend so much time talking "to" the child that they neglect the listening part of communication. Talking with children let them know that not only do we have something to tell them, but that we are also willing to listen to what they have to say.

Keep lines of communication open by listening attentively when the child talks to you

Encourage the child to talk to you. However, if you are busy, do not pretend to listen. Tell the child, "I'm busy now, but we will talk about it later." Be sure to follow through with the child. Never try to trick children. Answer questions honestly. Share your feelings and ideas but accept the child's fears, ideas and feelings. Never promise the child anything that you cannot deliver. Making an effort to keep our promises to children increases the effectiveness of our communication.

Use kind words and actions to encourage and support the child

Unkind words help to tear a child down and make the child feel bad. Kind, supportive words and actions tell children that they are loved and lead to positive self-esteem. Nurturing words and actions help to develop trusting relationships where problems can be discussed and solved. Remember that affection is also part of effective communication and that comforting a child and sharing smiles and hugs are powerful communication tools.

Tip: Pick a day and record how many times you say "No," "Stop," "Don't," "Quit," or "You know better." Work on your communication skills to replace these words with positive statements.

As parents we spend so much of our time talking to our kids, and then wonder why they don't seem to hear us. In heated moments, we find ourselves stuck in power struggles, but can't figure out what to say to stop the fighting. Sometimes we just don't know how to answer a tough question.

Why can talking with kids be so hard? "The basic challenge is that parents very often speak without understanding how their children receive the message," says Michael Thompson, Ph.D., co-author of *Raising Cain*. We often make an assumption that our kids understand. But then we wonder, 'Why didn't they do what I said?'"

While many parent-child conversations can lead to misunderstandings, becoming an effective communicator is not only possible - it can even be fun! In this guide you will find practical ways to communicate effectively with kids of any age, using words they can hear and techniques that make sense. The information is based on successful strategies that parents and experts (many of them parents themselves) have used with kids.

Remember: There is no script to memorize or order you have to follow. Think of these easy-to-employ ideas as tools you can pull out when you need them to help you and your child understand each other. And keep in mind that there are important times when NOT talking at all may be your best option.

Take a break and listen to your child

Specific actions — like making eye contact, kneeling down to your child's level and even tilting your head-show your child you are listening. They also help YOU stop and really listen. If you can't talk at that moment, you might say, "Let's talk in a few minutes; I'm in the middle of something."

Repeat what you heard

It's often useful to restate what you heard and put your child's feelings into words. You might say, "You wanted a turn on the swing right now, didn't you?" or, "You seem sad about going to day care today." These reflective statements acknowledge and give words to your child's feelings. However, do this carefully. If a child is in the middle of a tantrum, saying "You're really mad and out of control!" may aggravate the situation rather than help it.

Ask specific questions to gather more information

You might say, "Can you tell me exactly what happened?" If it makes sense to talk some more, you might ask, "What upset you the most?" Follow-up questions both acknowledge your child's feelings and get her talking about them. And they help you gather more information, so you can better understand.

See the situation through your child's eyes

You know how you feel when your boss or partner says, "That's ridiculous," or insists you really like something you know you hate? Kids feel the same way when parents say, "You don't really mean that," or "I can't believe you said that!"

Acknowledge your child's feelings

In response to your child's statement, you might simply say, "I'm glad to know that," or "I understand." At times, this acknowledgement is all your child needs to hear. Try not to contradict your child's statement immediately, even if you think he's wrong. Hear him out before saying no. If your child says, "I don't want to go to school anymore," instead of saying go," you might ask, "What's the worst thing about it?"

Listen to your child's request without judging or correcting it.

Good teachers give a child a chance to explain himself first, even if he's wrong. The same technique works at home.

Give yourself a moment to think about what your child is asking.

Even if your final answer will still be "No," you might say, "Let me think about what you're saying for a minute and get back to you."

Pause to consider your child's question.

This forces you to slow down and helps you not to make a snap judgment, even if the answer is, "No, we are not getting a bunny." Pausing makes your child feel heard, because you have stopped to consider her opinion; it also diminishes the chances of a power struggle.

Share your thinking out loud.

Your children will enjoy being included in your thought processes. If your child asks for a sleep over, you might say, "I know you want a sleep over, but your grandmother may want to see you this weekend when she visits. Let me talk to her." In this way your child knows how you arrive at your decision.

Allow your child's negative feelings to come out, even if they are hard to take.

Simply being there, without saying much, may soothe and comfort your child. Sometimes you just need to wait it out until the feeling is expressed.

Avoid attacking your child's character.

If your child acts out, instead of saying, "Bad girl, how dare you speak to me that way," you might say, "That kind of language is not OK." In this way, you are separating the behavior from the child. You don't want to imply that your child is intrinsically bad, or make her ashamed of her feelings.

Tell your child how her behavior makes you feel.

"Don't hide your feelings," advises John Gottman, Ph.D., author of *Raising an Emotionally Intelligent Child*. "In fact, your feelings may be the best form of discipline, as long as they are not used to attack your child." You might express the depth of your emotions with phrases such as, "I am very disappointed in what you did," or, "It makes me sad that you lied to me."

Tell your child how you feel about yourself.

In this way, your child knows you have feelings and learns how to express her own. You might say, "I had a bad day at work today, I'm in a crummy mood," or, "I blew it. I'm sorry I made a mistake." Be aware that if you spend too much time talking about how you feel, your child may feel overwhelmed (or bored) by your level of emotion. On the other hand, if you never articulate your feelings, your child may not feel permission to articulate her own.

Grant in fantasy what you can't give in reality.

If your child badly wants something that he can't have, encourage him to imagine what he wants, and talk about it. You might say, "What would you do if we could stop the car right now?" or, "I bet you wish Mommy was here right now. What would you want to do with her?" (And then, stand in for Mommy and do it, if the request is reasonable and possible.)

Use humor, but not at your child's expense.

Not every conflict needs to be resolved through serious discussion. Sometimes humor is the best way out. You might say, "Ouch, that hurts!" instead of "Don't talk to me that way, young man!" Rather than "Clean your room now!" you might say, "This place is a like a biology lab! I don't see mold yet, but it'll start growing soon!"

Try a playful approach, not a critical one.

If you're struggling over what your preschooler should wear, try, "Let's see what you can put on your doll and then find something like that for you." You could joke with your school-age child about "how dumb I am" instead of criticizing him for criticizing you. You could even suggest ten minutes of your child's favorite activity before getting down to homework.

Focus on the positive before bringing up the negative.

For example, if your child pulls a practical joke that makes a mess, you might say, "Clever. Ingenious. Now clean it up." If he brings home a test with mistakes, first comment on what he got right before discussing what he got wrong.

Admit your mistakes.

Ask your child for help in figuring out what to do. Kids love to hear parents admit they were wrong. You might say, "Am I making a mess of this? Should we try to figure it out a different way?"

Tell a funny story about yourself as a child.

Most kids love to hear stories about their parents growing up. You might tackle a tough topic by describing what happened to you in a similar situation when you were a kid. However, don't turn all conversations into stories about you. Constantly saying, "I know how you feel, let me tell you what happened to me," may annoy more than amuse.

Ask a child what he wants to happen or would like to change.

If your child complains about something specific, you might ask him to suggest some improvements. For example, if he says, "I hate music class because Mr. Block is so mean," you might first ask, "What's the meanest thing Mr. Block did?" Then, follow up and ask, "What do you wish your teacher had done instead?"

Use dialogue to find solutions.

By first letting your child vent negative feelings, and then asking him to imagine a different scenario, you are encouraging him not only to discuss the problem, but to become part of the solution.

Remember that you are bigger than your child, so get on her level.

Imagine what it feels like to look up at someone every time you speak or to try to catch someone's attention from floor level. To help your child hear you, get down where she is and make eye contact. This sends a signal that you are listening and that you care what she's thinking.

Offer limited choices.

Choices give kids a sense of power and control. Instead of saying, "Time to get dressed," you might say, "Do you want the red shirt or the blue one?" Offer two choices, not five or six. You might say, "Do you want peas or green beans?" or "Do you want to brush your teeth first or comb your hair?"

Speak as simply as possible.

A one-sentence answer may be much more effective than a long explanation. Children are often satisfied with a simple, direct answer that addresses their main concern. A lengthy explanation may confuse or bore your child.

Write notes.

Sometimes older kids respond better to a written note than to a verbal nag. You might post this note: "Please write down here what time you will be home!" Or, "Today is room-cleaning day." Some kids may enjoy writing lists and charts themselves as a way of solving problems with you.

Listen to your tone instead of your words.

At times, it's not what say, but the way you say it that makes an impact. Kids sense what their parents are feeling. Often, they are not listening to your words so much as looking at your face and reacting to the tone of your voice.

Talk to your child as though you're composing a song.

"Parent-child communication is composed of both music and lyrics," comments Michael Thompson. "When someone listens to music, he may focus on either the melody or on the lyrics. Children are always listening to the melody (or tone) of a parent's voice. Unfortunately, we, the parents, are often paying more attention to our lyrics."

Listen to yourself from your child's perspective.

If you feel a conflict brewing, ask yourself, "Would I like to be spoken to this way?" If you don't like the way you sound, ask yourself, "Am I mad about something without realizing it?"

Avoid leading questions.

Questions that include an answer, such as, "Don't you want to change your clothes before we leave?" or, "Wouldn't you like to apologize to your sister now?" are really orders, not queries. These questions are likely to provoke a sullen response, or a plain old "NO."

Ask valid questions.

Questions such as "What you do you like (or hate) most about school right now?" will produce real answers. A real question about food might be, "You haven't been eating much lunch lately, what would you like to have today?" In comparison, a leading question on the same topic would be, "You know you like peanut butter, don't you want some?"

Avoid general questions.

Whether you have a preschooler or a preteen, well-meaning but general questions such as "How was school?" often produce only one-word answers, such as "good," "bad" or "OK." General questions often lead to dead-end conversations.

Instead, ask specific questions to inspire productive conversations.

Refer to something that happened recently, such as, "Is Spanish class getting any easier?" These questions work because they draw on your child's unique experience and therefore elicit specific responses.

Find out what your child knows already.

If your child asks you a difficult question (about sex, death, politics, etc.), you might simply ask, "What have you heard?" This allows your child to tell you what she understands, or misunderstands , and perhaps what concerns are prompting her question.

Keep your answers simple.

Give answers that are appropriate for your child's age. One simple sentence may be enough.

"The flight attendant is showing us how to stay safe on the airplane."

Ask more questions.

For example, if your child asks you about people being injured on the news, you might say, "I feel sad those people got hurt. How do you feel?"

Talk again.

Be prepared for children to ask the same question many times. This means they are continuing to think about the issue and may need more information. You might save some information for later discussions.

Don't turn a statement into a question.

Instead of saying, "It's time to leave the playground in five minutes, OK?" simply say, "We're leaving in five minutes." Don't ask for your child's permission. However, you might want to briefly explain your logic, remembering that an explanation is not the same as a negotiation.

Offer choices only when there really is a choice.

Be clear about negotiable and non-negotiable situations. If your child refuses to go to school, you might say, "I know you don't feel like going to school today. We still have to leave in ten minutes."

Don't let discussions go on too long.

If there really is no choice about the outcome, too much talking just postpones the inevitable. If need be, walk away from your child or get involved in some other activity.

Learn how to talk to kids of any age. Listen through your children's ears and find out how much of your conversation kids really understand — and why they don't seem to pay attention when you want them to. Plus, learn about the hidden messages that underlie your kids' questions and arguments.

Babies & Toddlers: Ages 0-2
How They Communicate

Crying is one of a baby's first ways of communicating through sound. By the time a baby is four weeks old, her cries are differentiated. There is a unique cry for hunger, wetness, pain and missing companionship. Within a few months, babies also start to coo and gurgle with pleasure.

Within three to four months, babies realize that when they make noise, people respond. When a parent or caregiver responds to a baby's cries, the baby begins to trust her means of communication, because her needs are being met. In the second six months of life, babies begin to babble in the language of their parents and other caregivers.

Babies and toddlers do not understand words out of context. Instead, they understand words in combination with your gestures, tone and facial expression.

By 18-24 months, toddlers begin to use action words. These words express what they see or want, leaving out adjectives and other grammatical conventions. They may come out with short phrases such as "Mommy go," or "Shoes on." Babies and toddlers also speak through gestures and tone of voice. What they do physically may be as important as what they actually say.

Toddlers use words and short sentences to assert themselves. "No" and "mine" are used to claim space and take control of their new world. It is developmentally important for a toddler to say these words. When young children say "No" to parents, they are often saying "Yes" to themselves. Asserting their independence is an early, important step towards becoming their own person, separate from you.

How You Communicate

Touch, cuddle and croon to babies as a first form of communication. When babies cry, you can reassure them with your presence and a comforting, soothing tone. Babies respond the emotions you are communicating through what they see, hear and feel. They react to your sadness, tension, happiness or satisfaction.

Be aware that tone and body language make a difference. When a baby hears "Stop!" he will sometimes cry, because he is reacting to the sharpness and volume of your command. In the same way, a soft, loving "Good night" when you are tucking him into bed will comfort your child because of the soothing tone.

Stay physically connected as a way to communicate. Babies like being close to their parents. Wearing or holding them next to your body communicates reassurance and comfort; a carrier also allows you to move around and carry on with your life.

Don't be surprised if your baby cries when you are on the phone. A baby knows when you are not paying attention, and he knows how to get that attention back. His wailing can come at inconvenient times, but being aware of what's causing your baby's reactions may help you stay patient and deal with him in the moment.

Turn baby talk into a two-way conversation. Invite responses from your baby. Singing and chanting nursery rhymes are good ways to play with sound. They invite your baby to make a pleasing stream of sounds that eventually lead to talking.

Extend sounds and words to help children develop language skills. If your toddler says "Go home," you might extend his thought by saying, "You want to go home. We can leave in a few minutes."

Even if you are not sure how much your child understands, talk anyway! Like holding and kissing, words are an important way of staying in contact with your baby.

Preschoolers: Ages 3-5

How They Communicate

Between ages two and three, many preschoolers begin to use more complicated sentences. However, this does not mean that they understand all of an adult's words or abstract concepts. In fact, preschoolers are often very literal thinkers and interpret ideas concretely. Many are only beginning to think logically and understand sequences of events.

Preschoolers learn that they can use specific words to say what they mean. They have long known their parents' words have power over their lives and they are beginning to realize that their own words can make a difference as well. They create more powerful meanings using their growing vocabulary.

"No" and "Why" become common words for young preschoolers. Saying "No" is a way a preschooler claims her space. Saying "Why" is a wish to understand the world around her. "Why" is also a word preschoolers use to question authority. Underneath the question, they are saying "Why do you have power over me when I want to feel autonomous?"

Preschoolers like to participate in decisions. This gives them a feeling of control and independence. A preschooler might think, "I can take a different position from my mother, and I like it." Or, "By saying what I want, I am a big kid."

Preschoolers love to imitate other people's words. They often mimic comments, phrases and sophisticated statements. At times they misuse or exaggerate phrases, particularly during pretend play. A preschooler might say to a doll, "You are so bad you are going to jail for 100 years!"

Preschoolers like to hear about and describe the same event over and over. By telling and listening to stories, preschoolers begin to form opinions about the world and how they fit into it. They say "tell me again," because hearing a story many times makes them feel safe and secure. When the story is repeated, it also allows them to imagine new scenarios.

Preschoolers like to make up their own explanations. This helps them make sense of things they are only beginning to understand. For example, a preschooler might explain her sadness about winter being over by saying "When the snow melts, the winter is crying." Preschoolers may also embellish stories with wishful thinking.

Between three and five, preschoolers refine their understanding of cause and effect. Older preschoolers can understand simple explanations of cause and effect such as "The medicine will help you get well" and "If you eat healthy food, you will grow big and strong."

Preschoolers also talk through their bodies, their play and their art. In fact, verbal communication still may not be the dominant way many preschoolers either understand the world or express themselves.

How You Communicate

Give your preschooler your full attention. Even a quick but focused connection may fill your child's need for communication. If she says "Play with me," and you are not available, you might explain why or say, "I had a hard day at work today. I need three minutes to change. Then I can play with you." Preschoolers can understand your feelings — to a point — and will appreciate your honesty.

Be aware of your tone. Because preschoolers are new to sentence-making themselves, they may have a heightened awareness of your tone and body language.

Reflect your child's unspoken emotions. This helps put your child's feelings into words. If she didn't get a turn at the playground, you might say, "You wanted to play with the ball next, didn't you?" or "Boy are you mad!"

Enlist your preschooler's help in figuring out a problem. For example, you might say, "Did something in that movie scare you?" If your child doesn't answer, you might follow up by saying, "Could it have been the look on that character's face?"

Help your preschooler develop emotional awareness. Even if there is misbehavior — you can talk about it together. Most preschoolers can understand a sentence like "Sometimes, I get mad too. It helps me to go into another room and take some deep breaths."

Offer limited choices. Preschoolers gain a sense of control by making their own decisions. You might say, "Do you want to get dressed before or after breakfast today?"

Don't end your sentence with "OK?" unless you are ready for your child to say "No." Asking your child if an activity is OK can lead to a lengthy discussion and even a power struggle.

Grant a preschooler's wish in fantasy. If your child expresses sadness that a toy has to be shared, you might say, "Would you like it if you had the toy all to yourself? What would you do with it?" By expressing a wish and talking it through, even if it can't be granted, a child begins to calm down.

Create safe opportunities for preschoolers to express their BIG feelings. For example, if your child is extremely angry, instead of saying, "Stop yelling," you might say, "Go in the bathroom and scream as loud as you can for one minute."

Don't over-explain. Simple explanations may be more effective than long discussions. If your preschooler is having a tantrum, holding her close, or just staying nearby, may mean more than any words you can say.

School Age: Ages 6-11

How They Communicate

School-age kids begin to view the world in complex ways. At this stage, children often move from being concrete thinkers to being more reflective ones. They think more logically about world events, while still viewing them subjectively. They start to look at causes and begin asking more challenging questions.

Between the ages of 6 and 11, kids become purposeful. They think in advance about what they want and often have a plan for how to get it. Because their communication style is impulsive and driven by their desires, it may mask how deep, loving and wise they are inside.

School-age kids alternately feel dependent, resistant or even rebellious toward their parents. This confusing behavior can be quite nerve-wracking for parents. School-age kids may appear needy for days and then suddenly throw tantrums. They become insulted if their parents treat them in ways they consider babyish, even though at other times they still want to be babied.

School-age kids question, doubt and criticize their parents. They no longer consider Mom and Dad to be the sole authorities. This questioning is normal, and it means they are becoming critical thinkers. They may appear to distance themselves from, or even reject, the people they love most.

School-age kids begin to tailor their communication styles to their surroundings. Younger kids usually communicate with one style no matter where they are or who they are with. As school-age kids spend more time away from home, they often develop new patterns of speaking based on what their friends are saying or what they hear on television.

School-age kids may become private about their thoughts. No matter how positive a relationship a school-age child has with his parents, he may now begin to shut them out as his life outside the home begins to compete with his home life.

School-age kids develop a more sophisticated sense of humor. They enjoy telling jokes and puns and playing more advanced games. They can understand more grown-up media and analyze the rules and premises of the games they play.

How You Communicate

Find time to talk. With a school-age child, you won't have as many opportunities for conversation as you did with your preschooler. As your child grows up, she may turn to you less frequently, so you may need to make a special effort to spend time together.

Speak to your school-age child in a mature fashion. School-age kids want their "bigness" acknowledged. They may be offended if they feel they are being spoken to like babies (even if they happen to be acting like them). You might say, "I expect you to begin your book report. What time would you like to work on it?" instead of "How many times do I have to tell you to do your book report!"

Show your school-age child respect. One way is to ask your child for help in understanding her and her needs. If you acknowledge that your child has some information you don't, she will know that you respect her, even though you are making final decisions.

Ask your school-age child specific, rather than general questions. Instead of asking a question such as "How was school?" you might ask, "Did your teacher give you comments on your science project?" Also avoid leading questions. A query such as, "Do you think it's appropriate to talk to me that way?" often backfires. Instead, you might say, "I feel angry when you talk to me that way."

Listen to your school-age child without contradicting her. Instead of saying "That's ridiculous," you might simply say, "Hmm," or "Really." Then, ask specific questions based on the situation your child has described.

Repeat what you heard your child say, but in a more mature way. You can reflect her statement in the form of a question, implying, "Am I getting this right?" In this way, you are respecting your child's intelligence, making her feel understood and encouraging her to tell you more. You might say, "So, you think your gym teacher is stupid, but you don't want me to intervene? Can you tell me what you are upset about?"

Laugh a little and admit your mistakes. At times, humor is the best way to resolve a dispute, react to an upset or make a request of your school-age child. You can also ask your child for help in figuring out what to do. Kids love to hear parents admit they were wrong. You might say, "Am I making a mess of this? Should we try to figure it out a different way?"

Ask your child to help set her own limits. Don't be afraid to say "No" when your school-age child (or you) needs it. However, within reason, your child can make some rules, too. For instance, you might ask her to propose a reasonable time to begin her homework. "Discuss it and then back off," recommends Gillian McNamee, Ph.D. "Ask your child to be the boss of deciding what help is given, how much and when (in accordance with her teacher's instructions)." In this way, you help your child to feel in control of her world.

Keep talking even if your school-age child won't talk to you. "You will feel at times that you have lost your credibility with a school-age child," comments Michael Thompson, Ph.D. "If you take silence or impulsive remarks personally, things can go quite badly. But they are often simply trying to establish their independence."

When kids get mad, they get really mad. And parents, despite their best intentions, get mad too and often react by yelling back. One thing leads to another and a simple disagreement has turned into a battle of wills, with screaming, kicking and tears. What to do? First, try not to feel embarrassed. Remember that any child, with any sense of self, is likely to have a tantrum sometime, someplace. And parents everywhere are wondering how to cope.

"Children often start to have a tantrum because they don't feel heard," points out Michael Thompson, Ph.D., author of *Best Friends, Worst Enemies*. "They think what they want is for their parents to give in. But often, what they really want is for their parents to stop and listen." When you listen, experts agree that it's important to accept, rather than dismiss, your child's feelings - even if they're hard to take. "We live in an emotion-dismissing culture," says John Gottman, Ph.D., author of *Raising an Emotionally Intelligent Child*, "but if you build an awareness about your child's emotions and your own, particularly an awareness of smaller emotions, then it may not be necessary for emotions to escalate."

Let your child express negative feelings without judging them. Imagine if every time you were upset, some bigger, taller, frowning person looked down at you and said, "Don't feel that way," or "Don't tell me that." Would you feel like shutting up or shouting back?

Ask yourself, "Am I really listening to my child or waiting to tell him what I think?" "Children often start to have a tantrum because they don't feel heard. If you are thinking of what you will say while your child is talking, then you know you are not really listening," advises Michael Thompson, Ph.D.

Reflect your child's feelings. You might say, "Boy, are you mad!" to a younger child. To a school-age child you might try, "I can see how frustrated you are. Can you tell me what made you feel that way?" ("What" is always more important than "Why" — it asks for specifics.)

Slow down the process by saying, "I need a moment to think about this." If your child is being rude, or getting ready to have a tantrum, you can slow things down by giving feedback. You might say, "Ouch! That comment hurts my feelings." Or, "I can see you're upset. Let's talk."

Use this opportunity to problem-solve. If kids are fighting, you might say, "In this family (or house) we don't hurt people's feelings. Let's try to solve this problem another way." Then, ask each child for his idea of what would be fair. You might say, "You don't think it's fair that you have to go to bed before your sister. I understand. What do you think should happen?"

Ask your child to explain it again. Even if you disagree, you might say, "Explain to me again why it feels so unfair." This requires a child to settle down and articulate what he feels.

Acknowledge your child's effect on you. Many children will calm down if you acknowledge their impact, and get angrier if you don't. You might stop and say something like, "I've stopped the car," (or "I am off the phone") "and you have my full attention." Then, ask questions like "What don't I understand?"

Focus on your child's behavior, not his character. You might say, "Yelling in the kitchen is not OK right now," instead of "How many times do I have to tell you to stop yelling?" Discuss the consequences of his behavior. You might say, "I can see from your behavior that we may have to stop having play dates after school." This may be more effective than saying, "No more play dates for you!"

Set limits that your child will find comforting. A limit is not a punishment. Limits may help your child learn how to calm himself down. "Kids find the setting of limits comforting and soothing," comments John Gottman. "They need to know that you (the parent) are in control."

If you're overwhelmed, give yourself a time out. You might simply say, "I need a moment to calm down." When your child sees you calm down, she may calm down too. Nothing is quite as powerful for a child as a parent who just stops to think about his own feelings.

Try not to criticize your child for "pouting." It's normal to feel discouraged at times. Consider how you feel when you get criticized or don't get your way about something important.

Explain a time out or disciplinary action without attacking your child. If you give a time out, explain why. You might say, "You need a time out to cool down." Use a rational tone, otherwise your child might hear only your anger and not think about the consequences of her action.

Don't drag out a fight with too much discussion. If your child (or you) is feeling out of control or in a rage, a lot of talking may not help. In fact, it could prolong the conflict.

97

Avoid physical power struggles. Using your size and strength only heightens the conflict. Imagine a child is feeling furious and picks up a stick. If you grab it before she has time to give it up voluntarily, she might try to hit you with it. Instead, you can avert danger and acknowledge your child's power by saying, "Please put that down. You could hurt someone you love." (Obviously you would never allow someone to hurt or be hurt.)

Try not to take your child's strong feelings personally. Many parents feel frustrated or personally attacked if their child criticizes or explodes at them. "Don't take your child's strong feelings personally all the time," adds Michael Thompson. "'I hate you' is not actually a personal statement. What your child really may be saying is 'I hate your power.'"

Keep breathing and stay relaxed. "It's hard not to tense up when your child is getting out of control, but if you stay relaxed, she's more likely to follow," recommends Thompson. Sometimes we start holding our breath when things get tense. Instead, inhale, exhale and then talk through your own feelings in a clear and (if necessary) firm way.

Let the tantrum run its course as long as no one is being hurt. "This is really crucial," says Michael Thompson. "A child who is filled with raw feelings may not know how to manage them. But the child may feel reassured by your calmer presence. Then, you get back to the business of communicating."

Keep your own strong feelings separate from the tantrum. While it's often important to show your child what you feel, "entering" his tantrum with your own anger may only escalate the situation. Take a breath, speak calmly, even leave the room and give yourself a time out if you need to.

Try to comfort your child physically. Each child reacts to rage differently. Some will want to be held, others want to be left alone. If it seems right, you might try holding your child, if he will let you. If your child struggles ferociously, let go as long as no one will get hurt.

Try to avoid threats in the heat of the moment. "The moment you make irrational threats with punishments that do not suit the occasion, you are not talking about the topic anymore," advises Michael Thompson. "If you say, 'If you do that I will ground you,' the child starts to fight the grounding and the original issue is lost." Instead, offer a specific, reasonable consequence and explain why.

Seek professional help if you see a repeated, chronic pattern that you can't figure out. If defiance or anger escalates and becomes increasingly difficult to deal with, and if nothing works over a period of weeks or months, there may be an underlying issue that needs professional help. You can find a referral through a pediatrician, guidance counselor at your child's school, a friend, neighbor, community center or place of worship.

Remember: Other people's kids have tantrums too. Talk to your friends and find out what they do, what they say and how they survive!

We've all had times when we couldn't believe the things we've said to our kids. Most parents have blurted out something like, "You'll never learn!" or, "Stop crying now, just stop it!" Then we wonder how these things we swore we'd never say to our kids, that we hated our parents for saying to us, come out of our mouths!

"A lot about being a parent is managing feelings of helplessness," says Michael Thompson, Ph.D. "The tantrums of little children make parents feel helpless. When older kids stand up to you and criticize your character, that brings up a different kind of helplessness. And when our kids make us feel helpless, our buttons get pushed, and we say things we wish we hadn't."

Often the best way to deal with it is to admit you're wrong and apologize. "Kids often enjoy nothing better than for their parents to be wrong, and feel validated when their parents apologize," adds Thompson. So instead of beating yourself up when you hear your mother's voice come out of your mouth, take a breath and apologize. The following strategies may help you figure what you need to say when an apology is in order.

Apologize for your behavior, not for yourself. You might tell your child, "I've been thinking about what happened and I don't like what I said or did."

Give yourself a momentary time out. You might say, "I'm sorry, I'm not thinking clearly right now. Give me a moment and I'll get back to you."

Ask your child, "What could I have done differently?" Ask her for help in figuring out what to do, and be open to her suggestions. You might say, "Did I make a mess of this?" Kids love to hear parents admit they are wrong.

You might also ask, "What could you have done differently?" In a non-accusatory way, review what occurred. Use this opportunity to discuss what you and your child could do differently next time.

Next time, try joking instead of over-reacting. You might say with a laugh, "Are you going to drive me totally crazy again?"

Think specifically about how you might behave differently next time. What it is about your child's behavior that pushes your buttons? Is there something you can do or say that would change the way you react? You might try taking a deep breath before you speak, or walking out of the room until you figure out how you want to react. Think about this when you're calm: the heat of the moment may not be the time to fix this problem, particularly if it's become a pattern. Learn from your mistakes - and move on!

Start an agreement, not an argument. Phrase your requests so that your child can say "Yes." He will listen more readily if you pitch your idea in a way that appeals to his need for control and independence. If you say, "Would you like to set out the plates or the spoons?" you are more likely to get cooperation than if you say, "Set the table NOW!"

Get your child involved. If it's getting near bedtime, you might say, "How many minutes do you think you should have to finish this project and get in bed on time?" If you are discussing discipline, you might ask, "What do you think would be a reasonable consequence for hitting me?" or, "for not doing your chores?"

Explain your point of view. You could say, "We have to leave the playground because I have to make dinner." Once you explain what's on your mind, remain open to any response. If your child says, "I don't care, I'm not hungry," you might say, "But I am and so is your brother."

Know that negotiation doesn't mean giving in. When you negotiate to buy a new car, you're not giving in - you're bargaining. Keep in mind that negotiating is not about winning and losing.

Negotiate issues in age-appropriate ways. If your school-age child doesn't like peas, you might ask, "What vegetable would you like instead?" If your preschooler is not interested in eating at all, instead of arguing, you might consider playfully cutting a sandwich into interesting shapes to make it more appealing.

Respond to criticism with a reasonable question. If your child tells you to stop nagging him to clean his room or take a bath, you might say, "How would you manage this yourself? When would you like to do it?"

Take time to cool down. If your child is making you angry or just plain crazy, go into the other room and chill out before trying to talk. "Will an emotional response from you ease the conflict or dig a deeper hole?" asks Brown.

Write down solutions. Get the family together and appoint a secretary who makes a list of everyone's ideas. Discuss them openly but don't allow criticism of anyone's idea. Also consider doing your negotiation in writing. Penning notes to your older child (like "Room Cleaning 5 PM") might prompt more agreement than nagging would.

Let your child win sometimes. Pick your battles wisely and remember that changing your mind does not mean you are losing. You might say, "OK, I agree with you. But let's make a deal that next time you will listen to me before blowing up."

Remember, you have final say. You don't have to reach consensus in any negotiation. Sometimes, somebody just has to make a decision. It's perfectly OK for parents to make the final decision, as long as they have heard their children's point of view and tried to be fair.. "Children will come to respect that; they may not like it, but they will come to realize that it's fair."

Chapter #6

Your Ministry Within Your Church

Your Ministry within your church is important to the body of Christ. Each person has a valuable part to assuring the body operates functionally. All parts of the body are important, even if duties and responsibilities are different.

I Corinthians 12:12 says "For as the body is one, and hath many members, and all the members of that one body, being many, are one body: so also is Christ." (King James – I Corinthians 12:12)

Paul wants us to understand that God expects us to work together as one in order to make up the body of Christ. The true church does not dwell in the four walls we worship within, but it is the souls that create the members of God's church. This is why fellowship is important. Fellowship is an avenue for the body to come together in the name of Jesus. Although fellowship is important, God gives you the opportunity to grow spiritually under the leadership of your Pastor, so that you may function in the body of Christ skillfully.

Being a member of your church is your invitation to work for the Lord. Don't be a bench warmer when Jesus comes. Remember, it's not what you use to do, or how much work you use did in the past, but it's about, will you be caught working when Jesus comes?

Church Over-programming: 10 Reasons To Under-program Your Church

As church goers we are constantly inundated with opportunities for activity from other churches (which we don't want to turn down lest we appear uncooperative and carnal), but what all this so often amounts to is a church that is merely busy, and busy does not always equal diligent or successful. Homes become neglected, families members become disgruntle and it becomes extremely frustrating to find any type of balance. I know this is difficult for most Christians to discuss because they feel they are somehow going against God when they are not spending all day at the church. Many have been taught that unless they are at the church all week long, participating in every event, God will not be pleased with them. The truth is, God is expecting us to find balance, even with our work at church. Although it is extremely important, it too must take on priorities. Ministry accounts for all the areas in our life, not just inside the four walls of the church.

<u>10 reasons to under-program a church:</u>
1. You can do a lot of things in a mediocre (or poor) way, or you can do a few things extremely well.

2. Over-programming creates an illusion of fruitfulness that may just be business. A bustling crowd may not be spiritually changed or engaged in mission at all. And as our flesh cries out for works, many times filling our programs with eager, even servant-minded people is a way to appeal to self-righteousness.

3. Over-programming is a detriment to single-mindedness in a community. If we're all busy engaging our interests in and pursuits of different things, we will have a harder time enjoying the "one accord" prescribed by the New Testament.

4. Over-programming runs the risk of turning a church into a host of extracurricular activities, mirroring the "Type-A family" mode of suburban achievers. The church can become a grocery store or more spiritual YMCA, then, perfect for people who want religious activities on their calendar.

5. Over-programming dilutes actual ministry effectiveness. Because it can overextend leaders, increase administration, tax the time of church members, and sap financial and material resources from churches.

6. Over-programming leads to segmentation among ages, life stages, and affinities, which can create divisions in a church body. Certainly there are legitimate reasons for gathering according to "likenesses," but many times increasing the number of programs means increasing the ways and frequencies of these separations. Pervasive segmentation is not good for church unity or spiritual growth.

7. Over-programming creates satisfaction in an illusion of success; meanwhile mission suffers. If a church looks like it's doing lots of things, we tend to think it's doing great things for God. When really, it may just be providing lots of religious goods and services. This is an unacceptable substitute for a community on mission, but it's one we accept all the time. And the more we are engaged within the four walls of the church, whether those walls are literal or metaphorical, the less we are engaged in being salt and light. Over-programming reduces the access to and opportunities with my neighbors.

8. Over-programming reduces margin in the lives of church members. It's a fast track to burnout for both volunteers and attendees.

9. Over-programming gets a church further away from the New Testament vision of the local church. Here's a good test, I think: take a look at a typical over-programmed church's calendar and see how many of the activities resemble things seen in the New Testament.

10. Over-programming is usually the result of un-self-reflective reflex reactions to perceived needs and an inability to kill sacred cows that are actually already dead. Always ask "Should we?" before you ask "Can we?" Always ask "Will this please God?" before you ask "Will this please our people?" Always ask "Will this meet a need?" before you ask "Will this meet a demand?"

Your decisions are very important and you do not want to Minister hypocritically in the church. God expects you to use wisdom in knowing what areas to work in the church without neglecting other Ministry areas of your life.

Chapter #7

The Ministry Of Your Job

Our place of employment is very important to our financial gain and affords us the opportunity of upward mobility. On the job is where we often meet individuals that God has us to Minister too. Our ministry is not always through our words, but often through the life we live and how we deal with difficult situations. Difficult situations, as well as difficult people often bring about stress and anxiety. Finding balance at work will alleviate a great deal of stress in your life.

Balancing Your Workload On Your Jobs

Start by recording how you spend your time currently. Simply use a planner or diary to note down your activities throughout the day in order to monitor where your time is going. At the end of the week, set aside some time to review your schedule. Now, how much time was wasted? This is where you need to be strict. Consciously cutting out unproductive conversations, numerous tea/coffee breaks, or any of the other little time wasters in your schedule takes some will power but it is worth it. Of course, you still need human contact and a cup of joe every now and again, but being aware of how much time your are spending on those things will help you to control your activities.

Appointments: Unnecessary appointments may also have wasted your time. How many regular meetings do you have with colleagues? Again, you should be strict here, but how many of those were actually necessary or productive? Controlling your appointments is a vital step in time management.

Colleagues: Well-meaning colleagues can be a further source of wasted time. In the spirit of camaraderie, you should want to help your colleagues if there is a problem that needs your attention. If the task is not something directly related to your position, then perhaps refer them to someone who would be in a better position to help. Water cooler gossip is another source of time wastage. Pointless, or even friendly, conversations can easily fill your schedule if you don't employ strict time management.

Workload: Take another look at your schedule. How much time is spent on work that someone else could/should be doing? Menial tasks, such as photocopying, stamping letters, or filing work, are often duties of clerical or secretarial staff. Even if you have been doing these tasks for years, training or requesting that someone else takes on this duty (where appropriate) will save you much time in the long run (although you may have to spend some time to monitor and teach someone how to do it at first).

Managers: It's unfortunate that sometimes one's superiors contribute to wasted time. Within the proper bounds of respect and good humor, helping your manager to see how they defined tasks and unclear communication is a key source of time wastage. If your manager doesn't define duties clearly then you will end up going back to them with questions. Try to get clarity from the start.

Being prepared: Being well prepared for essential meetings and appointments will help you to save time. How many times have you attended meetings without a clear idea of what it is about, or without having read the necessary documentation beforehand? It's probably a safe bet that those very same meetings were unproductive (which probably led to a follow up meeting). If, on the other hand, you take the time to prepare for each scheduled appointment then it will be a success. Decisions can be made and actions assigned only if you have clear thoughts on the issue and are aware of what's going on.

Deadlines: Of all the things that are knocking your balance, deadlines are probably having the biggest effect. And it is probably the most difficult thing for you to change. Organizing your projects in terms of priority and not just the closeness of the deadline will help you to keep a balance.

What if the deadline is just downright impossible, though? In that case, you should reason with your superiors to get the deadline extended. Failing that, forcefully requesting more resources to achieve the task will make the deadline more practical. You could also consider getting the Deliverable altered so as to be more achievable, even if the due date doesn't change. Your only remaining weapon is just to make it clear from the start that the deadline is impossible, although as a dedicated worker you will of course put your all into it.

Communications: Being organized in terms of communications is also vital. Paperwork can easily get out of hand. A simple and effective system is necessary here. You only need two folders for paperwork - the 'to do' folder, and the 'to file' folder. Anything else can be thrown away. Taking immediate action when you receive paperwork is vital to being organized. Sort your paperwork into the appropriate folder and schedule time to deal with the folders regularly. Emails can be equally cumbersome. Studies have shown that keeping email programs open is actually disruptive to efficiency. Rather, you should check emails regularly (five or six times a day) and deal with the incoming emails appropriately. Having separate folders in your inbox for different types of emails will keep you organized.

Telephone calls can easily waste your time. Rather than waiting on hold, it is wise to find out an appropriate time to call someone, or even request that they call you. You could even schedule a specific time to call someone to avoid the problems of missed calls. You should also make sure that secretarial staff are aware of how to deal with calls. They should know when to refer the calls to your colleagues, and when it is appropriate to take a message rather than put the call through to you.

<u>Benefits</u>

Is managing your time really worth the hassle? Resoundingly, yes, it is. On a day-to-day level, it will make your routine more practical and organized. It will make your long-term view clearer, as you know that you are in control of upcoming projects and tasks. For your career, it will help you achieve your goals quicker. It even has health benefits. It's scientifically proven that we get highly stressed when we don't achieve tasks and goals that we wanted to reach. Stress, in turn, is detrimental to sleep, digestion and mental activities. On the other hand, a balanced workload and controlled use of time will negate stress and make you more capable.

<u>Top Tips</u>

1. Make a record - how are you spending your time? What can be cut out? Also, always write down your 'to do' list and organize it according to priority.

2. Managing communications - make effective telephone calls (don't stay on hold, leave clear messages etc.), keep a tidy inbox with multiple folders for different types of emails, don't let yourself be disturbed by colleagues if inappropriate.

3. Managing meetings - attend only meetings that it is necessary or advantageous to attend. Make sure you are prepared for it so that it achieves something (otherwise a follow-up meeting becomes a requisite - another timewaster).

4. Be organized - a tidy desk, a tidy to do list, and a tidy email inbox show a tidy and organized mind and person.

5. Prioritize - even if you have multiple projects on the go and numerous tasks to achieve, a clearly defined list of priorities will keep you on top of things and will help you to meet deadlines.

6. Delegate tasks - don't be afraid to pass duties onto other capable people. The time spent teaching someone else to do one of your tasks is soon made up for.

7. Say no - sometimes well-meaning colleagues, or people outside of your company, make demands on your time unnecessarily (meetings, conferences, solving other people's problems etc.). A polite 'no' will help you to keep control of your time.

8. Maintain a record - a diary or planner will help you to keep an eye on where your time is going. If it is being spent badly, you can change things. Making a written note of how you spend your time is one of the key steps. Don't miss it out.

Working With Difficult People

Your work Ministry includes working with difficult people. Here are four steps for dealing with difficult people, biblically:

<u>Self-inspect:</u> make sure it's not YOU. Matthew 7:2 "For with what judgment ye judge, ye shall be judged: and with what measure ye mete, it shall be measured to you again."

<u>Speak the truth in love to the difficult person:</u> Matthew 5:16 "Let your light so shine before men that they may see your good works, and glorify your Father which is in heaven."

<u>Don't take vengeance, but practice goodness:</u> Romans 12:19 "Dearly beloved, avenge not yourself, but rather give place unto wrath: for it is written, Vengeance is mine; I will repay, saith the Lord."

<u>We must forgive:</u> definition of forgiveness means to pardon, cancellation of debt, to cease from resentment, to no longer look for restitution or payback. Please note that forgiveness is a given, but trust is earned."

Who is the most difficult person you work with? Does it feel to you like they spend each evening plotting and planning on how to ruin the next day for you? Does it drain your energy just thinking about this person? You're not alone. It seems that everyone of us has a 'difficult to deal with' person in our life. They take a lot of energy just to ignore, and many of us wish they would just go away. If you can identify with this scenario, finish the rest of this sentence: "I would be more effective working with my difficult person if ..."

<u>What is your if?</u>

Now go back and look at what you wrote. Is your answer dependant on them doing something to change? Why do you think they would be willing to change to make your life easier? You're right, they won't. So how are we going to be more effective when working with this person? There are three things that you can change. Now go back and look at what you wrote. Is your answer dependant on them doing something to change? Why do you think they would be willing to change to make your life easier? You're right, they won't. So how are we going to be more effective when working with this person? There are three things that you can change.

<u>1. The System:</u> Perhaps this person is difficult because they are a 'stick to the rules' kind of person and you aren't. It can be very frustrating to you that this person is so stuck on a system you don't agree with. If you could just change the system it would make your life a lot easier, don't you think? Of course, changing the system is an extremely time-intensive proposition with no guarantee of any success. There are people, like Erin Brockovich, who are able to change the system but most people decide that the effort does not equal the payoff. If this is your situation, you may chose to avoid trying to change the system. I'm not saying that it won't work - I am saying that it will take a lot of your time and efforts before you see any dividends. It may be easier to take another approach with your difficult person.

<u>2. The Other Person:</u> *You've* probably heard the old cliché, "If you plan on changing your spouse when you get married, it makes for a very interesting first marriage." It's not so easy to change the other person because there is no incentive for them to change. Why should they? What they are doing is currently working just fine, isn't it? Consider a co-worker that listens to his music at a very loud volume. He likes it that loud, it helps him drown out all the other noise in

the office. You despise the type of music he listens to, and it is far too loud for you to concentrate. You've asked your co-worker to turn it down every day for the past three months and it has now escalated into an all out war between the two of you. You are trying to get your difficult person to see that his music is too loud and you cannot concentrate. You are trying to change his perspective on the volume. Why should he turn it down? He likes it just the way it is. Trying to change the other person is often like hitting your head against a brick wall .. it just doesn't work very well. There is no incentive for the other person to take your perspective.

3. You: Of course, you do have one hundred percent control of what you do. You could try to change your perspective on the situation. Let's assume that your difficult person is Mary, and Mary loves to complain about the company you work for. She says things like "they don't appreciate us", "I'm doing all the work around here and never get any recognition", and "this is an old boys' club and women will never get in senior management positions". Basic whining and moaning, all the time, day in and day out. At first, you agreed with some of the things she said, and occasionally got pulled into the negativity yourself. After a while you realized how destructive this was to your attitude and you tried to convince Mary that she was wrong. This, of course, just intensified the situation and the negativity seemed to get worse. You've probably moved into the same 'zone' that many of us do when confronted with Mary - saying "You're right, this is a terrible place to work", hoping that your agreement will make her go away faster.

Did it work? Not really. What Mary wants is attention and acknowledgement. You are giving her both of those things. We need to change what we are doing to get a different result.

"If you keep on doing what you've always done,
you'll keep on getting what you've always got."

You've heard that before, and it is completely true. If we want to change the way Mary is acting, we need to change what we are doing, and not give her what she wants. People are difficult because they are getting something out of the deal. They may be getting attention, agreement or even success because of it (think of aggressive drivers). If we want them to do something different (remember the opening question?) then we need to do something different.

The next time Mary says "I hate this company", don't argue with her or agree with her, give her what she doesn't want (agreement, attention etc.) and say something like "I LOVE working here!" Don't worry about if you agree with what you are saying or not, give her something other than what she wants. She wants to feel bad about where she is working. She wants to complain. She wants to be negative. Don't give her what she wants.

This is work! Sometimes a lot of work too, especially if you happen to be in a negative mood that day and agree with her. Don't give into the temptation. Be 100% consistent in this approach. For two weeks this will be very difficult for you. I promise that if you are consistent and not give Mary what she wants, then she will change her behavior with you. The next time you are asked the question "I would be more effective working with my difficult person if ...", the right answer lies within you. You can change what is happening with that person. It takes time, effort, persistence and patience. The result is worth the effort!

Daily Devotion

Why is reading the Bible and daily devotions something important for Christians? Well the reason they are important is because we need to spend time with the Lord. Think about it this way, we spend time with those who are important to us, our significant other, friends, family. We spend time with them because we enjoy being in their company and because we want to know them better. Well this is the same reason we ought to have a daily time set aside to spend with Jesus to get to know him better. Prayer and reading the Word of God will accomplish many things in our spirits.

1. It will bring us closer to Christ
2. It will transform our hearts and minds and make us more like Jesus.
3. It will reveal the Will of God to us for our own lives.

There are other reasons as well. The Bible is important for it is where we learn the character of God. The NT is where we learn about the teachings of Jesus and the Apostles which form the foundation of our faith upon which all else is built.

The fact is Devotions are often a hard thing to do. We are busy and so many demands on our time will if we let them totally push spending time alone with God out of our lives. We all say we love Jesus, so we should logically want to spend time with him and get to know him. Remember being a Christian is really about our personal relationship with the Lord. In order to have a close relationship with someone you need to spend time with them. I encourage every Christian who reads this to try and start daily devotions and if need be find a partner to help one another keep daily devotions.

Satan will use all means at his disposal to undermine our relationship with God. And his greatest tactic is to make us so busy we feel we don't have time to spend alone with the Lord. The passage in Revelations where Jesus says "Behold I stand at the door and knock, and whoever hears and opens the door I will come in and eat with him and he with me" was written to Christians not unbelievers. Somehow he had been crowded out of their hearts and was asking to come back in. Today many of us have crowded the Lord out of our hearts too. We wonder why we don't feel close to him as we once did. Look at what takes your time, and make time for the Lord today, and each day forward. Then you will begin to be renewed in your walk and your faith.

Chapter #8

The Ministry Of You!

There are probably a few hundred reasons that might motivate you to care for yourself and to be healthy. Here are five, actually four, reasons that motivate me at a really deep level and I think that these are reasons why God would want us all to be motivated by.

1. It glorifies God

2. You're taking care of your body - His temple

3. It's being a good witness

4. You'll have more energy – be better equipped for what God has planned for you

5. I need your help with a 5th reason?

It Glorifies God:

The Bible says in 1 Corinthians 10:31 that whatever we do we're to do it to the glory of God. It also tells us in Isaiah that we were created and formed by God to glorify Him. This is our primary purpose in life – to glorify God. We do that when we care for our body and live a healthy lifestyle.

Our Body is God's Temple and for us to Care For:

One scripture that reminds us that our body is God's temple is 1 Corinthians 19-20. God's Holy Spirit lives inside a believer. After we accept Jesus into heart, God gives us His Spirit to help us live the kind of life He wants us to live. Since God actually lives in us, Paul tells us in verse that our body is His temple. Since God "bought" us with a high price, Jesus' death, than we are obligated to care for our body which is His temple.

Being Healthy is Being a Good Witness:

Acts 1:8 reminds us that we are to be witnesses for other people. People look for us to be models of the Christian faith. We ought to desire to live our lives in a way that represents our faith well. Taking care of our health is one way that we can be a good witness.

You'll Have More Energy to Do God's Work:

Ephesians 2:10 helps us see that we are God's masterpiece, created to do the good things that He had planned a long time ago for us to do. We all know that the more fit and healthy we are the more energy we will have. The more energy that we have, the more we can put into whatever task we are doing. We'll also be better able to sustain ourselves for the long haul. What we believe determines what we do. I suspect that if you believe what I've written above, and you value your relationship with God, it's likely that you are taking good care of your body and your health.

You must remember that your body is the temple of the Holy Ghost. Proverbs 6:19-20 "What? Know ye not that your body is the temple of the Holy Ghost which is in you, which ye have of God, and ye are not your own?" God is expecting you to take care of his temple, which is your body. Take time to eat healthy, exercise, and rest. Feed your body spiritually healthy food, not carnal junk food. Read your word and find time for intercession with God.

Taking Care Of You: Christian Codependency

You can overcome Christian codependency by learning how to take care of yourself. Christian codependency promotes misconceptions about when God thinks it is okay to put yourself before others. We have to care about ourselves and others. One of the best ways to determine if you should put someone else's request or need before your own is to consider your motive. Here are some reasons you might be compelled to neglect your own needs for others:

- Obligation - You believe you have to.

- Guilt - You will feel bad.

- Fear - You are afraid of the repercussions

- Pride - You want people to think well of you.

- People-pleasing - You fear disapproval.

- Obedience - You believe God wants you to.

- Choice - You want to.

Obligation, guilt, fear, pride, and people-pleasing have something in common: They are all unhealthy reasons. Rather than making the right choice for you, you allow yourself to be influenced by others. It isn't what you really want to do and the outcome is typically resentment.

II Corinthians 9:7 says, "Each man should give what he has decided in his heart to give, not reluctantly or under compulsion, for God loves a cheerful giver" (NIV). Choice allows you to own your decision and prevents you from being resentful.

Obedience to God is the other good reason. We can and should at times sacrificially give when we believe God is directing us and when it involves our witness and the reputation of our faith. I know the times when my selfish nature is fighting with the Holy Spirit to not give in to God's leading to sacrificially give, but this isn't a common occurrence. It can't be all the time or you go back to an unhealthy place where you are neglecting yourself.

There is a time to put yourself first. If you are in the check-out line at the grocery store, you can occasionally let someone go in front of you, but you can't keep letting one person after another go in front of you or you will never get home to make dinner. There is definitely a time to put yourself before others. Relationship Prayer: God, help me to recognize my motives when I want to put someone before myself. Help me to do it out of choice and obedience to you. Relationship Challenge: Pay attention to why you want to put others before yourself. Try to do it of choice or obedience to God. God cares about your motives. If you do put someone before yourself, He wants it to be for the right reasons. Overcoming Christian codependency helps you to learn how to take care of yourself while still caring about others in ways that please God.

Dealing With Anxiety

There are a number of healthy ways of coping with anxiety that may help your anxiety go down in intensity, become less frequent, and/or become more tolerable.

1. Deep Breathing

Deep breathing can be an important coping skill to learn. It may sound silly, but many people do not breathe properly. Natural breathing involves your diaphragm, a large muscle in your abdomen. When you breathe in, your belly should expand. When you breathe out, your belly should fall. Overtime, people forget how to breathe this way and instead use their chest and shoulders. This causes short and shallow breaths, which can increase stress and anxiety. Fortunately, it is not too late to "re-learn" how to breathe and help protect yourself from stress. Practice this simple exercise to improve your breathing and combat anxiety.

2. Progressive Muscle Relaxation

Using relaxation exercises can be an effective way to reduce your stress and anxiety. One relaxation exercise called progressive muscle relaxation focuses on a person alternating between tensing and relaxing different muscle groups throughout the body. In this way, relaxation is viewed like a pendulum. More complete relaxation of your muscles can be obtained by first going to the other extreme (that is, by tensing your muscles). In addition, by tensing your muscles (a common symptom of anxiety) and immediately relaxing them, the symptom of muscle tension may become a signal to relax over time. You can learn a basic progressive muscle relaxation exercise in this article.

3. Using Mindfulness to Cope with Anxiety

Using mindfulness for anxiety can be very helpful. Mindfulness has been around for ages. However, mental health professionals are beginning to recognize that mindfulness can have many benefits for people suffering from difficulties such as anxiety and depression. In a nutshell, mindfulness is about being in-touch with and aware of the present moment. So often in our lives, we are stuck in our heads, caught up in the anxiety and worries of daily life. This exercise will introduce you to mindfulness and may be helpful getting you "out of your head" and in touch with the present moment.

4. Self-Monitoring

Self-monitoring can be a helpful way of getting a handle on your anxiety symptoms. We are all "creatures of habit." We often go about our day without thinking, being unaware of much that goes on around us. This may be useful in some situations, but other times, this lack of awareness may make us feel as though our thoughts and emotions are completely unpredictable and unmanageable. We cannot really address uncomfortable symptoms of anxiety without first being aware of what situations bring up these feelings. Self-monitoring is a simple way of increasing this awareness.

5. Using Social Support for Anxiety

Over and over again, it has been found that finding support from others can be a major factor in helping people overcome the negative effects of a traumatic event and PTSD. Having someone you trust that you can talk to can be very helpful for working through stressful situations or for emotional validation. However, simply having someone available to talk to may not be enough. There are several important pieces to a supportive relationship that may be particularly beneficial in helping someone manage their anxiety. Learn more about what makes up a good supportive relationship in this article.

6. Self-Soothing Exercises for Anxiety

When you are experiencing anxiety, it is important to have ways of coping with those feelings. For example, seeking out social support can be an excellent way of improving your mood. However, the anxiety associated with symptoms of PTSD can sometimes occur unexpectedly, and social support may not be readily available. Therefore, it is important to learn coping strategies that you can do on your own. Coping strategies focused on improving your mood and reducing anxiety that you can do on your own are sometimes described as self-soothing or self-care coping strategies.

7. Using Expressive Writing for Anxiety

Using journaling to cope with and express your thoughts and feelings (also called expressive writing) can be a good way of coping with anxiety. Expressive writing has been found to improve physical and psychological health. In regard to PTSD in particular, expressive writing has been found to have a number of benefits including improved coping and posttraumatic growth (or the ability to find meaning in and have positive life changes following a traumatic event), as well as reduced PTSD symptoms, tension, and anger.

8. Using Distraction to Cope with Anxiety

Purposeful use of distraction techniques can actually be of benefit in coping with emotions that are strong and feel uncomfortable, such as anxiety and fear. Distraction is anything you do to temporarily take our attention off of a strong emotion. Sometimes, focusing on a strong emotion can make it feel even stronger and more out of control. Therefore, by temporarily distracting yourself, you may give the emotion some time to decrease in intensity, making it easier to manage. Learn some distraction techniques in this article.

9. Behavioral Activation for Anxiety

Anxiety and avoidance go hand-in-hand. While the avoidance of anxiety-provoking situations may help reduce our anxiety in the moment, in the long-term it may prevent us from living a meaningful and rewarding life (especially as this avoidance grows bigger and bigger). Behavioral activation is a great way of increasing your activity level, as well as the extent with which you engage in positive and rewarding activities. Through behavioral activation, you can reduce your depression and anxiety.

Dealing With Depression

Because our life becomes so complex with the many challenges we face, it is vital to stay close to the Lord so that we do not fall into a state of depression. Walking around sad, gloomy and dejected is not what God desires for your life.

2 Corinthians 4:8-10 says "We are troubled on every side, yet not distressed; we are perplexed, but not in despair; Persecuted, but not forsaken; cast down, but not destroyed; Always bearing about in the body the dying of the Lord Jesus, that the life also of Jesus might be made manifest in our body." (King James Bible)

Please understand that it is not God's plan for us to suffer with Depression. The bible gives us a clear understanding of what types of challenges we should expect in our day-to-day life and how we should FEEL when it happens. In other words, we may feel under attack, but we should not have great anxiety and stress about it. We may feel puzzled concerning the matters we deal with, but we should not feel like there is no hope. We may feel harassed, but we should not feel abandoned or deserted. We may be put down, but not destroyed. If you have to deal with the spirit of depression you must deal with it wisely so that you may defeat the plan of the enemy.

Depression is a state that affects mind, emotion, and body, creating a dysphoric mood, lethargy or anxiety in the body, and thoughts of hopelessness and, in a significant number of cases, suicidal ideation. Depression is a feeling of profound sadness, and/or poor self-image, and/or hopelessness and helplessness. It usually includes anhedonia and anergia (lack of pleasure and lack of energy), and may be irritable and agitated, meaning a dysphoric mood is present without lethargy.

Therapy for Depression

The Psychotherapy Model views depression as a normal response to human experience and survival. Rather than medicating the depression away as a permanent solution, the Psychotherapy Model approaches a person's depression with intense curiosity in an effort to help the person to understand and heal the source of the depression. Through the process of focusing internally a person can understand, unravel, and transform their depression. Psychodynamic approaches often view depression as a defense mechanism, a form of coping or self-protection which relies on "giving up" or "shutting down" to avoid greater emotional risk or pain (see case example: Tommy). And there are other psychological and emotional reasons for depression. Whatever the cause, depression can be improved, if not resolved completely, with therapy. Indeed, research shows that some people may be more predisposed than others to develop depression in response to life events. The familial inheritance identified in depression is both genetic and learned. Whether one is predisposed to depression or not, there is nonetheless a great benefit in addressing depression with therapy.

Depression and Different Stages of Life

Depression should not be confused with normal grief in the aftermath of a major loss, although extended grief may lead to true depression. Depression that is mild and chronic, with fewer symptoms, is known as dysthymia. Depression may present differently based on age or cultural factors. Adolescents tend to show an irritable and agitated depression; older adults may or may not be irritable; certain cultural groups may mask their feeling to varying degrees; women are known to be more likely to admit to depression than men. Depression is one of the most common reasons people seek therapy.

Depression's Effect on the Body

Those experiencing depression may have great difficulty mustering the energy necessary for even the most basic tasks, such as getting out bed, preparing food, or bathing. Depression often includes intense, unrelievable fatigue. Depression may be somaticized, leading to complaints about back pain, muscle aches, nausea, and headaches. Depression may lead to sudden tearfulness without an apparent trigger.

Depressive Thoughts

Depression always includes negative thoughts, sometimes with great severity. Individuals who are depressed may perseverate on thoughts like "I'm no good," "no one cares about me," "life is pointless," or "I'll never feel better." People with depression may have great guilt or shame, sometimes with an identifiable etiology, sometimes not. Worries are frequently present. In the most severe cases, thinking may be minimal, and the person with depression may border on a comatose state. Suicidal ideation is common.

Feelings of Depression

Depression involves the emotions of sadness and grief, and often anger, fear, shame, and other negative emotions. Affect may be strong, with tearfulness, tension, and possibly anger may be present, or affect may be restricted and in severe cases, flat.

Relationships & Depression

Depression usually interferes with a person's ability to communicate, express emotion, and to experience emotional and sexual intimacy in relationships. A person who is depressed may be unable to receive comfort from others, believing they do not deserve it or it is insincere. Their lethargy, irritability, or anhedonia may make giving love near impossible. Depressed people often isolate; at the other end of the spectrum they may be overly dependent, attached, or needy. Depression may have passive-aggressive elements that disrupt relationships. Depressed people are often uninterested in normally pleasant social activities, and may be unable to work due to lethargy or fearfulness.

Correlated Psychological Issues

Depression may co-occur with any other mental disorder, and is commonly linked with anxiety. Depression may alternative with manic or hypomanic states in Bipolar disorder or schizoaffective disorder. Depression is often linked to a lack of social support, recent loss, financial stress, and familial depression. Suicide risk is always a concern and must be assessed frequently. Depression must be distinguished from appropriate, short-term grief in the face of loss. Depression can be a major symptom of post-traumatic stress. Depression is also associated with substance abuse, especially with alcohol and other central nervous system depressants. People may self-medicate with such substances to manage depression, making their symptoms worse in the long term.

Medication for Depression

The most popular medical treatment of depression is medication. Several classes of medications have been developed to improve mood. All have a good chance of significant side-effects, in some cases including insomnia and sexual problems. For severe depression, medications can be helpful in stabilizing a person, helping one to get out of bed in the morning, and making talk therapy more effective. Medication can be a lifesaver, for those who have been considering suicide. However useful these medications may be at symptom reduction, they fail to address the emotional and psychological causes of depression, which often underlie the formation and maintenance of anxiety.

Dealing With Past Trauma: Inner Healing

This is one of the most vital and important areas of deliverance ministry that we cannot overlook. While it is important to cast out demons, it is just as important, if not more important, to minister to the emotional wounds. Emotional wounds are one of the most common reasons that deliverances can fail or demons seem to keep coming back and regaining inhabitation within the person. I need to make it clear that if you are going to be in the deliverance ministry, it is an absolute necessity that you learn about emotional wounds and how to bring the person to the point where they can receive inner healing from the Holy Spirit.

Our goal is not to forget a hurtful event or trauma, but to receive healing for that event, where the Holy Spirit removes the stinger from it. When we look back upon a healed wound, we can see it in a different way, because it has been healed and is no longer painful to look back upon Identifying emotional wounds. The first thing we need to do is identify the problem, and realize the need for inner healing. Below is a common list of common symptoms to look for in somebody who has an emotional wound:

Inner rawness: there's often a sense of inner rawness and hurt that doesn't seem to go away.

Irritability: it's easy to become irritable with others, even if they aren't doing anything wrong!

Little or no tolerance: there is a low tolerance issue with others, where you expect and demand from them.

Feelings always rising up: feelings of anger, hate, resentment, etc. seem to "rise up" within you at the slightest offense from others.

Overly sensitive about an event in your past: If there are events in your past which cause you to become very sensitive or angry, or even cause you to lash out, then it is likely revealing a deep emotional wound tied in with that event or memory.

Hard to forgive: it becomes very difficult, if not impossible to love and therefore forgive others. It can also be hard to forgive and love yourself. It can even be hard to forgive and love God, even though He has done nothing wrong against you!

Hard to feel loved: it is hard to clearly see and realize the love of others and God in your life. You may be surrounded by people who love you, but it can be difficult to fully feel and receive that love. There seems to be a wall up that blocks the flow of love into your life.

Lashing out: when there's an inner wound that has festered, it becomes easy to lash out or have sudden outbursts of anger, hate, resentment, etc. You may find it easy to lash out at people who love you, and have done you no harm.

Feelings of anger towards God: when a person has been wounded, it becomes easy to blame God for their troubles and hardships. This is the last thing that you want to do when seeking to be healed, because it virtually puts a wall in your mind that can block the healing power of the Holy Spirit to operate. Although He desires to heal your wound, He will not override your freewill, and if you hold hate in your heart against Him, it can block His efforts to heal your wounds.

Self-hate: many times when a person is hurt from past abuse, they will begin to think that they were. This is not true. Abuse is never acceptable, even if a child was being out of order. Parental love disciplines and corrects, but never abuses.

Easily frustrated: because an inner turmoil that an inner wound causes, it is easy to become easily frustrated with everyday chores and responsibilities.

Escapism: as a result of inner turmoil, it is easy to desire to escape or suppress reality. This can be in the form of overeating, drinking, smoking, porn, spending binges, etc. When a person indulges in escapism, addictions can form, and open the door to spirits of addiction, which makes the addictions virtually impossible to break.

Cutting: a person who is a cutter usually has an alter inside the person who is holding much pain, and needs to release the pain or it honestly feels that it deserves the pain (self-hate/religious bondage).

Retaliation urges: because of built-up hate and anger as a result of unforgiveness, somebody who has a festering inner wound will find it easy to retaliate or snap back at those who offend them or step on their toes.

Irresponsible behavior: inner pain has a way of consuming a person's mind, and eventually this can take on a careless approach to life. It is hard to feel good about yourself if you have an inner wound, and if you don't feel good about yourself, it will begin to show in your lifestyle. Irrational expectations of others: somebody who has been wounded may set high expectations for those around them. They feel that others ought to hold up to unrealistic standards, and are very intolerable to any mistakes made. They find it hard to forbear (put up with) one another as the Bible commands of us (see Colossians 3:13).

Perfectionism: a person who has an emotional wound may also be performance driven. Perhaps they felt like no matter what they did, they could never please a parent or authority figure, and later on in life, that rejection wound causes the person to be a performer to the point where they are never satisfied and burned out by their efforts.

Feelings of hopelessness: I believe this is also a common result of unresolved inner wounds. Since the love of God is blocked in your life, it becomes hard to see why He would love or care for you, and therefore you become an easy target for feelings of hopelessness.

Drivenness: when you suffer from an emotional wound, it can create a sense of void in your life's meaning, thus driving you to find meaning and purpose and happiness. This could be in the form of college degrees, careers, financial success, etc. Instead of appreciating the person who God has made (YOU!), you find yourself chasing what you think will bring true happiness and purpose to your life.

Obsessive Compulsive Disorder or OCD: it is my belief that Obsessive Compulsive Disorder (OCD) often involves emotional wounds that were never fully healed. This is especially true with people who have bondages to self-hate, self-resentment, self-unforgiveness, etc.

Hostility towards God, self, and others: because of bound up emotions, a person can tend to feel hostile towards God, other people in their life, or even themselves. This is usually rooted in a form of bitterness against God for not preventing something from happening to you, bitterness against somebody who has wronged or harmed you emotionally, or bitterness against yourself for failures that you've fallen into yourself. Be honest with yourself! If you had a headache, would you go to the doctor and tell him, "There's something wrong with me, but I don't want to think about it long enough to figure out what it is! I don't know what's wrong with me! I don't know if it's a headache, a stomachache, a runny nose, or an ingrown toenail!" You would never do that when seeking physical healing, would you? Then why do we so often do this very thing when we are seeking inner healing? We know that there's a problem, a wound, but we don't want to even peek into our pasts to figure out what is really wrong! If you're going to receive healing for an emotional wound, you need to first be honest with yourself and what has happened. Let's get started by answering some basic questions: Who is it that you hate or blame? Be honest with yourself; there's somebody in your past that you are holding something against. Be specific, and go back as far as you can. If you can figure out when this wound began, and who is responsible, it is the first step to receiving healing for the wound. What did they do to you? Make a list of everything that was done to you, which you still hold against them in your heart. What might be a list of things which you still hold onto in your heart? What things can't you seem to easily forget? I'm not referring to a list of people whom you haven't forgiven, but rather a list of people/events where you just cannot seem to release it from your heart. Don't try to cover up their mistake and say that it was alright. If they did you wrong, then there's no getting around that. Being honest about what was done to you is very important.

What things have you done, that you deeply regret? Make a list of things that you still, to this day, regret doing. If you have any feelings of self-hate, self-unforgiveness, etc., then you need to be honest and figure out why you hate yourself.

Is there anything in your past that you feel excessively embarrassed or ashamed of? This is a common cause for self-hate. If there are things which you still haven't forgiven yourself of, then now is a good time to make a list of those things, so that you can effectively forgive and release the hate held secretly within your heart against yourself. It is vital that we get right down to the roots, and lay out the specific reasons why there are wounds that have not yet healed. Spiritual infections, like natural infections, will fester and grow worse when in the dark; it is important to bring the issues to the light, so they can no longer fester, but receive the healing light of Christ into those areas of the mind and emotions. If you cannot be honest with yourself, and bring these things out into the light, then you're only hindering the healing power of the Holy Spirit from ministering to those wounds and bringing about healing in your mind and emotions.

Keys to inner healing: the first thing that you want to settle is any feelings of guilt and shame, especially any feelings that God is somehow disappointed or angry with you. When dealing with a physical wound, what is the first thing you do? Cleanse it from germs so that it can properly heal. When dealing with spiritual or emotional wounds, carrying around baggage (guilt, shame, fear, etc.) makes the healing process much more difficult. Getting yourself to the point where you know that God loves, forgives, and accepts you, is one of the foundations to receive inner healing. Knowing that God isn't angry or disappointed in you creates an atmosphere where you can freely turn your burdens over to Jesus, and trust Him to take care of them. Carrying around a burden of shame is a sure way to hinder the inner healing process because it mentally separates us from the healing work of Jesus. If we want to freely receive healing for our damaged emotions, then we need to settle it in our minds that God is not angry with us, and stand on God's Word about our sins being forgiven and washed from us by the Blood of Christ.

One of the biggest keys to receive healing for damaged emotions depends on your perception of God, and how He feels about you and your healing. You must realize that he is the source of your healing, and deliverance... and NOT your problems! Blaming God for your problems will put up an invisible wall, which will hinder His healing power from flowing into your mind and emotions. The Holy Spirit will not override our freewill, and when we blame Him, our freewill is putting our hand up in His face. It is important that our freewill allows His work and does not blame Him for the bad thing(s) that have happened to us. It is important to realize that God is for you, and not against you. He desires to see you healed and restored to wholeness even more than you do!

Open up those wounds, and give the pain to Jesus. What you want is to open up those wounds before the light (Jesus), so that they can be healed. As long as you hold them in darkness, they will never fully heal. If you had a physical wound, and it turned into an infection, and you merely put a bandaid over the wound, would that solve the problem? Of course not! You need to take that mask off, expose it to the light, and apply the healing and germ-killing light of Christ into that wound so that it can heal.

God's Word tells us to cast our cares upon Him, for He cares for us (see 1 Peter 5:7). We need to realize that Christ has taken our pain on the cross, and if we will transfer it to Him, He is waiting to heal our wounds. The Holy Spirit has shown me this very important key to inner healing:

Why should we carry something that Christ has carried for us on the cross? Surely he hath borne our grief, and carried our sorrows (grief, pain, affliction): yet we did esteem him stricken, smitten of God, and afflicted. But he was wounded for our transgressions, he was bruised for our iniquities: the chastisement of our peace was upon him; and with his stripes we are healed.

Isaiah 53:4-5 - The word "sorrows" in this passage, actually translates to grief, pain, or affliction. When Jesus shed His blood, He carried our inner pain and wounds, so that we don't have to! God's Word tells us that He cares for us, and because of this fact, we are told to cast all - not some, but ALL - of our cares upon Him (see 1 Peter 5:7).

Being thankful for Jesus carrying our sorrows is another key to break-through. If you choose to carry your own sorrows, it is usually because (a) you don't really realize or believe that He carried your sorrows, or (b) you haven't taken the time to think about or understand what Jesus did. Anytime when we seriously look at what Christ did for us, it's impossible not to be thankful for such a gift that He's so lovingly purchased for us! Being thankful will make you eager to take advantage of what Christ has lovingly carried for you.

I want you to picture Jesus standing there beside you with tears in His eyes, feeling the hurt and suffering that you're going through. We are told to cast our cares and concerns upon Him - why? Because He CARES for us! Picturing Jesus standing there beside a situation with tears in His eyes can be very powerful. John 11:35-36 tells us that, "Jesus wept. Then said the Jews, Behold how he loved him!" Casting all your care upon him; for he careth for you.

1 Peter 5:7 - Developing a thankful attitude is another big key to receiving healing for our emotional wounds. Thankfulness leads to trust, if you are thankful for what God's given you, then you will find it easy to trust Him in those areas of your life. Thankfulness is also a big key to overcoming rejection issues, how is that? Because when you begin to look at all that Christ has done for you, it is impossible to feel rejected by your heavenly Father, which is one of the big keys to healing rejection. God's Word actually commands us to be thankful: And let the peace of God rule in your hearts, to the which also ye are called in one body; and be ye thankful.

Colossians 3:15 - Not only are we commanded to be thankful, but the Bible also tells us what can happen when we are unthankful: Because that, when they knew God, they glorified him not as God, neither were thankful; but became vain in their imaginations, and their foolish heart was darkened.

Romans 1:21 - An unthankful heart is prone to unforgiving, unloving, resentful, and all sorts of hateful feelings against others. It is a poison to our emotional health and ability to receive the healing that God wants to bring to our wounds and hurts. Those who are unforgiving and judgmental towards others have forgotten what God has done for them. Anybody who truly thankful for how God has treated them, would go about treating others the same way and He treated them.

Begin to be thankful for the little things which God has created for you to enjoy. Little things such as the birds singing in the trees or your pet cat or dog - they were made for us to enjoy! It is hard, if not impossible to be thankful and unforgiving at the same time. When we realize what Christ has done for us, and are thankful for such an expensive gift that has been purchased with Jesus' own blood for us, then we will naturally forgive those who wrong us, that love is contagious and will flow through us. We cannot honestly look at what Christ has done for us, and not overflow with thankfulness in our heart! Becoming thankful is a huge key to breakthrough if you struggle with unforgiveness.

Fear is often a tool of Satan because when we puts our trust in God, tremendous amount of peace and healing can then take place. Fear will keep a person holding onto what must be released into Jesus' hands. This is another reason why we must come to know the true good and loving nature of God towards His children. Knowing that God is a good God and has your best interest in mind, paves the way to being able to trust Him with the concerns in your life. You need to know that you can trust God with your needs, He understands them, and desires to help you!

Another key to receive inner healing, especially from a background or root of rejection, is coming to a place where you know that God loves you dearly and has your best interest in mind. If you have a hard time believing that God is good towards you and has your best interest in mind, then I highly recommend Gloria Copeland's book entitled, "Blessed Beyond Measure." Satan and evil spirits are always eager to make a person feel as if God is angry with them. It puts the person on the edge of their seat and makes them afraid of God, which causes them to feel discouraged in their relationship with Him, and tend to give up on spending time with Him and drawing near to Him (the source of their healing!). It's no wonder Satan wants us to feel like God is somehow angry or disappointed in us! Try this: if you have struggled and felt like God is angry with you, then try to imagine that God sees you, knows where you've been, and yet still looks favorably on you? It will loosen up the tenseness on your whole system once you begin to see things as God wants you to see them. Once you can imagine it, then turn to God's Word, and learn of how He really does look upon you with favor and hope! He's always calling us back to repentance, so that He can restore our relationship with Him. I can't tell you how powerful that imaginations can be when used for God's glory instead of Satan's. This is a powerful key to freedom and healing for many!

Another key to inner healing is not to meditate or continue to think about what was done to you. Once you give that to the Lord, don't continue to think about how badly you were wronged. You will cause emotional wounds to fester when you choose to continue thinking about what was done to you. Don't get me wrong, we are to face what was done to us, head on, honestly, and don't deny what was done to us, but once we give all the pain and hurt to Jesus, then we need to leave it there. If you have two dogs, and you feed one but leave the other to starve, then which one will be around? The one that you feed of course! We need to make a solid choice not to dwell/feed upon what was done to us, as it will reinforce the reason as to why we are hurt or angry. This is a very important key to receiving healing from emotional wounds.

As absurd as this sounds, you need to revisit the pain! By going back to the place where the pain was formed, and revisiting that wound in your soul, it will allow you to truly and fully forgive, thus pulling the pain up at its root. The job can be half-done if you simply say, "I forgive them" without thinking of what you are really forgiving them of. When you can revisit that pain, and forgive out of the love in your heart, then your healing will come naturally! It may also help to picture Jesus standing there besides you while you were being wronged, and think about how He felt about what was done to you. You shouldn't have to keep forgiving the same person for the same offense that took place 10 years ago; we need to reach the point of pain, and forgive at the scene of the accident. I'm not saying that we must revisit the same physical place, but rather the memories and place in your mind where the abuse or pain took place.

Are you problem focused? Or solution focused? Those who keep focused on the problem rather than the solution will begin to see the problem as larger than the solution. Are we paying more attention to the problem than we are the solution? Is your problem bigger than God's solution? Jesus came to bring solution, and by us accepting the solution, it makes use of His labor and blood which brings Him much glory, but by paying more attention to the problem, we ignore the solution that Jesus provided and make a mockery of what He went through for us. Being problem focused creates an atmosphere where depression, unforgiveness, irritability, and hopelessness can breed.

You cannot experience inner healing as long as you are focused on the problem. If you want to receive healing, you must stop focusing on the problem, and begin meditating on the solution.

Stop listening to the devil! The devil and his evil spirits work diligently to aggravate the wound to keep it from healing. This work is done by keeping the person reminded of how badly they were wronged or what was done to them. The devil seeks to remind you about why you are angry or hateful towards that person who has wronged you. Demons will do this same thing when trying to develop bondages of fear in a person; they seek to remind the person about why they are fearful. This is why it is vital to stop listening to the voice of the devil, because his goal is to aggravate the wound and make it fester into an even deeper infection.

It can be tempting to desire hatred over healing! When a person has been wounded, they will often choose to retain the feelings of hate and resentment, than to be healed of their wound and see God make everything alright. Do you really want to be healed? Or would you rather hold on to feelings of hate and resentment inside your heart against that person(s) who has wronged you? Would you rather see them suffer and punished for their wrong, or would you rather be healed yourself and let off the hook for your mistakes that you've made in life? Remember, Jesus made it clear that if we want to be forgiven and let off to hook for our failures in life, then we need to let others off the hook and give them what we want God to give us, that is, His mercy and forgiveness!

Stop blaming the person who wronged you, because it wasn't what they did to us or what they are doing to us that is keeping us in bondage, it is our own reactions to what was done to us which holds us in spiritual prison. It is our own anger, hate, resentment, and unforgiveness which will keep us behind spiritual bars! We need to take responsibility for your own failures. One of the reasons that we have a hard time forgiving is because we would have nobody else to blame for our problems. It is important for us to take responsibility concerning our own failures, and give up those things which do not honor the Lord in our hearts. We aren't responsible for what was done to us, but we are responsible for how we chose or choose to react to what happens. Until we can realize our own failures and take responsibility for what we've allowed into our minds and lives, then it can be a blockage to our emotional healing. Blaming others will hinder the healing power of the Holy Spirit in our lives, therefore it must be dealt with before healing can freely flow into our mind and emotions. Remember, it is not what was done to us that keeps us in bondage; it is our reaction to what was done to us which causes all the spiritual bondage and torment! When a woman is raped, it isn't the rape which causes her spiritual bondage, but rather the way she reacted to it; the hate and resentment that is felt afterwards is what gives Satan a foothold. What if the person who has wronged us is still doing it today and has no repentance in their heart? What they are doing to us cannot keep us in bondage, however, how we choose to react to what they are doing can hold us in bondage and torment spiritually.

Perhaps Satan's best-kept secret to prevent a person's soul from healing, is to cause them to feel like God is somehow disappointed in them, or even angry with them. If the enemy can cause a person to feel like God is not eager to forgive or be merciful to them, this is a sure roadblock to anybody's healing process. This causes a person to distance themselves from the very person (Jesus) that desires to heal them. You cannot distance yourself from God and receive healing to your emotions at the same time. Drawing neigh to Him is a huge key to receiving healing. When we are close to him our relationship brings us comfort. God's word tells us that He is the one who gives us a sound clear mind of love and power (see 2 Timothy 1:7). Jesus tells all those who are heavy laden (people who are carrying emotional and mental baggage) to come unto Him, and He will give them rest (see Matthew 11:28-29). One of the biggest keys to inner healing, is to come unto Jesus, but Satan's way of preventing that, is to make the person feel like God is angry with them. This has a lot to do with our perception of our relationship with God. If we don't perceive ourselves as being made right with God, it will cause all sorts of spiritual problems and seriously prevent the inner healing process.

Another one of the biggest keys to inner healing is tearing down walls that prohibit the healing power and light of the Holy Spirit to reach the wound to bring healing. The Holy Spirit is very eager and ready to heal our wounded emotions, but He's also a gentleman and won't override our freewill. He honors our freewill so much, that He would even let us choose to reject Jesus and end up in hell ; He won't even force us to go to heaven! Our freewill can choose to take down our emotional walls or to hold them in place. What are these walls that I am referring to? They are our own reactions to what was done to us. When we react in anger, bitterness, resentment, and choose to give place to the devil in our hearts, we are putting up walls around our wounds that will prohibit the light of Christ from healing them. That is why it is vital that we take responsibility for our reactions to what was done to us. We are not writing off or discrediting what was done to us, but simply not allowing walls to go up which will prevent the Holy Spirit from healing our wounds.

Transparency is very important when seeking healing for emotional wounds. What heals our wounds? The healing light of Christ! What does light require to pass through? Transparency! If you want God's healing light to heal your damaged emotions, then you must be transparent with Him. For the light requires transparency to pass through.

Be truthful and transparent with Christ and He will be able to bring complete healing in your life. Some people have denied their feelings of bitterness and resentment that they don't even recognize that they are sick inside and need healing. Everyone else seems to notice dysfunctional issues that they exhibit, but them.

It is important to make sure that you have forgiven yourself, and are loving yourself as Christ loves you. It is vital that you see yourself as God sees you, as cleansed, washed with the Blood, and your past failures actually removed from your account. If you continue to walk around beating yourself up as if you haven't been forgiven, then you are actually denying the work that Christ has done for you on the cross! Many times, those who have emotional wounds are in bondage to guilt and condemnation, and coming to the realization that their sins are forgiven, is perhaps one of the single most powerful keys to receive healing from emotional wounds.

One helpful thing is to find somebody to talk with about your problem who will love and pray for you. There is tremendous healing power in bringing something out into the open and sharing it with a fellow believer who loves you and will pray for you. The Bible tells us that we need to confess our faults (which I believe also applies to our wounds and weaknesses) to one another and pray that we are healed:

"Confess your faults one to another, and pray one for another, that ye may be healed, The effectual fervent prayer of a righteous man availeth much." (King James Bible James 5:16)

If you want to receive mercy in your situation, then you need to be merciful to those who have wronged or hurt you.

Jesus tells us in Matthew 5:7, "Blessed are the merciful: for they shall obtain mercy." Do you want to receive mercy in your situation?

Have you been merciful in your heart towards those who have wronged or wounded you? Could the very reason that you aren't receiving mercy, is because you're not being merciful? Mercy and forgiveness begin in a person's heart, as Jesus says in Matthew 18:35, "So likewise shall my heavenly Father do also unto you, if ye from your hearts forgive not everyone his brother their trespasses."

Finger pointing or blaming others is an outward manifestation of the root of bitterness. This is called resentment, and it goes hand in hand with refusing to accept personal responsibility for something. Somebody who has been raped or abused usually finds it easy to blame the person who wronged them and perhaps even blame God for allowing it to happen, while they are overlooking the fact that the hate, resentment, and unforgiveness are built up inside of them, which is the very thing holding them back from being healed. Jesus has commanded us (a requirement, not an option) in John 15:12, "This is my commandment, That ye love one another, as I have loved you." When we allow resentment and unforgiveness reign in our hearts, we are disobeying that command which Jesus gave us, and allowing hatred to fill our hearts instead. It's no wonder that Satan and evil spirits take advantage of such negative emotions!

Another important step to the overall healing process is to seek deliverance from any spirits that have entered in through the wound. Demons will often enter in through trauma or abuse, and must be removed in order to ensure complete healing.

Dealing With Grief

Losing someone or something you love is very painful. After a significant loss, you may experience all kinds of difficult and surprising emotions, such as shock, anger, and guilt. Sometimes it may feel like the sadness will never let up. While these feelings can be frightening and overwhelming, they are normal reactions to loss. Accepting them as part of the grieving process and allowing yourself to feel what you feel is necessary for healing.

There is no right or wrong way to grieve, but there are healthy ways to cope with the pain. You can get through it! Grief that is expressed and experienced has a potential for healing that eventually can strengthen and enrich life.

What is grief?

Grief is a natural response to loss. It's the emotional suffering you feel when something or someone you love is taken away. You may associate grief with the death of a loved one, and this type of loss does often cause the most intense grief. But any loss can cause grief, including:

- A relationship breakup
- Loss of health
- Losing a job
- Loss of financial stability
- A miscarriage

- Death of a pet
- Loss of a cherished dream
- A loved one's serious illness
- Loss of a friendship
- Loss of safety after a trauma

The more significant the loss, the more intense the grief. However, even subtle losses can lead to grief. For example, you might experience grief after moving away from home, graduating from college, changing jobs, selling your family home, or retiring from a career you loved.

Everyone grieves differently

Grieving is a personal and highly individual experience. How you grieve depends on many factors, including your personality and coping style, your life experience, your faith, and the nature of the loss. The grieving process takes time. Healing happens gradually; it can't be forced or hurried – and there is no "normal" timetable for grieving. Some people start to feel better in weeks or months. For others, the grieving process is measured in years. Whatever your grief experience, it's important to be patient with yourself and allow the process to naturally unfold.

Myths and Facts About Grief

MYTH: The pain will go away faster if you ignore it.
Fact: Trying to ignore your pain or keep it from surfacing will only make it worse in the long run. For real healing it is necessary to face your grief and actively deal with it.

MYTH: It's important to be "be strong" in the face of loss.
Fact: Feeling sad, frightened, or lonely is a normal reaction to loss. Crying doesn't mean you are weak. You don't need to "protect" your family or friends by putting on a brave front. Showing your true feelings can help them and you.

MYTH: If you don't cry, it means you aren't sorry about the loss.
Fact: Crying is a normal response to sadness, but it's not the only one. Those who don't cry may feel the pain just as deeply as others. They may simply have other ways of showing it.

MYTH: Grief should last about a year.
Fact: There is no right or wrong time frame for grieving. How long it takes can differ from person to person.

Source: *Center for Grief and Healing*

Are there stages of grief?

In 1969, psychiatrist Elisabeth Kübler-Ross introduced what became known as the "five stages of grief." These stages of grief were based on her studies of the feelings of patients facing terminal illness, but many people have generalized them to other types of negative life changes and losses, such as the death of a loved one or a break-up.

The five stages of grief:

- **Denial:** "This can't be happening to me."

- **Anger:** "*Why* is this happening? Who is to blame?"

- **Bargaining:** "Make this not happen, and in return I will _____."

- **Depression:** "I'm too sad to do anything.

- **Acceptance:** "I'm at peace with what happened."

If you are experiencing any of these emotions following a loss, it may help to know that your reaction is natural and that you'll heal in time. However, not everyone who is grieving goes through all of these stages – and that's okay. Contrary to popular belief, you do not have to go through each stage in order to heal. In fact, some people resolve their grief without going through *any* of these stages. And if you do go through these stages of grief, you probably won't experience them in a neat, sequential order, so don't worry about what you "should" be feeling or which stage you're supposed to be in.

Kübler-Ross herself never intended for these stages to be a rigid framework that applies to everyone who mourns. In her last book before her death in 2004, she said of the five stages of grief, "They were never meant to help tuck messy emotions into neat packages. They are responses to loss that many people have, but there is not a typical response to loss, as there is no typical loss. Our grieving is as individual as our lives."

Grief can be a roller coaster

Instead of a series of stages, we might also think of the grieving process as a roller coaster, full of ups and downs, highs and lows. Like many roller coasters, the ride tends to be rougher in the beginning, the lows may be deeper and longer. The difficult periods should become less intense and shorter as time goes by, but it takes time to work through a loss. Even years after a loss, especially at special events such as a family wedding or the birth of a child, we may still experience a strong sense of grief.

Common symptoms of grief

While loss affects people in different ways, many people experience the following symptoms when they're grieving. Just remember that almost anything that you experience in the early stages of grief is normal, including feeling like you're going crazy, feeling like you're in a bad dream, or questioning your religious beliefs.

- **Shock and disbelief** – Right after a loss, it can be hard to accept what happened. You may feel numb, have trouble believing that the loss really happened, or even deny the truth. If someone you love has died, you may keep expecting them to show up, even though you know they're gone.

- **Sadness** – Profound sadness is probably the most universally experienced symptom of grief. You may have feelings of emptiness, despair, yearning, or deep loneliness. You may also cry a lot or feel emotionally unstable.

- **Guilt** – You may regret or feel guilty about things you did or didn't say or do. You may also feel guilty about certain feelings (e.g. feeling relieved when the person died after a long, difficult illness). After a death, you may even feel guilty for not doing something to prevent the death, even if there was nothing more you could have done.

- **Anger** – Even if the loss was nobody's fault, you may feel angry and resentful. If you lost a loved one, you may be angry at yourself, God, the doctors, or even the person who died for abandoning you. You may feel the need to blame someone for the injustice that was done to you.

- **Fear** – A significant loss can trigger a host of worries and fears. You may feel anxious, helpless, or insecure. You may even have panic attacks. The death of a loved one can trigger fears about your own mortality, of facing life without that person, or the responsibilities you now face alone.

- **Physical symptoms** – We often think of grief as a strictly emotional process, but grief often involves physical problems, including fatigue, nausea, lowered immunity, weight loss or weight gain, aches and pains, and insomnia.

Coping with grief and loss tip 1: Get support

The single most important factor in healing from loss is having the support of other people. Even if you aren't comfortable talking about your feelings under normal circumstances, it's important to express them when you're grieving. Sharing your loss makes the burden of grief easier to carry. Wherever the support comes from, accept it and do not grieve alone. Connecting to others will help you heal.

Finding support after a loss

- **Turn to friends and family members** – Now is the time to lean on the people who care about you, even if you take pride in being strong and self-sufficient. Draw loved ones close, rather than avoiding them, and accept the assistance that's offered. Oftentimes, people want to help but don't know how, so tell them what you need, whether it's a shoulder to cry on or help with funeral arrangements.

- **Draw comfort from your faith** – If you follow a religious tradition, embrace the comfort its mourning rituals can provide. Spiritual activities that are meaningful to you – such as praying, meditating, or going to church, can offer solace. If you're questioning your faith in the wake of the loss, talk to a clergy member or others in your religious community.

- **Join a support group** – Grief can feel very lonely, even when you have loved ones around. Sharing your sorrow with others who have experienced similar losses can help. To find a bereavement support group in your area, contact local hospitals hospices, funeral homes, and counseling centers.

- **Talk to a therapist or grief counselor** – If your grief feels like too much to bear, call a mental health professional with experience in grief counseling. An experienced therapist can help you work through intense emotions and overcome obstacles to your grieving.

Coping with grief and loss tip 2: Take care of yourself

When you're grieving, it's more important than ever to take care of yourself. The stress of a major loss can quickly deplete your energy and emotional reserves. Looking after your physical and emotional needs will help you get through this difficult time.

- **Face your feelings.** You can try to suppress your grief, but you can't avoid it forever. In order to heal, you have to acknowledge the pain. Trying to avoid feelings of sadness and loss only prolongs the grieving process. Unresolved grief can also lead to complications such as depression, anxiety, substance abuse, and health problems.

- **Express your feelings in a tangible or creative way.** Write about your loss in a journal. If you've lost a loved one, write a letter saying the things you never got to say; make a scrapbook or photo album celebrating the person's life; or get involved in a cause or organization that was important to him or her.

- **Look after your physical health.** The mind and body are connected. When you feel good physically, you'll also feel much better emotionally. Combat stress and fatigue by getting enough sleep, eating right, and exercising.

- **Don't let anyone tell you how to feel, and don't tell yourself how to feel either.** Your grief is your own, and no one else can tell you when it's time to "move on" or "get over it." Let yourself feel whatever you feel without embarrassment or judgment. It's okay to be angry, to yell at the heavens, to cry or not to cry. It's also okay to laugh, to find moments of joy, and to let go when you're ready.

- **Plan ahead for grief "triggers."** Anniversaries, holidays, and milestones can reawaken memories and feelings. Be prepared for an emotional wallop, and know that it's completely normal. If you're sharing a holiday or lifecycle event with other relatives, talk to them ahead of time about their expectations and agree on strategies to honor the person you loved.

When grief doesn't go away

It's normal to feel sad, numb, or angry following a loss. But as time passes, these emotions should become less intense as you accept the loss and start to move forward. If you aren't feeling better over time, or your grief is getting worse, it may be a sign that your grief has developed into a more serious problem, such as complicated grief or major depression.

Complicated grief

The sadness of losing someone you love never goes away completely, but it shouldn't remain center stage. If the pain of the loss is so constant and severe that it keeps you from resuming your life, you may be suffering from a condition known as *complicated grief*. Complicated grief is like being stuck in an intense state of mourning. You may have trouble accepting the death long after it has occurred or be so preoccupied with the person who died that it disrupts your daily routine and undermines your other relationships.

Symptoms of complicated grief include:

- Intense longing and yearning for the deceased
- Intrusive thoughts or images of your loved one
- Denial of the death or sense of disbelief
- Imagining that your loved one is alive
- Searching for the person in familiar places
- Avoiding things that remind you of your loved one
- Extreme anger or bitterness over the loss
- Feeling that life is empty or meaningless

The difference between grief and depression

Distinguishing between grief and clinical depression isn't always easy, since they share many symptoms. However, there are ways to tell the difference. Remember, grief can be a roller coaster. It involves a wide variety of emotions and a mix of good and bad days. Even when you're in the middle of the grieving process, you will have moments of pleasure or happiness. With depression, on the other hand, the feelings of emptiness and despair are constant.

Other symptoms that suggest depression, not just grief:

- Intense, pervasive sense of guilt.
- Thoughts of suicide or a preoccupation with dying.
- Feelings of hopelessness or worthlessness.

- Slow speech and body movements
- Inability to function at work, home, and/or school.
- Seeing or hearing things that aren't there.

Can antidepressants help grief?

As a general rule, normal grief does not warrant the use of antidepressants. While medication may relieve some of the symptoms of grief, it cannot treat the cause, which is the loss itself. Furthermore, by numbing the pain that must be worked through eventually, antidepressants delay the mourning process.

When to seek professional help for grief

If you recognize any of the above symptoms of complicated grief or clinical depression, talk to a mental health professional right away. Left untreated, complicated grief and depression can lead to significant emotional damage, life-threatening health problems, and even suicide. But treatment can help you get better.

Contact a grief counselor or professional therapist if you:

- Feel like life isn't worth living
- Wish you had died with your loved one
- Blame yourself for the loss or for failing to prevent it
- Feel numb and disconnected from others for more than a few weeks
- Are having difficulty trusting others since your loss
- Are unable to perform your normal daily activities

Crisis Management

What is a traumatic experience?

A traumatic experience is an event in which an individual experiences, or witnesses, an actual or threatened serious injury or death. It is normal for people to experience emotional and physical aftershocks or stress reactions following a traumatic event. Sometimes these aftershocks appear immediately after the event. However, sometimes it takes a few hours, days or even weeks before stress reactions appear. An individual's response may include intense fear, helplessness, or horror. Depending on the severity of the event, the signs and symptoms of these reactions may last a few days, several weeks or months, or longer. The way an individual copes with crisis depends on his or her own history and prior experiences.

Sometimes traumatic events are so painful that professional assistance may be necessary in order to cope with them.

WHAT IS CRISIS INTERVENTION?

Crisis intervention offers immediate, intensive and brief professional assistance to people who have had a traumatic experience. The purpose is to help individuals cope and return to a previous level of physical or emotional functioning without being at risk of endangering themselves or others. This short-term professional support attempts to deal with the immediate crisis or problem. Prompt and focused interventions help prevent the development of a serious long-term disability. Crisis intervention also encourages the development of new coping skills to help the individual function more effectively.

TYPES OF CRISES

People filter threatening experiences through their own unique ways of thinking and feeling. Depending on the trauma and one's "filter," some people may have less of a reaction while others may develop more severe symptoms. A number of crises may occur that can affect different groups of people, such as students, employees, or society as a whole. At one end of the continuum these crises could include a strike, assault, physical injury, accident, death, suicide, robbery, homicide or rape. Other events that affect a broader spectrum of people include fire, natural disasters, riots, terrorism, and racial incidents. Crisis intervention offers the immediate help that an individual in crisis needs in order to reestablish equilibrium.

SECONDARY TRAUMA

People at risk for secondary traumatization are those other than the actual victims who are affected by the traumatic event. This may include friends, family and acquaintances of the victim, or people who have simply heard about the trauma or crisis. People who help trauma and crisis victims are sometimes at risk for secondary trauma as well. This may be because of consistent exposure to human suffering and possibly feeling responsible for the safety of the victim.

SYMPTOMS AND REACTIONS

People whose normal lives are disturbed by a traumatic event find that their sense of security and safety is shattered. They also find that their responses to life and other people are either greatly exaggerated or no longer exist. The following are some of the symptoms one may encounter:

EMOTIONAL REACTIONS

Intense emotion and reactivity: People may feel intense anxiety, pain, fear, shame, grief, horror, anger and shock. They may also have difficulty relaxing or falling asleep.

Numbness: When people are overwhelmed, they may experience shock and protect themselves through detachment, denial and disbelief. They feel isolated and disconnected.

Depression: People may have difficulty concentrating or remembering. They may also experience diminished interest in everyday activities and have crying spells. A sense of despair and hopelessness may be very evident.

Flashbacks: People often re-experience the traumatic event over and over again. The feeling of not having any control is heightened. They may feel tortured by the invading thoughts and memories.

Nightmares: These are like flashbacks but they occur in dreams. As a result, people may have difficulty sleeping. Re-experiencing the trauma intensifies feelings of panic and helplessness.

Triggering events and people: Often, people will attempt to avoid anything associated with the trauma. However, events that remind them of the trauma may trigger feelings initially triggered by the trauma itself.

POSSIBLE PHYSICAL REACTIONS:

- Aches and pains such as headaches, backaches, etc.

- Weakness, dizziness, and fatigue most of the time.

- Heart palpitations, profuse sweating and chills

- Changes in sleep patterns

- Changes in appetite and digestive problems

- Being easily startled by noises and/or unexpected touch.

- Increased susceptibility to allergies, colds, and illnesses.

- Increased alcohol consumption and/or substance abuse.

HOW TO BETTER COPE

- Recognize your own feelings. Also understand that your feelings are a normal reaction to an abnormal situation.

- Talk about the experience. Talk is healing.

- Reach out to friends and family for support. Try to connect with others, especially those who may have shared the same stressful experience. Form a support group.

- Set small realistic goals to help tackle obstacles. Take one day at a time and be kind to yourself.

- Get as much physical activity as possible. Exercise or learn relaxation techniques or meditation in order to relax and feel rejuvenated.

- Structure you time. Schedule breaks for yourself. Redefine your priorities and focus your energy on them.

- Get involved in something that is personally meaningful and important every day.

- Give yourself time to heal.

- Give someone a hug - touching is very important.

HOW TO HELP FAMILY MEMBERS AND FRIENDS COPE

- Listen and empathize. Be supportive and non-judgmental. Be flexible with roles and chores

- Offer and ask for support from family, friends, and campus community.

- Respect a family member's need for privacy and be more tolerant. Give each other space.

- Set priorities and focus your attention on them with other family members.

- Give yourself and your family members time to heal at their own pace. Make healing a family issue.

- Reassure children and the elderly. Reinforce the feeling of safety.

- Validate each other. Show appreciation, give hugs and offer praise.

- Use rituals that can reaffirm family bonds and help the healing process (e.g., leaving flowers at an accident site or organizing a memorial service).

- After some time has elapsed, focus and talk about how each person has changed or grown as a result of the experience

Forgiveness: No More Grudges

Holding on to grudges can affect your health in a very negative way. Resentments or grudges can be a major stumbling block to your happiness and personal growth and yet, so many people are holding on to these intrusive feelings and thoughts. When you develop a grudge, you are harming your physical health and emotional well-being because it becomes a poison that takes over your whole life. Forgiveness is a productive way to move forward, detach from the past and let go of lingering hurts so you can experience a healthier, more promising future. What causes you to hold a grudge? Usually, it is the people closest to you that you resent because they have violated your trust through a lie, betrayal, deceit or abuse. However, resentment comes at a big cost to you.

When you can't let go of hurt and anger, it snowballs and grows. That feeling takes hold making it difficult to enjoy your present life or appreciate your good fortune. Resentments define who you are and how you act and they hurt only you. When you hold on to a grudge, it makes you bitter, which depletes you of your strength, reduces your ability to make good choices and compromises your overall mental and emotional health.

Here are some common behaviors that indicate you may be holding on to a grudge:

Passive-aggressive behavior: While often very subtle, this behavior is focused on getting back at the person you are angry at through indirect means. Holding back necessary information, tense silences, or saying there's nothing wrong when obviously you are really angry are typical indicators of passive aggressive manipulation.

Sarcastic remarks: These remarks indicate there is still strong emotion behind what you're thinking, even though you may be saying you're "just kidding." Short, abrupt comments: Comments of this nature suggest your intolerance and annoyance. They usually are delivered with a certain intonation in your voice.

If you are besieged with intrusive thoughts and negative feelings and believe you are justified to feel this way, you are heading toward a lifetime of misery, anger and torment. These one-sided dialogues with yourself make it harder to move on or work on developing a forgiving, letting go attitude.

Ask yourself the following questions to get some insights into your own behavior: To what extent will you do things to annoy him/her? How long are you willing to hold on to your resentment? What benefit do you get from keeping these negative feelings current? Forgiveness starts by making a decision to forgive. That decision frees you to let go of the old hurts. You give yourself permission to release the negative emotions associated with that other person and choose to not let their past actions hurt you anymore. The healing choice is yours .

Unless you forgive others, your feelings of resentment, hurt and humiliation will continue being an active part of your life. Unless you forgive yourself, your feelings of guilt and shame will continue to entrap you!

Every experience in life - good or bad - can be a teaching lesson for you Consider your lesson in forgiveness as a vehicle for personal growth. This means getting in touch with what you learned from this experience so you never repeat the same harmful pattern again. With this understanding, all experiences become stepping stones for enhancing your growth, rather than sources of pain and despair.

Martin Luther King once said, "We must develop and maintain the capacity to forgive. He who is devoid of the power to forgive is devoid of the power to love. There is some good in the worst of us and some evil in the best of us. When we discover this, we are less prone to hate our enemies."

Seven Keys To Forgiveness

Where is nothing like seeing a person who lives their life under the weight of unforgiveness, anger and bitterness. They cast a shadow where ever they go. But with the right information anyone can take back their power and live free of the torture they have been under. There are seven keys to forgiveness that will help you on this journey to living free and empowered.

1. You have to have been the injured party. Some people believe that they can forgive what was done to others, but that is untrue. Only the party that was injured can really forgive. Some people take on the offenses of others, which is a whole separate issue.

2. Forgiveness does not mean that you are giving the other person the right to be back in your life. Some things are too egregious to even conceive of having a person be part of your life. Some have been taught that forgiveness is restoring them the position that they were in previously, which is technically true. But what if the meaning could be interpreted differently. What if it could be an emotional restoration as opposed to a physical one. Forgiveness is not a means to throw off common sense in regard to your safety and well being.

3. Forgiveness has to be unconditional. There can be no promises or things that have to be done. When you forgive, the matter is closed. Forgiveness is an act of grace for something that perhaps does not deserve it. Which is why the injured party is the only one that can really give it. Forgiveness has to be an all or nothing deal. If there are terms they may ultimately be moved by whoever is the emotionally stronger party, which can lead to further complications.

4. Forgiveness is for the sake of the forgiver. It is their empowering act. It is not reliant on someone asking forgiveness, but many will not want it, have the opportunity to ask for it, or even know they injured someone with a word or deed. The forgiver is doing it to get rid of the effects of unforgiveness such as lack of trust, anger, bitterness or even physical illnesses that are caused by unforgiveness. Unforgiveness gives the injurer the power over someone else, but forgiveness breaks it.

5. Forgiveness can take time. It is wishful Hollywood thinking that forgiveness just happens at the mention of a word. In little things that might be true, but in larger things the experience does not hold up. The solution is not so simple because it requires that every time you are tempted to remind the party of what they did or you find yourself acting out of unforgiveness they you remind yourself that you have forgiven that party for that. How long it takes depends on the injured party and the seriousness of the injury.

6. Forgiveness assists in personal and spiritual growth. It is a freeing act in so many ways. When you can forgive then you are more likely to ask for forgiveness from those you have harmed, and they will be more inclined to give it. It is an act of grace, mercy, and humility to forgive someone for anything. Most would even say that it is against our nature, but the benefits of forgiveness far outweigh living bound to another person.

7. Forgiveness is a choice, and individual decision, not a feeling. Feelings line up with what your mind and heart tell it to do. You can be ruled by your feelings and stay bound to a person that

might not even be alive anymore, or you can choose to forgive and move on.

Resentment: An Unhealthy Way To Live

Resentment is that deep feeling of displeasure or anger that we have toward someone because of a past offense. It is our painful memory of past hurts. Resentment **is** the great enemy of right relationships. It destroys friendships and turns friends into enemies. But the most damaging effect of resentment is the destruction of the one who holds it.

A pastor was called to the bedside of a dying man. He was a man whom nobody liked. He was hard, bitter, and sullen. He lived in a tumble-down shack on the edge of town. When he went into town, he made it clear that he didn't want to speak to anyone, and he didn't want anyone to speak to him. Even the children ran from him .

People wondered what had made him so bitter and mean. Some thought he had a guilty secret. Others were sure that he had committed some terrible crime and that he was a fugitive from justice. But they were all wrong.

The simple truth was, when he was a young man, a friend had done him a grievous wrong. He was so angry about it that he said, *"I'll remember it until my dying day."* And he did. He said to the pastor who sat at his bedside, *"I've gone over it every morning. I've thought about it every night. I've cursed that man a hundred times a day."* Gasping for breath, he continued, *"I see now that my bitterness has eaten out my soul. My hate has hurt nobody but myself. God knows that it has turned my life into hell."*

You don't want to have a life like this man. To die in bitterness and hatred because of someone else?

Why do we Hold Resentment?

Of all the evil, destructive things that can happen to us, resentment is one of the worst. It is like a deadly germ, working constantly to gain power over us to destroy us. No right-thinking person would harbor and nourish a deadly germ in his body, knowing that this germ would eventually kill him. Yet many Christians hold on to the sin of resentment which is far more destructive than any germ.

Seeing that resentment is such a deadly sin, we might well ask, *"Why do we hold on to resentment?"* There are a number of reasons:

- We feel justified in our resentment.

One reason why it is difficult for us to recognize the poisonous nature of resentment is that it seems right to us. We feel that we are justified in our resentment. We say to ourselves, *"It is only natural to resent so-and-so."* In order to justify our resentment, we often build in our mind a false image of the other person. We push aside the whole picture of what that person is and all the good and decent things he may have done and focus on his offenses against us.

- It makes us feel superior.

When someone does something that offends or hurts us, we take a superior attitude toward that person. We say to ourselves, *"I would never do a thing like that!"* We like this feeling of superiority, and therefore we hold on to our resentment.

- We like to "keep score."

Sometimes we hold on to our resentments in order to have something to offset any future offenses we may commit. We want to be able to say, *"Maybe I was wrong in that matter, but you did such-and-such to me."*

- We enjoy our resentments.

Strange as it may seem, we keep our hurts alive for the pleasure we get out of them. We enjoy nursing our wounds and feeling sorry for ourselves after someone has offended us.

Resentment grows into Bitterness

Resentment is one of the most unusual of all sins in that it is meant to punish the other person; yet it is far more hurtful to us than it could ever be to the other person. Sometimes the other person may not even be aware of having done anything wrong. Therefore our resentment does not harm at all, but it is very destructive to us. If we hold on to resentment, it can grow into bitterness. Bitterness affects our health, our mind, our personality, and our relationship with God. Let us consider these things:

1. Bitterness affects our health.

Bitterness is poison to our body. Resentment, bitterness, hatred, and unforgiveness can cause ulcers, high blood pressure, and dozens of other diseases. It has been estimated by some doctors that as much as 90 percent of our illnesses are caused by anger, fear, resentment and bitterness.

Holding bitterness in your heart can cause you to lose sleep and to be tired most of the time. It will take away the enjoyment of your food. It will kill your happiness. In time, it will show in your eyes and in your face. A doctor said,

> "The moment I start hating a man, I become his slave. I can't enjoy my work anymore because he controls my thoughts. My resentments produce too many stress hormones in my body and I become fatigued after only a few hours of work. The work I formerly enjoyed is now drudgery. Even vacations cease to give me pleasure.... I can't escape his tyrannical grasp on my mind."

2. Bitterness affects our mind.

It has been proved that bitterness can and does bring on depression. People who have a tendency to be depressed much of the time are often people who hold resentment against a loved one or relative who injured them earlier in life. If you are one of these people, you will never know lasting victory over depression until you get rid of that bitterness.

3. Bitterness affects our personality.

The more we resent someone, the more we think about him. And the more we think about a person, the more we become like him. It is a fact that, when you focus your emotions on someone, you tend to become like that person.

A teenager was bitter against a relative. When it was suggested by a youth worker that she should forgive that relative, the teenager said, "I'll never forgive that person as long as I live."The youth worker casually replied, "I'm sorry to hear that.""Why?" asked the teenager.

"Because in twenty years, you will be just like that relative," replied the youth worker. This thought so horrified the teenager that she said quickly, "Oh, no! In that case I'll forgive her."

Bitterness affects our relationship with God.

When we pray the Lord's Prayer, we say something like this, *"Forgive us our trespasses as we forgive those who trespass against us."* When you pray this, you are saying, *"God, please forgive me of my sins just like I forgive other people of their sins against me."* If you don't forgive other people, you are actually asking God not to forgive you.

Forgiveness sets us free

The only thing that can set us free from resentment and bitterness is forgiveness. But no not many people truly understand what forgiveness is. Forgiveness is not trying to overlook sin or to pretend it never happened. Forgiveness is not trying to forget. Forgetting comes after forgiveness, not before.

What is forgiveness? Forgiveness is bearing the wrong or injury yourself and choosing to remember it no more. Forgiveness means that you give the person who wronged you a clean slate so far as you are concerned.

Forgiveness is costly. The one who forgives pays the price of the injury or evil that he forgives. In order for Christ to forgive us, He had to pay the penalty of our sins. This is why He died on the cross. It is costly to forgive, but it is more costly *not* to forgive. You may have remembered a certain injury or offense a long time. You may be thinking of it right now. That person may indeed have done you a great injustice, but that injury did not do you nearly the harm you have done yourself by holding that resentment.

How to Turn from Bitterness to Forgiveness?

The following steps will show you how you can give up your bitterness:

Recognize that God is the Judge.

People need to be judged for their wrong deeds, but you and I are not the ones to judge them. Judgment belongs to God. The Bible says,

"Beloved, do not avenge yourselves, but rather give place to wrath; for it is written, 'Vengeance is Mine, I will repay,' says the Lord." Romans 12:19

God tells us not to try to "get even" or to avenge ourselves, but rather to forgive. When we forgive someone, we are turning that person over to God, recognizing that He alone has the right to judge and punish people for their wrongdoing.

Confess your sin to God.

The other person may have done you a grievous injury. If so, he is responsible to God for this. But, if you are holding bitterness, you are sinning, and you are responsible to God for your sin of bitterness. To deal with this sin, you must confess it to God and ask Him to cleanse you with the precious blood of His Son.

Pass the sentence of death upon resentment and bitterness.

Resentment and bitterness are not minor vices. They are among the deadliest of all sins. We must pass the sentence of death upon them or they will pass the sentence of death upon us. Holding bitterness is *"living after the flesh,"* and the Bible says, *"If you live according to the flesh, you will die..."* (King James Bible - Romans 8:13)

Because we were crucified with Christ, we have the right to refuse anything that belongs to the old life. This means that we can refuse and reject the sin of bitterness. We have the right to ask the Lord to put it to death by His Spirit. We can pray,

"Lord Jesus, I was crucified with You. Because of this, I have the right to refuse any sin that belongs to my old life. Right now, I refuse and reject this bitterness, and I ask You, by Your Holy Spirit, to put it to death."

Forgive even as Christ has forgiven you.

Forgiveness involves a choice on our part. We must choose to forgive. We may not feel like forgiving the other person, but God deals with our choices, not our feelings. You may say, *"But suppose that person doesn't ask for forgiveness or even admit that he was wrong? How can I forgive him?"*

So far as we know from the Scriptures, no one ever came to Jesus and asked to be forgiven of his sins. Yet Jesus did forgive people. He forgave them in a very special way. He forgave them unilaterally. The word *"unilateral"* looks like a very difficult word, but it is really not hard to understand. It means *"one-sided."* To forgive someone unilaterally means that you forgive him from your side, regardless of what he does. He may not ask for forgiveness. He may not even know that he needs to be forgiven. But you can choose to forgive him anyway. The ones who crucified the Lord Jesus did not ask for forgiveness, but Jesus forgave them anyway. He prayed, *"Father, forgive them, for they know not what they do."* Forgiveness flowed out from His heart to those who did not ask for it or deserve it. This was unilateral forgiveness.

When we came to the Lord for salvation, we did not confess every sin that we had ever committed. We did not ask His forgiveness for each sin. Yet the Lord received us and forgave us of every sin we had ever committed. Now He commands us to forgive others, even as He forgave us. The Bible says,

"Therefore, as the elect of God, holy and dearly loved, clothe
yourselves with a heart of mercy, kindness, humility, gentleness,
and patience, bearing with one another and forgiving one another,
if someone happens to have a complaint against anyone else. JUST
AS THE LORD HAS FORGIVEN YOU, SO YOU ALSO FORGIVE OTHERS."
Colossians 3:12-13 (NET Bible)

Although the other person may not ask for forgiveness or even admit that he was wrong, you can still forgive. You can forgive unilaterally. Trust the Holy Spirit to make your forgiveness real.

Forgiving others and getting rid of bitterness is the result of our working together with the Holy Spirit. We cannot do it by ourselves, and the Holy Spirit will not do it apart from our choice. We must work together with Him. We choose it, and we trust Him to do it.

"For if you live according to the flesh, you will die; but if by the Spirit
you put to death the deeds of the body, you will live." Romans 8:13

We must ask the Holy Spirit to enable us to forgive and forget! We can "forgive" someone and then repeatedly "reinstate" their sin by dwelling on it. By refusing to forget it, we keep the resentment alive. May God enable us to forgive as He forgives—to forgive and forget. God says,

"Their sins and their iniquities I will remember no more." Hebrews 8:12

Clara Barton, founder of the American Red Cross, was asked on one occasion if she was still speaking to so-and-so. *"Why shouldn't I?"* she replied. Her friend who had known years ago of an offense which this person had committed against Miss Barton reminded her of the offense. Her response was, *"Oh, I distinctly remember forgetting that offense."*

Dealing with our Feelings

An important part of turning from bitterness to forgiveness is dealing with our feelings. We can choose to forgive and mean it with all our heart, but the hurt is still there. To be fully free from resentment and bitterness, we must deal with our feelings. Is there a way by which we can deal with our feelings? Yes, there is! The way to deal with our feelings is to change the way we look at a matter. We cannot change the facts of a past situation, but we can change the way we look at the matter. Remember, we are controlled by the way we inwardly see and believe things to be.

Consider Joseph: We have already seen how Joseph's brothers hated him and sold him as a slave. The facts of the situation could not be changed. What had happened, had happened forever. Yet Joseph was not resentful toward his brothers. How did Joseph manage to have good feelings toward his brothers after all they had done to him? He put a proper meaning on those circumstances. He saw God's hand in all that had happened to him. He realized that God had used all those circumstances for his good. He said to his brothers, *"You meant evil against me; but God meant it for good."* (Genesis 50:20) The story of Joseph teaches us this great truth: **God** *can bring good out of a bad situation if we trust Him.* God does not cause evil, but He can use it to bring about His purposes. The Bible says,

"We know that all things work together for good to those who love
God...." Romans 8:28

Notice that this verse does not say that we "see" or that we "understand," but that *"we **KNOW** that all things work together for good to those who love God."* We may not see or understand how all things are working together for our good, but we can know it because God says so. Concerning our situation, we cannot change the facts. What has happened, has happened, and we cannot change it. But we can trust God to bring good out of the situation.

When we believe that God is using all things, even those things which seem bad to us, for our eternal good, we see things in a different way. We can actually thank God for the things that happened to us. This takes the hurt out of past offenses and sets us free from resentment.

Spiritual Warfare: How To Forgive Others

Wounds can fester into infections if left untreated. That's exactly how unforgiveness works. Whatever was done to us pierced our skin, but if we keep prying it open and looking at the wound, it won't be able to heal... instead, because it is continually exposed to the dirty air, it becomes infected. That infection in the spiritual realm is welcoming to unclean spirits, which fester the wound even more. If something isn't done, the person ends up facing demonic harassment and torture, and becomes a very bitter and unhappy person.

You may be saying, "This person has NO clue what they've done to me! They don't deserve anything at all! Much less MY forgiveness!" They certainly don't deserve your forgiveness, much less God's... but none of us deserve what Jesus did for us either. Those who killed Jesus didn't deserve anything at all, but look at what He said just before He died, "Father, forgive them, for they know not what they do!" Look at the deep and rich mercy and love that Jesus has towards us... none of us deserve it! But He loves us for who we are, not because of what we've done. He wanted a relationship with us so much that He gave His life for it! When we grasp what Jesus has done for us, it makes it a lot easier to pass that grace along to others. We aren't letting them off God's hook, we are merely releasing our souls from bondage that un-forgiveness brings us under. You aren't forgiving them for their benefit, but for your own good! Your soul, not theirs, is what is being held in bondage because of the feelings you've allowed yourself to harbor inside. Why should you allow what they've done to continue to bring you under bondage? I wouldn't! I would let that poison out of my heart... give it to the Lord and seek Him to heal the wounds they have caused.

Forgiving others is sometimes very hard, but it is essential if you want to break out of the bondage that it's brought you under. Forgiving others opens you up for the Lord to begin healing your soul (inner healing). Since unforgiveness blocks us from receiving God's forgiveness of our sins (Matthew 6:15), it puts up a wall between us and the source of our healing.

The steep price of unforgiveness

I have seen so many people in spiritual bondage due to unforgiveness. It is a common source of bondage and demonic harassment, as Jesus warns us about in *Matthew 18:34-35*, "*And his lord was wroth, and delivered him to the tormentors, till he should pay all that was due unto him. So likewise shall my heavenly Father do also unto you, if ye from your hearts forgive not every one his brother their trespasses.*"

There is nothing less than a strong literal warning that a person can fall into the hands of demonic spirits for torment and harassment if they are unforgiving and bitter inside. I have seen It again and again, it is not an uncommon scene to find a person harassed by demons because of bitterness in their heart. Bitterness is also known in the Bible as spiritual poison:

Acts 8:23, "For I perceive that thou art in the gall (poison) of bitterness, and in the bond of iniquity."

Unforgiveness not only gives demons the right or ability to torment us, but it also prevents God from forgiving our own sins! Now this is serious, this means that when we cry out for God's help, but have unforgiveness in our hearts, He looks down and our sins are before Him. It puts up a wall in our relationship with our heavenly Father. Jesus was very clear that if we are to be forgiven, we cannot be unforgiving towards others: *Matthew 6:15, "But if ye forgive not men their trespasses, neither will your Father forgive your trespasses."*

Beyond this, bitterness is also a very common means for a born again believer to become spiritually defiled, that is, polluted or unclean spiritually: *Hebrews 12:15, "Looking diligently lest any man fail of the grace of God; lest any root of bitterness springing up trouble you, and thereby many be defiled."*

Notice the word 'many' in the above verse... this is a very common means for people to become defiled and open themselves up for spiritual harassment from the enemy.

Give to God the things that belong to Him

Unforgiveness is actually taking something that belongs to God, and taking matters into our own hands. God's Word tells us clearly that we should allow God to bring His wrath upon that person, and let Him have the room to repay those who wrong us: *Romans 12:19, "Dearly beloved, avenge not yourselves, but rather give place unto wrath: for it is written, Vengeance is mine; I will repay, saith the Lord."* Those who have wronged us will reap what they sow. If you chose to forgive somebody, they may be off your hook, but that doesn't mean they are off God's. God's Word tells us clearly that what we sow, we shall reap: *Galatians 6:7, "Be not deceived; God is not mocked: for whatsoever a man soweth, that shall he also reap."*

What unforgiveness actually is

Unforgiveness is actually a form of hate against another person. If a person hates somebody, it is a sign that the person is lacking love in their heart. Why? They are not firmly rooted and grounded in the love of Christ, and Christ's love is not flowing through them. As simple as that sounds, that's how it works. What somebody may have done against us is one thing, but if you take Satan's bait of unforgiveness to heart, it will do much more harm than they did. Do you want to continue to allow their mess to trouble you even more? Have they not done enough damage? Allowing yourself to hang onto hard feelings and become bitter is only causing your wound to become even more infected spiritually. Honestly tell yourself, what good is it doing you to hold onto the hurt and bitterness that the enemy has tried to plant within you? It is doing nothing but harm, and is holding you in bondage spiritually. The only reason you are holding onto those feelings is because it feels good inside. Don't let this fool you, bitterness is known in the Bible as spiritual poison:

Acts 8:23, "For I perceive that thou art in the gall (poison) of bitterness,
and in the bond of iniquity."

The reason Satan wants you to hold onto that bitterness is because it is poison to your soul. Jesus said that the devil came to steal, kill and destroy. Satan wants to do just that to you. Know wonder Satan makes unforgiveness 'feel good'... he wants your soul to be poisoned! Don't let him do this to you... stop him dead in his tracks! Release yourself from those hurt feelings, and let them go... stop holding onto those feelings, and let that poison out of your soul!

Benefits Of A Healthy Diet

Part of your Ministry is to take care of YOU. One way you can do this is by enjoying the benefits of a healthy diet. Maintaining an overall healthy diet not only offers your body the energy and nutrition that it needs to function, but offers several health benefits as well. Below is a list those foods that are the best for you body, and the health benefits that those foods provide.

Fruits And Vegetables: Health Benefits

Eating a diet high in fruits and vegetables as an overall healthy diet may...

- Reduce risk for stroke and other cardiovascular diseases.
- Reduce risk for type 2 diabetes.
- Protect against certain cancers, such as mouth, stomach, and colon-rectum cancer.
- Reduce the risk of coronary artery disease.
- Help decrease bone loss and reduce the risk of developing kidney stones.

Nutrients

- No fruits or vegetables have cholesterol, and most are naturally low in fat and calories.
- Vegetables are a great source for potassium, dietary fiber, folic acid, vitamin A, vitamin E, and vitamin C.
- Fruits are a great source for nutrients such as potassium, dietary fiber, vitamin C and folic acid.
- Diets rich in potassium may help to maintain healthy blood pressure.
- Dietary fiber helps reduce blood cholesterol levels and may lower risk of heart disease. Fiber is important for proper bowel function. Fiber-containing foods such as vegetables help provide a feeling of fullness with fewer calories.
- Folic acid (folate) helps the body form red blood cells. Women of childbearing age who may become pregnant and those in the first trimester of pregnancy should consume adequate folic acid, including folic acid from fortified foods or supplements.
- Vitamin A keeps eyes and skin healthy and helps to protect against infections.
- Vitamin E helps protect vitamin A and essential fatty acids from cell oxidation.

- Vitamin C helps heal cuts and wounds and keeps teeth and gums healthy.
- Vitamin C also aids in iron absorption.

Whole Grains

Grains, especially whole grains, provide several health benefits. Grains provide essential nutrients and helps reduce the risk of developing chronic diseases.

Health Benefits

Eating a diet high in grains, especially whole grains, as an overall healthy diet may ...

- help with weight management.
- reduce constipation.
- reduce the risk of coronary artery disease.

Nutrients

- Grains provide many nutrients such as dietary fiber, B vitamins and minerals.
- Dietary fiber may help reduce blood cholesterol levels and lower risk of heart disease.
- B vitamins are essential for your metabolism by helping your body release energy from protein, fat and carbohydrates.
- Folic acid helps the body form blood cells and is especially important for women of childbearing age who may become pregnant.
- Magnesium from whole grains helps build bones and release energy from muscles.

Eating Disorders: Stress

Anyone can develop an eating disorder. However, approximately 90% of eating disorders take place in women. Teens and those in their 20's form the most likely age groups in which eating disorders take place. If you suspect that your loved one is struggling with an eating disorder, consider contacting an eating disorder treatment center today for assistance. Also, eating disorders may be more common among those with depression or perfectionism.

Although many people assume that those with eating disorders are thin and underweight, even those of an average weight can have eating disorders. The three most popular types of eating disorders are anorexia, bulimia, and binge eating disorder. Anorexia treatment, binge eating disorder rehab, and bulimia help are all unique programs which may be available at eating disorder treatment clinics.

Those with anorexia are typically underweight while those with bulimia constantly fluctuate between being slightly underweight to slightly overweight. Bulimia may be the most difficult eating disorder to notice upon first looking at a person because an average weight is often present. People with binge eating disorder are typically overweight or obese. Binge eating disorder is the most common form of eating disorders and affects approximately 2 men for every 3 women.

What are Triggers?

Triggers are certain instances which contribute to the rise of an eating disorder. These events alone do not cause eating disorders but may increase the rate of onset and worsen one's current condition. There are a number of different triggers that can take place, each of which can cause a number of different reactions. When eating disorders result from or exacerbate due to these triggers, eating disorder treatment is highly recommended. At eating disorder treatment clinics, therapy is offered which helps the individual deal with underlying issues and triggers that have initiated their eating disorder. Bulimia programs, anorexia treatment, and binge eating disorder help centers, all are available in the recovery process.

What Types of Triggers cause Eating Disorders?

Triggers of eating disorders may include but are not limited to:

- **Sudden changes** – A sudden change like moving into a new home, graduating from school, or losing one's job may trigger the onset of an eating disorder.

- **Cruel teasing** – The harmful remarks of a friend or even a stranger can drastically alter one's mood and encourage an eating disorder's development. In serious cases, eating disorder treatment at an eating disorder residential center should be sought out.

- **Stress** – Over-eating and stress often are connected to one another in some way. When a person is stressed out, a desire to eat high-calorie foods can arise. Unfortunately, fat cell formation is higher when a person is under stress.

- **Death of a loved one** – Experiencing the death of a close friend, partner, or family member can be unbearable to some. Eating disorders are just one way that people negatively deal with feelings brought about by such an instance. Therapy provided in eating disorder treatment can help a person to develop more positive coping skills.

- **Verbal abuse** – This form of abuse may be especially damaging coming from a parent or partner. Other negative methods of coping with this abuse include drug and alcohol use or other high-risk behaviors.

- **Exposure to media** – Constant bombardment of overly-thin women in the media and advertisements for weight-loss methods puts and unhealthy mindset in a person, especially in the minds of women. In men with bigorexia, exposure to muscular men may trigger this type of eating disorder.

- **Sexual abuse** – Often times, sexual abuse creates feelings of hatred towards the body. In females, they may wish to maintain a child-like figure and restrict food in order to reach this goal.

- **Competition in sports** – The desire to compete well in sports, as well as pressure from coaches to stay thin may contribute to the onset of an eating disorder.

VICIOUS CYCLE

It probably would not surprise you that stress is a primary predisposing factor to an eating disorder (ED), but did you realize an eating disorder itself is a source of stress and poor nutrition causes stress?

The person with the eating disorder gets trapped in a vicious cycle of stress that is difficult to break. Stress causes the eating disorder and the stress of the eating disorder and nutrient deficiencies perpetuate the stress as well as the illness.

Scientific studies have shown that psychological stress may worsen the symptoms of almost every known medical condition. This certainly is applicable to eating disorders. Furthermore, studies have shown that learned and practiced stress management skills and good nutrition can impact and dramatically improve people's health and well-being.

If stress causes eating disorders and eating disorders cause stress, then any treatment plan or prevention education program must focus on helping people reduce their stress through effective coping skills. This page will explain the connection between EDs and stress, explain why prolonged stress is unhealthy, and offer tips for reducing stress.

WHAT YOU NEED TO KNOW

- Poor nutrition adds to your stress

- Good nutrition, moderate exercise, adequate sleep, practicing stress reduction techniques and activities, and perhaps medication treatment will allow you to think clearly, feel more in control, be more energetic, feel more relaxed, and to have the focus required to work towards your recovery.

STRESS CAUSES

Perhaps stress more than any other factor, ultimately leads to an eating disorder. If there was no stress or conflict, the individual would not need to use eating disorder behaviors as a coping mechanism.

There are limitless possibilities and combinations of stressors that can predispose someone to an eating disorder, including work, school, finances, family and relationship problems, and media and cultural pressures. All of these issues become sources of stress that the individual desperately wants relief from. Unfortunately, people turn to unhealthy addictive behaviors, such as eating disorders to cope with stress.

People turn to eating disorders subconsciously as a way to soothe themselves and gain a sense of control (albeit a false sense of control). The anorexic has a false sense of emotional relief by restricting food, the bulimic feels a false sense of emotional relief and release through purging, and the binge eater finds a false sense of solace physically and emotionally during binge episodes. Although these behaviors may in the short-term seem effective in making one feel better, over time these unhealthy behaviors take on a life of their own and end up causing more stress than the original stressors.

CAUSE STRESS

Eating disorders are the source of stress for various reasons. First, nutrient deficiencies, lack of adequate calories, and dehydration cause physical stress to the body.

People with eating disorders often have nutrient deficiencies:

- The anorexic deprives the body of adequate calories and nutrients by restricting food intake

- The bulimic purges, thereby ridding the body of nutrients consumed

- The bulimic and binger typically binge on carbohydrates high in sugar and fat, thereby depriving themselves of nutrient rich foods

The self-imposed rules and rituals of people with eating disorders cause them a great deal of stress. Third, individuals with eating disorders try to keep their eating disorder behaviors a secret, because they consider their behaviors shameful and embarrassing.

Those with eating disorders often withdraw socially, develop relationship problems, have difficulty expressing themselves, are self-conscious about their weight and appearance, place too high expectations on themselves, and are high achievers and perfectionists. All of these things add to their stress.

PROLONGED STRESS

When people are stressed, their bodies are wonderfully and automatically "activated" to prepare the body for the perceived threat. Their bodies go into a "fight or flight" response to deal with the danger. To prepare the body to deal with the stressor, the body releases the hormones Adrenaline and Cortisol into the bloodstream. While the stress response is a natural and beneficial process meant for short-term activation, prolonged stress requiring continuous activation of the stress response can be unhealthy for the body.

Prolonged stress can result in such symptoms as headache; upset stomach; lack of or increased appetite; indigestion; acid reflux; muscle tension in the neck, face, or shoulders; heart racing; elevated blood pressure; anxiety; depression; and fatigue. Besides these symptoms, prolonged stress lead to other diseases, such as cardio-vascular disease and type2 diabetes.

Prolonged stress puts the stress response into "overdrive" causing too much Cortisol to be released into the body. Too much Cortisol can lead to cravings of food high in sugar, sodium, and fats, which can lead to the over consumption of these foods and ultimately weight gain.

Elevated levels of Cortisol produce a rise in sugars in the bloodstream. Additionally, too much Cortisol, a fat-storing hormone, and elevated sugar levels signal the body to store fat especially in the abdomen. Therefore, if you need to lose weight for health reasons, prolonged stress is definitely not helping matters.

STRESS DEPLETES NUTRIENTS

Stress depletes the body of essential vitamins and minerals, so it is especially important to eat well-balanced meals and snacks after being stressed. This is what happens:

- A person experiences stress

- This triggers the body to release stress hormones

- Stress hormones excrete nutrients such as the essential minerals of calcium, magnesium, iron, and zinc from the body

- This process in turn helps the body more effectively deal with stress by reducing stress-related symptoms and mood swings and helping muscles to relax

- The body needs to replenish nutrients used

GOOD NUTRITION

Poor nutrition elevates stress levels, while good nutrition makes it easier for the body to deal with stress. A wholesome nutrition plan involves consuming adequate calories, vitamins, and minerals and eating proteins, vegetables, fruits, whole grains, dairy, and oils (unsaturated fats).

When you experience fatigue, a lack of concentration, and feel irritable, it is more difficult to handle stress and situations that might not otherwise be stressful and anxiety provoking become stressors. On the other hand, good nutrition gives you more energy, improves your concentration, and helps you stabilize your mood. With this in mind, you can understand why breakfast is considered the most important meal of the day.

Many people drink caffeinated and/or sugary beverages or eat sweets to boost their energy. This energy boost from refined sugar is only short-lived. Eating protein and carbohydrates low in refined sugar provides a longer lasting, more sustainable energy level. There is nothing wrong with or bad about eating sweets and drinking sweetened and caffeinated beverages in moderation, but consider your goal when making food choices – do you need a quick fix or longer-lasting endurance?

EMOTIONAL EATING

The emotional eater eats in response to his or her feelings, not in response to physical hunger. The emotional eater may eat in response to feelings of stress, sadness, happiness, anger, anxiety, and feeling overwhelmed and depressed. Considering most of the time we are experiencing either negative or positive emotions, this can lead to a lot of munching and

Most of the time emotional eaters and bingers eat carbohydrates high in fat and sugar due to the soothing affect these foods bring them physically and emotionally. Eating in response to one's emotions, not physical hunger, can result in the consumption of too many calories from foods high in sodium, sugar and fats.

Learning to eat in response to physical hunger, not emotions, is important. Eat when physically hungry and stop when comfortably full. When the temptation to eat in response to emotions occurs when you are physically satisfied, try distracting yourself with something else, such as calling a friend, doing a craft, exercising, or practicing a relaxation technique.

MINDFUL EATING

People with eating disorders need to learn how to be a "mindful" eater. To become a mindful eater one must have a healthy relationship with food and their body. Eating should be both physically and emotionally satisfying.

Qualities of the mindful (or intuitive) eater include:

- Trusts self to make appropriate, nutritionally sound food choices and be in control over eating.
- Eats when physically hungry; stops eating when physically satisfied.
- Eats a variety of foods from each of the food groups.
- Chooses and consumes foods that are appealing.
- Is flexible about food choices.
- Adapts to eating whatever is available or served.
- Enjoys food but is not preoccupied by thoughts of food.
- Experiences freedom from food rituals and rules.
- Is non-judgmental about food. For example, does not label food as "safe/good" and "unsafe/bad".
- Is okay with eating foods high in sugar, fat, and sodium in moderation.
- Does not experience feelings of guilt after eating.
- Sometimes eats for reasons other than physical hunger, such as emotional eating, availability of food in social situations, or just because it tastes good — and is okay with it.

STRESS MANAGEMENT PLANNING

Any stress management plan must begin with good nutrition. Good nutrition gives the body the needed nutrients it needs to function at an optimum level. Next, a stress management plan requires an understanding on what causes you stress. Once you understand what causes you stress,. You can develop a plan for how you will deal with tat stressor in the future. Obviously, you cannot predict every stressful situation, but you can look for connections on what has caused you stress in the past to predict your future stress triggers. This information will give you insight into what stress relief method to use and when to use it to help you relax.

To prepare yourself for dealing with stress, start practicing some stress reduction techniques to find out which one's you feel comfortable with. Then, train yourself to automatically switch into your stress reduction mode when you feel stressed or anxious.

NUTRITION TIPS

Nutrition tips for reducing stress:

- Eat breakfast, lunch, and dinner (especially breakfast)
- Eat meals and snacks at regular intervals; avoid long periods without food. This helps sustain a consistent level of energy and endurance
- Eat nutritionally well-balanced meals
- Eat adequate amounts of food from each of the food groups
- Eat healthy snacks
- Regularly hydrate yourself with water
- Minimize caffeinated and sugary beverages and sweets

LIFESTYLE TIPS

- Consider these tips for reducing stress in your life:
- Good nutrition
- Adequate sleep
- Moderate exercise
- Practice time management skills, including prioritizing
- Setting time aside for relaxation, recreation, and vacations
- Go to therapy and/or a support/therapy group
- Do not be afraid to say "no" to opportunities to take on more responsibilities

ACTIVITIES

Consider what types of recreation you enjoy and do these regularly. Here is a list of activities for you to consider using to reduce your stress:

- Reading
- Watching movies
- Crafts
- Hobbies
- Gardening
- Renovating and decorating home

- Being in nature, such as through hiking or camping

- Singing; being in a choir

- Painting or drawing

- Going to the beach

- Planning and going on a vacation or weekend-get-away

STRESS MANAGEMENT TECHNIQUES

Start practicing some of the stress management techniques listed below to discover what methods work best for you and you enjoy.

DEEP BREATHING - Take several deep diaphragmatic breaths by inhaling through your noise (counting to 5 to yourself) and then exhaling through your mouth (counting to 8 to yourself).

VISUALIZATION or GUIDED IMAGERY - Imagine a tranquil scene and use all of your senses to experience it, such as a sunset on a beach or a stream and waterfalls in a forest. You may use a CD or tape to lead you through a guided imagery.

MEDITATION – One form of meditation you can practice for 5-20 minutes is to focus on a word, phrase, a sound or nothing at all in order to distract yourself from other thoughts, center yourself, and relax. Some may use this as a spiritual exercise by focusing on a scripture passage or word of spiritual significance.

MUSCLE RELAXATION – Tense and relax all of the muscle groups in your body. For example, tense and relax all the muscles in your face, holding a tight grimace 10 seconds, then completely relaxing for 10 seconds. Repeat procedure for other muscles in your body.

HYTHMIC EXERCISES - While any exercising can help reduce stress, non-strenuous, focused, rhythmic exercise done for the purpose of reducing stress and centering self can help you achieve a more tranquil state. As you exercise, focus on your rhythmic movement, your breathing, how your body feels, and experience your senses taking in the surroundings. Rhythmic exercises include jogging, walking, rowing, cycling, and swimming. For example, if you are riding a bike, concentrate on the movement of your legs pedaling, your inhaling and exhaling, the feeling of the warmth of the sun and the wind against your face, etc.

MINDFULNESS - "Mindfulness is the here-and-now approach to living that makes daily life richer and more meaningful," says Claire Michaels Wheeler, MD, PhD, author of *10 Simple Solutions to Stress*. Mindfulness involves having the wonder and curiosity of a child, it is without judgment, it is detail-oriented, and requires focusing only on the activity of the moment. Use all of your senses to take in the environment, whether you are outside in nature or inside interacting with family or friends. Stop and smell the roses!

MUSIC – The right music can lower your blood pressure, relax your body, and calm your mind. Unlike other stress relief techniques that require focused quiet time, music can be listened to as you go about your daily activities. Soothing music can help make your daily tasks more enjoyable, help relieve your stress, can inspire you, and give you emotional strength for the day. Listen to music you enjoy that relaxes you at a modest volume.

MASSAGE – Massage offers many health benefits in addition to providing relief from various aches and pains, muscle tension, and stress. The soothing effects of massage create a sense of well being. You can either have a massage by a masseur or do a self-massage. For details on how to give yourself a self-massage, do a search on the topic on the internet.

SQUEEZE A STRESS BALL – When feeling stressed try squeezing a stress ball to relieve tension. Squeezing a stress ball is also good for exercising your hand muscles, such as after typing. A gel or foam-filled stress ball is squeezed in the palm of your hand and can be manipulated by the fingers. Consider buying a stress ball at a store on the internet.

TAKE A BREAK – Taking a break or time out allows you time to refresh yourself, whether it be a break from work or a time out from the intensity of a conversation or other activity. Ideally, you will return from the break more alert, clear-minded, and energetic.

WRITE ABOUT IT - Sometimes it is helpful to put your feelings and thoughts in writing. This helps you to express and organize your feelings in a safe, private way and gives you time to consider the best way to deal with your emotions and situation. Venting your emotions through writing will help you compose yourself in preparation for later verbalizing your issues should you need to take such action.

COMPOSE YOURSELF - Rather than blurting out a response, take a moment to compose yourself before responding to someone who has upset you by taking a deep breath to inhale and exhale or counting 1-10 to yourself.

EXPRESS YOUR FEELINGS – Express your feelings! Don't bottle your emotions up inside as this only produces resentments, grudges, and misunderstandings. If someone or something is bothering you, express this. If someone has hurt your feelings, communicate this using "I statements", such as "I feel … when you …" instead of using "you statements". "You statements" such as "You make me feel …" usually makes the other person feel blamed and results in him or her being defensive.

SOCIALIZE – Socializing is essential to your mental health. Talking and doing activities together provides a distraction from stress and lessens its intensity. Talking allows you to air your thoughts and feelings. The feedback from others can give you a fresh perspective. Be open to receiving their support, encouragement, and help. Be a good listener and be ready to help and support others, too. If you are feeling stressed, call or visit a friend. If you are feeling seriously stressed and/or depressed, consult a therapist.

TAKE ACTION

Don't wait until you are stressed to practice stress reduction techniques. Use stress management techniques as an ongoing way to prevent and reduce stress. It is easy, especially when depressed, to read this but not act upon it. Make a commitment to reducing your stress in some specific ways. Start today!

SIGN OF STRENGTH

Men are less likely than women to admit to being stressed and are less likely to reach out for help when stressed. Generally, men think that asking for help is a sign of weakness. On the contrary, taking action to deal with stress or any problem requires great strength and courage. Striving after personal growth and improvement is an admirable quality in any person.

CAREGIVERS & STRESS

A discussion about EDs and stress without mentioning the stress experienced by caregivers over their affected loved one's eating disorder would seem remiss. Parents, partners, and entire families often are profoundly affected and stressed by a loved one's eating disorder.

Living with a person with an eating disorder can be extremely difficult with all of their rules and rituals, secretive behaviors, mood swings, depression, irritability, social withdrawal, and their controlling nature.

Unlike other life-threatening illnesses, those with eating disorders are often in denial of their disease and unwilling to seek treatment. This causes a sense of helplessness and hopelessness about how to reach out and help a loved one – and this causes them a great deal of stress.

STRESS MANAGEMENT TIPS FOR CAREGIVERS

Here are some stress management tips for caregivers:

- Practice stress management techniques, skills, activities, and a stress reduction lifestyle
- Model and practice good nutrition and moderate exercise
- Communicate your feelings to your loved one, but do not pester
- Do not be an enabler by conforming to the unreasonable demands and control of the person with the eating disorder
- Do not share the shame of the child's eating disorder by avoiding discussions about it to him and those whom you can confide in for help and support
- Give equal attention, care, and love to all family members despite your worries

- Learn about eating disorders, so you better understand the disease
- Be willing to participate in a loved one's therapy sessions, if asked
- Join a support group, such as N.A.M.E.D.'s Online Support Group for Concerned Others
- Consider counseling for yourself to get support for dealing with your situation

Self Esteem Issues

Self esteem is THE major challenge of our era. It lies at the heart of many of the diverse issues and challenges we face in life. In fact, it is precisely because low self esteem does not seem to be the problem, that it is so very insidious. Many people who suffer from low self esteem attribute their life challenges to wholly different causes. It does not even occur to them to relate their problems to how they regard themselves at the deepest level. Instead, they blame their problems on a mean boss, racial or sexual prejudice, a talent for choosing abusive love partners and so on. In this way, the problem is externalized. However, doing this merely moves a person further away from the real problem, and consequently from the solution. Thus by disguising itself as some other more immediately visible issue, low self esteem is never tackled and overcome. It remains to rear its ugly head again. Whatever challenge you face, you can rest assured that someone else has had it even worse, and yet gone on to triumph. If so, what prevents you back from doing the same? The answer must inevitably be - yourself. YOU are the primary force shaping you life. If others faced similar external challenges and triumphed, then external circumstances are NOT the primary determiners of your life.

People with NO apparent self esteem problems may still be susceptible at a subtle level. For example, failing to shoot for your dreams when you were young, and settling for a safe route to an unchallenging existence, can damage how well you regard yourself. In later life, it could manifest in short temper, cynicism when others DO try to better themselves, and even physical illness. However, it seems hard to pinpoint the exact problem.

At the heart of compromises such as these is the fact that you did not believe in yourself sufficiently. In other words, self esteem issues, often inherited from your parents, appeared at this early stage.

There are many causes of low self esteem. We gain our predominant world-view by the age of five. In other words, whether you consider the world to be a safe or dangerous place, and whether you will react to events in a primarily positive or negative manner, is determined by this age. Parents are the prime shapers of our young psyches at this time. However, schools, society, and our peers also play an important role. Our later experiences in life merely reinforce the core impressions we gained at this very early age.

As the role of parents is so vital, they need to be FAR more conscious of the consequences for their child of EVERYTHING they do, say, or even think. Moreover, this care must begin whilst the child is still in the womb! Parents are too often far too casual about how they bring up their children. They unconsciously pass on their own limitations to them as a result.

What can you do to improve your self esteem? The first thing is to understand the difference between self-esteem and self-image. Self-image forms as a result of comparisons you make between yourself and those around you. It is the judgment you make of yourself - the image you have of yourself. Sadly, it is often negative as you can usually find someone better than you at almost everything. Self-image in turn affects self-esteem. An easy way to understand this difference is to look at young children. They have perfect self-esteem BECAUSE they have no self- image. They are not continually judging themselves against externals and falling short.

The key is NOT to work upon self-image. This is what many people try to do. However, working on self-esteem is the heart of creating radical change. When you work from the inside out, how you feel about yourself in comparison with externals must eventually improve as well. The key to improving your self-esteem is to take conscious control of your self-talk. Negative self-talk is the prime cause for creating and maintaining negative self esteem. The things you say to yourself in your mind, as well as the meaning you attribute to events in your life, combine to create the reality you end up live. Most people's self-talk is roughly 95% negative. They see the worst in themselves and in everything that happens. Putting a stop to such self-destructive thinking is vital. It is our thoughts and expectations that shape and produce what we become. The quality of our lives is a direct result of them.

One excellent way to combat and overcome negative self-talk is through using positive affirmations. The principle behind them is that the brain cannot entertain two contradictory notions at the same time. Eventually one of the two contradictory notions must win out and cause the other to collapse completely. The belief that finally wins out is the one that you invest with the most emotional energy and constancy of thought.

Affirmations such as:

"I like myself"

"I am a positive person and I create a positive life"

"I am a wonderful person of immense value who deserves to be loved"

Others like these will do absolute wonders. Note how all good affirmations are framed in the positive. Never frame an affirmation in the negative, e.g. "I am NOT a negative person". The subconscious literally cannot see the word "not" and will therefore interpret and act upon the affirmation as if you said "I AM a negative person"!

Create a series of affirmations like this and resolve to use them throughout the day. You can write one or more of them out ten, twenty or more times a day. You should also take every opportunity to say them out loud to yourself. Always do so with enthusiasm and gusto; really feeling the positive emotions surging through your body. This is the true key to making affirmations work in improving self esteem. Putting all your emotional energy behind them gives the affirmations the power to destroy negative self-talk and low self esteem.

An extremely powerful way to use affirmations is to record yourself speaking them quietly onto a tape, perhaps with some soothing background music that you like. Then you can play this tape quietly in the background at every opportunity. You have effectively created your own subliminal tape! Try playing this to yourself when you sleep at night, using an auto-reverse walkman. The results in your life will be truly tremendous.

Recognition of the problem is halfway to the solution. There are many effective ways to remedy low self esteem. However, the key to success in life is to recognize the existence of the problem in the first place! Therefore, consider where self esteem issues may be lurking in your life, but manifesting as apparently external problems. The key attitude for success in life is to take total responsibility for what happens to us. We must work upon ourselves continually in order to manifest what we want. Creating high self esteem is one of the best things you can ever do to totally transform every aspect of your life.

Self-Esteem issues in women are factors that often block their otherwise tremendous potential. Women are capable of doing amazing things. They only need to tap their inner powers and potential. This potential is there in each and every woman, whatever race, culture or community she may belong to.

You as a woman have an inherent inner beauty within you, a warm and loving nature that is naturally nurturing, caring and giving. The love that you can give is boundless and you can do wonderful things with this love. Laurie Beth Jones of The Path says "If you are parenting, teaching or healing others consider your mission amongst the most important in the world." All you need is to take a look at Florence Nightingale or Mother Teresa or Oprah Winfrey and you will know how women are able to cut across all boundaries and borders in loving, sharing and giving. Sometimes women are their own worst enemies.

Even though women have traditionally been home makers and now they are going all out to do all the things that they never did before, like working in offices, getting top positions in companies, getting ahead in the fields that once belonged only to men, they can say they have arrived; but have they really? Sometimes, they feel so superficial within themselves. Is this what they really want, then why the emptiness within? Why the feelings of incapability, feelings of not being loved, anger, jealousy and fear? So self-esteem counts here. Self-Esteem issues in Women play a major role in their life to feel good about themselves. Why do they endorse thin, skinny models, lay a huge emphasis on exterior beauty to their children even their own girl child become anorexic and bulimic, and believe that being fair of skin is a sign of great beauty?

They welcome other people's judgment at the drop of a hat and are completely devoid of their own personal beliefs. This is sheer hogwash. They have to learn to get over these lame insecurities. They have to bury the dirt and come out smelling roses. Life is beautiful, when you know how to enjoy it, without negative emotions caused by low self-esteem.

The Healing Begins With You

Remember, the healing begins with you. First learn to love yourself and only then can you love others. Your mind will be enriched and empowered to take your life into your own hands. The best way to love you is to love the God within you.

How to Raise Girls with Healthy Self-Esteem

Although women have made gains in education and employment in the equal rights war, they're still losing the self-esteem war. Girls' self-esteem peaks when they are about 9 years old, then takes a nosedive. Here is a look at why girls' self-esteem plummets and what can be done to prevent it.

What do we know about girls' self-esteem?

Self-esteem is related to how we feel about ourselves: it's not just how we look but how we feel about how we look. And it's not just how successful or smart others say we are, but how confident we feel about our talents and abilities. Consider the following in order to understand the internal and external pressures girls feel and how these pressures affect the development of their self-esteem:

- Eating disorders, low self-esteem, and depression are the most common mental health problems in girls.
- 59% of 5–12th grade girls in one survey were dissatisfied with their body shape.
- 20–40% of girls begin dieting at age 10.
- By 15, girls are twice as likely to become depressed than boys.
- Among 5–12th graders, 47% said they wanted to lose weight because of magazine pictures.
- Health risks accompany girls' drop in self-esteem due to risky eating habits, depression, and unwanted pregnancy.
- Girls aged 10 and 12 (tweens) are confronted with "teen" issues such as dating and sex, at increasingly earlier ages. 73% of 8–12–year olds dress like teens and talk like teens.

When and why does girls' self-esteem drop?

- Starting in the pre-teen years, there is a shift in focus; the body becomes an all consuming passion and barometer of worth.

- Self-esteem becomes too closely tied to physical attributes; girls feel they can't measure up to society standards.

- Between 5th and 9th grade, gifted girls, perceiving that smarts aren't sexy, hide their accomplishments.

- Teenage girls encounter more "stressors" in life, especially in their personal relationships, and react more strongly than boys to these pressures, which accounts in part for the higher levels of depression in girls.

- The media, including television, movies, videos, lyrics, magazine, internet, and advertisements, portray images of girls and women in a sexual manner—revealing clothing, body posture and facial expressions—as models of femininity for girls to emulate.

The sexualization of girls and mental health problems

In response to reports by journalists, child advocacy organizations, parents, and psychologists, in 2007 the American Psychological Association (APA) created a Task Force to consider these issues. The Task Force Report concluded that the sexualization of girls is a broad and increasing problem and is harmful to girls' self-image and healthy development. Sexualization is defined as occurring when a person's value comes only from her/his sexual appeal or behavior, to the exclusion of other characteristics, and when a person is sexually objectified, e.g., made into a thing for another's sexual use. The report states that examples of sexualization are found in all forms of media, and as 'new media' have been created and access to media has become omnipresent, examples have increased.

The APA Task Force Report states that sexualization has negative effects in a variety of domains:

- Cognitive and emotional health: Sexualization and objectification undermine a person's confidence in and comfort with her own body, leading to emotional and self-image problems, such as shame and anxiety.

- Mental and physical health: Research links sexualization with three of the most common mental health problems diagnosed in girls and women—eating disorders, low self-esteem, and depression or depressed mood.

- Sexual development: Research suggests that the sexualization of girls has negative consequences on girls' ability to develop a healthy sexual self-image.

How can parents help their daughters develop healthy self-esteem?

Although the media, peers, and pop culture influence children, parents still hold more sway than they think when it comes to having an impact on a daughter's developing self-esteem. Here's how parents can help:

- Monitor your own comments about yourself and your daughter.

- Get dads involved. Girls with active, hardworking dads attend college more often and are more ambitious, more successful in school, more likely to attain careers of their own, less dependent, more self protective, and less likely to date an abusive man.

- Watch your own stereotypes; let daughters help fix the kitchen sink and let sons help make dinner.

- Encourage your daughter to speak her mind.

- Let girls fail - which requires letting them try. Helping them all the time or protecting them, especially if done by dad, can translate into a girl feeling incapable or incompetent.

- Don't limit girls' choices, let them try math, buy them a chemistry kit. Interest, not just expertise, should be motivation enough.

- Get girls involved with sports/physical activity, it can reduce their risk of chronic diseases. Female athletes do better academically and have lower school drop-out rates than non-athletes. Regular physical activity can enhance girls' mental health, reduce symptoms of stress and depression, make them feel strong and competent

- Watch television, movies, and other media with your daughters and sons. Discuss how images of girls are portrayed.

- Counteract advertisers who take advantage of the typical anxieties and self-doubts of pre-teen and teenage girls by making them feel they need their product to feel "cool." To sensitize them to this trend and to highlight the effect that ads can have on people, discuss the following questions (adapted from the Media Awareness Network) with children:

  1. Do you ever feel bad about yourself for not owning something?

  2. Have you ever felt that people might like you more if you owned a certain item?

  3. Has an ad make you feel that you would like yourself more, or that others would like you more if you owned the product the ad is selling?

  4. Do you worry about your looks? Have you ever felt that people would like you more if your face, body, skin or hair looked different?

  5. Has an ad ever made you feel that you would like yourself more, or others would like you more, if you changed your appearance with the product the ad was selling?

It is within the family that a girl first develops a sense of who she is and who she wants to become. Parents armed with knowledge can create a psychological climate that will enable each girl to achieve her full potential. Parents can help their daughters avoid developing, or overcome, negative feelings about themselves and grow into strong, self-confident women.

Christ Esteem

What is self-confidence? What does self-confidence look like in people? How does understanding God's love impact our self-confidence? Self-Confidence A.K.A. Self-Esteem defined...It is how you feel about yourself. If you mostly like yourself and feel that you are a good person, your self-esteem is high. If you mostly feel bad about yourself, your self-esteem is low.

1. For a Christian self-confidence is who we are in Christ. The Holy Spirit is our Christ-esteem or Christ-confidence.

Acts 2:38, *Peter replied, "Repent and be baptized, every one of you, in the name of Jesus Christ for the forgiveness of your sins. And you will receive the gift of the Holy Spirit. (NIV)*

2 Corinthians 1:21-22, *Now it is God who makes both us and you stand firm in Christ. He anointed us, 22 set his seal of ownership on us, and put his Spirit in our hearts as a deposit, guaranteeing what's to come. (NIV)*

2. Learn to live with who you are.

Like everyone you have things you like and don't like about yourself. None of us human beings are perfect. You have it much better than you realize. The grass is not greener in someone else's life.

Phil 4:11 *I am not saying this because I am in need, for I have learned to be content whatever the circumstances. (NIV)*

3. Maintain a healthy lifestyle.

Exercise, rest, study God's word, pray, work, play, learn new things, think positively, and eat right. But don't overdue any one thing.

1Cor 6:19-20, *19 Do you not know that your body is a temple of the Holy Spirit, who is in you, whom you have received from God? You are not your own; 20 you were bought at a price. Therefore honor God with your body. (NIV) Philip. 1:6, being confident of this, that he who began a good work in you will carry it on to   completion until the day of Christ Jesus. (NIV) Phil 4:8 Finally, brothers, whatever is true, whatever is noble, whatever is right, whatevers pure, whatever is lovely, whatever is admirable, if anything is excellent or praiseworthy, think about such things.(NIV) Phil 4:5, Let your moderation be known unto all men. The Lord Is at hand.(KJV)*

4. Live the same outside as inside. Get real and stay real. Don't be a hypocrite. Inventory your mind often.

If it is wrong according to God's word it is wrong and don't do it. Just because the world says that smoking weed is ok does not mean it is ok. It is against the law and it is more harmful to the body than cigarettes. Some call it the Pot Smoking Club(PSC) mentality and it is harmful. When you do hypocritical things you make yourself feel low. Stop yourself now and get real.

Romans 12:2, Do not conform any longer to the pattern of this world, but be transformed by the renewing of your mind. Then you will be able to test and approve what God's will is-- his good, pleasing and perfect will. (NIV)

5. Believe in yourself and what God can do through you.

I'm constantly in prayer and allowing the Spirit to give me guidance during counseling sessions and other life situations. I can tell being in prayer and allowing the Holy Spirit to work makes me very effective. Recognize negative feelings and deal with them daily, don't ignore and stuff your feelings.

Phil 4:13, I can do everything through him who gives me strength. (NIV)

2 Cor 10:5, We demolish arguments and every pretension that sets itself up against the knowledge of God, and we take captive every thought to make it obedient to Christ. (NIV)

6. Communicate. Talk with others about how you feel and find out how others feel.

You may find out that you are not the only one who feels a certain way or who has done a certain sin. When you communicate you build better friendships, reduce conflict, and learn about others. Also be aware of your body language when you are communicating. Your body language is communicating something, is it what you really want to communicate about your confidence?

James 5:16, Therefore confess your sins to each other and pray for each other so that you may be healed. The prayer of a righteous man is powerful and effective. (NIV)

7. Make good choices. React calmly and rationally to all situations.

Try to be calm as a cucumber. Sometimes you need to sleep on an idea before you carry it out. When you face choices your self-esteem is at risk. Will you regret and be sorry about your decision the next day? Or will you look in the mirror and say well done or good job?

I Tim 5:22, Do not be hasty to share in the sins of others. Keep yourself pure. (NIV) Proverbs 19:2, It is not good to be hasty and miss the way. (NIV) Eccl 5:2, Do not be quick with your mouth, do not be hasty in your heart to utter anything before God. God is in heaven and you are on earth, so let your words be few. (NIV)

Steps to making good choices:

a.) Understand the choice you are about to make. Ask others about the choice. Get advice. Pray about it and ask for God's peace to help you pick the right choice.

b.) Brainstorm ideas for making your choice.

c.) Test your brainstormed ideas with worst and best case scenarios.

d). Pick a solution.

e.) Act on your choice.

8. Be trustworthy and responsible.

When you are responsible people come to you and trust you to do what you say you are going to do.

Galatians 5:22-23, But the fruit of the Spirit is love, joy, peace, patience, kindness, goodness, faithfulness, 23 gentleness and self-control. Against such things there is no law. (NIV) Romans 15:13, May the God of hope fill you with all joy and peace as you trust in him, so that you may overflow with hope by the power of the Holy Spirit. (NIV)

9. Stay busy doing things you enjoy. Have hobbies. Learn to entertain yourself.

Don't expect others to entertain you. Develop your own style and be happy about it. Secular wisdom says that *"An idle mind is the devils workshop."*

10. Don't think of yourself more highly than you ought.

This temporarily increases your self-esteem until others start pulling away from you because we all know that most people do not like a conceded person. *Romans 12:3 , For by the grace given me I say to every one of you: Do not think of yourself more highly than you ought, but rather think of yourself with sober judgment, in accordance with the measure of faith God has given you. (NIV).* If you Review these steps and scriptures often to increase your Christ-esteem.

The Power Of Staying Positive

Positive thinking dramatically increases your chances of success in any endeavor. Our thoughts are not simply ethereal pieces of information that enter our minds and then disappear. The words and ideas that we think can shape our lives and drive us toward success and happiness or failure and distress. How you think and feel can have a profound effect on your ability to recognize opportunity, how well you perform, and the outcome of the goals that you've set for yourself. When you maintain an optimistic outlook and make an effort to harbor only positive thoughts, you begin to create the circumstances conducive to you achieving what you desire. You feel in control and few of life's challenges seem truly overwhelming because it is in your nature to expect a positive conclusion. An optimistic mind is also an honest one. Staying positive does not mean that you ignore difficulties or disregard limitations. Instead, it means spending time focusing only on the thoughts that are conducive to your well-being and progress.

Positive thinking dramatically increases your chances of success in any endeavor. When you're sure that you are worthy and that achievement is within your grasp, you start to relax and look for solutions rather than dwelling on problems. You are more likely to imagine positive situations or outcomes and disregard the thoughts related to giving up, failure, or roadblocks. What the mind expects, it finds. If you anticipate joy, good health, happiness, and accomplishment, then you will experience each one. Thinking positively may sound like a simple shift in attention, and it is, but it is a mind-set that must be developed. Whenever a negative thought enters your mind, try immediately replacing it with a constructive or optimistic one. With persistence, you can condition your mind to judge fleeting, self-defeating thoughts as inconsequential and dismiss them.

It is within your power to become as happy, content, or successful as you make up your mind to be. Staying positive may not have an immediate effect on your situation, but it will likely have a profound and instantaneous effect on your mood and the quality of your experiences. In order for positive thinking to change your life, it must become your predominant mind-set. Once you are committed to embracing positive thinking, you'll start believing that everything that you want is within your grasp.

Control techniques require you to become aware of your surroundings. Negativity is one of the leading causes of stress. Therefore, the power of being positive is where you will gain your strength. By practicing these techniques and re-energizing from stress on a regular basis you should be able to continue to place control and balance in your everyday activities. When we are negative we are taking the weight of the world on our shoulders and fighting losing battles. It is essential to eliminate negativity from our surroundings.

- **Environment**—Open your eyes and your ears with the people you come into contact with or who call you on the phone. Really listen to what they are saying. Have you ever known someone who is constantly on the verge of crisis, someone who always has to be the center of attention, this is known as the Queen Bee syndrome someone who is overbearing, impatient, or rude? Have you listened to conversations or engaged in conversations in which the other person is constantly saying negative things? Keep your mind focused to pick up on these occurrences for a day. Note how much negativity is around you in your environment then you will   use your control techniques to pull away from those negative situations and not let yourself be drawn to them.

- **Smile** – Yes it's true, when you smile outside you can feel it inside even if you are not in a good mood. Control techniques have a lot to do with attitude and how you perceive a situation at any given time. Observe the way someone looks when they are being rude or impatient. What characteristics shine through when you are looking at the person who is unsatisfied, discontent, and negative? Visualize how you must appear to other people when you are caught up in these negative behaviors. Is it an appealing picture? If you want to have a charismatic personality, one that stands above the rest, then controlling stress and eliminating negativity are important factors to alter your character and develop a unique personality that people value and respect.

- **Sleep** - Be sure you are getting your eight hours of sleep at night so that you wake refreshed. Not getting the proper amount of sleep will lead you to be moody and irritable which will make you more susceptible to increased feelings of stress. If you have problems sleeping see sleep tips for many ideas to resolve this issue.

- **Keep the Control** - If you are dealing with another individual one on one, then even though you may not be able to retreat to a different location, use any excuse to turn away (for example, reach behind you for a piece of paper or look in a drawer to locate a pen) and regain control of the situation. One control technique that is readily available is deep breathing. By taking deep breaths you are alerting your body to relax. Remember, you can choose how to react, and this is not only a challenge but an opportunity to practice calming effects and maintaining control. Nobody can steal your peace unless you choose to surrender it to him.

- **Be Positive** - With each individual experience (or, as we call it, challenge) there is always a way to view it from a positive perspective by referring to your control techniques and keeping that optimistic attitude.

For example: Did you ever feel that you were in control of a situation but, due to someone else's error, a wrench was thrown into your work, causing you to have to backtrack and make allowances for that person's error? You may be frustrated and complaining of their incompetence. This happens quite a bit when you need to depend on others to complete a project. To alleviate your negative thoughts, you may want to ask yourself, "Is this person truly incapable, or are they so overwhelmed with tasks that they have become forgetful?" You may find it better to give them the benefit of the doubt and even see if you can lend them a hand or see if someone else can help them in an effort to lighten their load. Learn more from the Power of Positive Thinking to better improve your personal and professional relationships and assume control over your circumstances.

- **Break It Down** - You may also want to consider making to-do lists. This control technique will allow you to break things down into bite size pieces and easier to accomplish. It's also satisfying to watch your progress by crossing things off the list upon their completion. Placing tasks on paper immediately reduces your stress and puts all of the control in your court. You decide what tasks need to be addressed and when. You also ensure that even if you do them sporadically, like running errands during your lunch hour at work, that nothing will be overlooked or neglected.

- **Smell the Roses** – We control all of our reactions by the thoughts we entertain in our minds. Every moment of every day is part of your life. So many times we rush through our days to get to the other end and the middle is nothing but a blur of activities. We need to use control techniques to introduce a thought process that reminds us to enjoy the moments. Place a small sticker or picture of a rose (or some other reminder) randomly in areas that you spend large increments of time throughout the day, use this as a reminder to stop and absorb the moment, maybe take a five minute break, remind yourself to smile and take some deep breaths to relax. Train your body to slow down and smell the roses.

- **Tomorrows** - Don't do today what can be put off until tomorrow. No, I don't mean procrastinate, just remember that not everything has to be completed by the end of this day, that's what tomorrows are for. Control techniques mean you are holding the controls. Don't strap yourself into so many obligations or goals in one day that you must rush through your day just to get everything accomplished. I hope these control techniques will start you heading in the direction of eliminating negativity in your life and becoming a more positive individual. The benefits are endless.

Chapter #9

Time Management

When life is busy, or all your energy is focused on a special project, it's all too easy to find yourself "off balance," not paying enough attention to important areas of your life. While you need to have drive and focus if you're going to get things done, taking this too far can lead to frustration and intense stress. That's when it's time to take a "helicopter view" of your life, so that you can bring things back into balance.

This time, like all times, is a very good one, if we but know what to do with it. - *Ralph Waldo Emerson*

Managing Goals

It is very important to have goals in your life. Goals (or things that you want to accomplish in the future) can give your life purpose and direction, as well as motivate healthy behaviors focused on improving your life.

However, goals can also be very overwhelming and a source of stress, especially if you are struggling with posttraumatic stress disorder or some other mental health disorder. Sometimes people set goals that are too lofty, difficult to attain, or too far off in the future. This can bring about a sense of helplessness and hopelessness, increasing risk for depression and low motivation. In addition, sometimes goals can send the message that the where you are right now is not good enough, potentially bringing about feelings of shame and guilt.

Therefore, you have to be careful when you set goals. It is important that goals are approached in a way that improves your mood and quality of life, as opposed to increasing distress. Listed below are some tips on how to make goals less stressful. In addition to reducing distress, by following these tips you may also increase your likelihood of achieving them.

Break Your Goals Down into Smaller Goals

Large goals can often feel unattainable and far away. Therefore, it can be helpful to break down that larger goal in a series of smaller goals that you can achieve in the near future. Think of these smaller goals as the stepping stones that will eventually take you towards the larger goal you have set for yourself.

Think About What is Driving Your Goals

When we set large goals that may take some time to achieve, we can sometimes forget why we set that goal in the first place. As a result, we may lose motivation in attempting to achieve that goal. To counter this, try to think of why you set this goal. What kind of values are driving

169

your pursuit of this goal? For example, let's say that you set the goal of getting a college degree. You may have set this goal because you value education. Likewise, you may have set this goal because you value family and know that a college education may open up a number of opportunities for more financial security for you and your family.

Reward Yourself For Making Progress in Achieving Your Goals

Oftentimes, once someone achieves a goal they quickly move on to the next goal. Take some time to recognize your achievements. Reward yourself. Take yourself out to dinner or buy yourself a gift. Do something that marks the progress you have made.

Give Yourself Permission to Change Your Goals

Sometimes in the pursuit of a goal we may realize that we no longer want that goal. Our interests may have changed or other goals may take priority. It can be hard to not complete a goal, especially after a lot of hard work has gone into pursuing that goal. Give yourself permission to focus attention on other goals. You are not giving up. You are simply just changing your focus. You will face worse consequences (low motivation, lack of interest) if you stick with the old goal despite not desiring it anymore.

Watch Out For Perfectionism or High Standards

No one is perfect and setting high standards can make goals feel even more overwhelming and difficult to attain. Setbacks will happen. This is okay. The most important thing is that you approach these setbacks with self-compassion (don't beat yourself up or blame yourself, that will only increase your distress) and re-commit to the pursuit of your goal.

Let Others Know About Your Goals

Some goals can take a tremendous amount of effort. Therefore, enlist the help of others. It can also be helpful for others to know what goals you are pursuing because they can keep you focused and committed at times when you may feel your motivating waning. Other people can also provide social support to help with anxiety and stress that may come about from pursuing a goal.

By following these tips, you will be much more likely to achieve your goals, increase your self-confidence, and improve your quality of life. Goals can be very helpful; however, goals can bring about stress, anxiety, and other pleasant emotions, especially if you are already managing the demands of a mental health disorder. Therefore, it is very important to make sure that you are moving towards goals in a way that minimizes distress and maximizes success.

Managing Your Home

Think you're the only disorganized person in your neighborhood? The National Association of Professional Organizers reports that we don't use 80 percent of the stuff we keep. We wear 20 percent of the clothes we own, while the other 80 percent hangs there just in case, and 25 percent of adults say they pay bills late because they lost them. If you have stacks of papers, frazzled mornings or lost car keys, use the following ideas to help you organize your family and home!

Evenings/Mornings:

1. Make lunches, set out clothes and put everything you need for the next day in a designated area the night before. Have kids pack homework and books in their backpacks to be ready for the next day.

2. Place your purse, briefcase, cell phone and keys in a designated area every day so you always know where they are.

3. Decide on a breakfast menu the night before. If the family is to have cereal, set out the cereal boxes, bowls and spoons.

4. Make a "to do" list for the next day and prioritize the tasks. (Be sure to refer to it regularly!)

5. Fill the gas tank the day before so you won't have to worry about getting gas if you are running late the next morning.

Bathrooms:

6. To organize countertop clutter, purchase a plastic tub with a handle on top. Place all of your accessories (such as hair spray and lotion) in the tub and place under the counter. Take the tub out when you are ready to use it, and put it back under the counter when you are finished with it.

7. To organize your bathtub/shower, place your soaps, body wash, shampoos and conditioners in shower caddies. Many different kinds of organizers are available at both discount and department stores -- including those that hang from the shower head pipe and others that have several shelves attached to a long pole you put in the corner of the tub.

8. To help keep your shower doors clean, buy a water squeegee (like you use on your windows) and keep it in the shower. When you are done taking a shower, just wipe down the doors with the squeegee for a clean and dry shower door. Many of the squeegees come with a hole in the handle, which is convenient for hanging it up in the shower with a suction cup.

9. Install a simple magnetic strip in your medicine cabinet and hang tweezers, nail clippers and scissors from it.

10. Store reading material in a decorative magazine rack. As you add new magazines, recycle or give away the older ones to keep the magazine rack from overflowing.

11. Throw away old or unused items in your bathroom: Makeup, lotions, old razors, sunscreen and perfume. Return old medications (including prescriptions) to your local pharmacy for safe disposal.

12. If you are out of space in your bathroom cabinets for towels, roll them up and display them in a decorative basket next to the shower or bathtub.

13. Install hooks on a wall or the back of your bathroom door for towels and robes.

14. Use drawer organizers for makeup, jewelry, ponytail holders and other loose items. (Plastic silverware trays, found in the kitchen aisle, are inexpensive and fit the bill.)

15. Place a shelving unit above the toilet for storing extra towels, washcloths and other accessories.

16. Put a clock in each bathroom so there are no excuses for being late.

Closet:

17. Place baskets in your closet for laundry and dry cleaning.

18. Sort through, bag and donate anything you don't wear anymore to a local charity. This includes clothes that are no longer in fashion, no longer fit, or you haven't worn in a year. Also, get rid of those worn-out and/or uncomfortable shoes you no longer wear.

19. Separate your clothes by season. If you have a tall closet with several rows of hanging rods, place the current season's clothes on the lowest level, and move out-of-season clothes up to the tallest rods.

20. Categorize your clothes by purpose: Work, casual, cold- or hot-weather wear and formal.

21. Gather all of your unused wire hangers (remember Joan Crawford!) and take them to the dry cleaners to recycle.

22. Hang scarves on a hanger or scarf rack, and belts and ties on hangers or racks.

23. Use a shoe rack to keep shoes organized. Recycle old shoe boxes that clutter the floor. (You don't need to keep every pair of shoes in your closet all year long, either!)

24. Install hooks on the closet wall to hang up hats, handbags and tote bags.

25. Store clothes that you want to save in a vacuum-sealed plastic bag. These bags compress the clothing, making it much easier to fit under the bed or in a closet. Save only the clothes that you think will be worn!

Kitchen:

26. Organize your cabinets into several categories such as plates, glasses, plastic containers, kid's plates and sippy cups. Place the plates on one shelf, the glasses on another , and so on. This way, when you empty the dishwasher, you or other family members will always know where everything goes.

27. Group your foods together in the pantry, keeping like items together, for easy access and inventory assessment.

28. Put all those mix packets (gravy, Jell-O, sauces) in a basket on a shelf.

29. Buy a pretty spice rack that works best for your kitchen cabinets. Place frequently used spices on the front of the rack and all others toward the back , and alphabetize each set.

30. Dedicate one cabinet or drawer to all of those plastic and Tupperware containers. Purchase stackable containers to maximize your space.

31. Save your countertop space for items you use daily. Display only the cookbooks that you really use, and, if possible, store your mixer/food processor, utensil holder, canister set, knife block, etc. in your pantry instead of on the counter.

32. If you have a collection of clipped recipes that are filling drawers and taking up countertop space, purchase a three-ring binder in a color that matches your decor, plastic sheet protectors (to protect your recipes), paper and a set of dividers with tabs. Glue each recipe onto a piece of paper (use the front and back of each piece of paper) and then place into a sheet protector. Categorize recipes (breakfast, dessert etc.), label the tabs, and place the recipes in the binder. An additional tip: If you buy a binder that has pockets, store clipped recipes that you want to try in the pockets before adding them to your collection.

33. Reuse those mounds of plastic grocery bags at the market. You might save a nickel or so each at some stores, plus you'll cut down on waste.

34. Get in the habit of cleaning out your refrigerator every time you bring home groceries. Dispose of old or inedible food and anything your family's just not going to eat.

Kid's room:

35. Is laundry a hassle? Put a basketball hoop over your child's laundry basket to encourage slam-dunking of dirty clothes.

36. Place a two-compartment hamper in your kids' room so she can sort light clothes from dark when undressing.

37. String a clothesline across your child's room to clothespin up her favorite artwork.

38. Hang a mesh hammock or fish net from the ceiling to store stuffed animals, dolls or action figures.

39. Add a bookshelf and help your child organize all those books.

40. Buy the kids their own alarm clocks (ideally with battery backup) and teach them how to get up on time.

Miscellaneous:

41. Make sure everything in your house has a place. Teach all family members to mind their own messes. For example, if you take it out, put it back; if you open it, close it; if you throw it down, pick it up; if you make a mess, clean it up; and so on.

42. Put wastebaskets in every room and place several unused trash bags in the bottom of each one. This will eliminate countless trips to retrieve new trash bags and give all family members a place to throw away their trash.

43. Place a decorative basket on the coffee table in which to keep remote controls.

44. Use a plastic caddy (instead of shelf space) to store cleaning supplies, and simply tote it from room to room.

45. Keep baskets or tubs in every room for fast toy pickup. For kids' out door toys, purchase a weather-proof bench-style storage box. Gather all outdoor balls and store it in the garage in a large, mesh drawstring bag.

46. Each night before bedtime, have all family members pick up clutter for 10 to 15 minutes. Make a game out of it and see who can pick up the most things in the shortest amount of time.

47. Create a family message center on the refrigerator or other prominent place and use it for shopping lists, reminders, calendars and phone messages.

48. Make a master grocery list on your computer from a spreadsheet or Word document. Categorize the groceries into sections such as frozen, dairy and so on. In each category, list the items you buy most frequently. Organize the grocery list according to the way your favorite grocery store's aisles are set up.

Print copies and keep one handy for the current week. When you see you are low on a product or when you're preparing your grocery list for the week, simply highlight the items you need. Keep the document current by adding new items and/or deleting items you no longer buy. Create a space on the page for miscellaneous items where your family members can write down what they need that are not on your regular list.

49. Shopping the Web beats hitting the brick-and-mortar stores, even for groceries. You'll avoid lines, traffic and lugging stuff home, and you can shop anytime you like.

50. Create an inbox on your desk for papers (bills, permission slips etc.) that need your attention. Clear it out daily.

51. Use one power strip (many can be mounted on a wall) as home base for all of your rechargeable goodies: Cell phone, Blackberry/iPhone, camera, iPod, handheld video games, etc. You'll never have to hunt for an outlet or ask someone to call your phone to see where you left it.

52. Have a lot of visually indistinct items, such as chargers for electronic items? Label them! You won't waste time looking for the right cord to charge the video camera, and when the scissors are left out on the table, you'll know who they belong to.

The goal of organizing isn't to make your home pristine, but rather to make your life more calm and functional. Work with the above ideas and you will end up with less clutter, a neater home, improved productivity and, most important of all, more quality time for yourself and your family.

Organize Your Life And De-clutter

1. **Begin With The Goal In Mind**. What do you want to accomplish? Down to 100 things? Use everything at least once every month? Every six months? I recommend you start off with the goal of only keeping things you are committed to using this year. Also set limits on how much seasonal clothing you're willing to keep. The easiest way to do this is to see how much storage space you already have (or are willing to have). Have an overflowing closet? Perhaps commit to only keeping what fits in the closet, or purchase some drawers. You don't have to get rid of items, but I recommend having a place to store everything. Unsurprisingly, if you pick up a copy of my free personal development course, personal development 101, we similarly start by determining what it is you want in life.

2. **Set The Ground Rules.** Before you come across an item, decide on the criteria you'll use to decide whether it stays or goes. How many "backup" items do you need? What's the plan, will you donate, or try to sell the excess clutter? I recommend picking a donation area and just taking clutter immediately there. Too often if we say we'll try to find a good home for it, the clutter ends up in a no man's land tucked away in a corner. We'll rationalize we're not "keeping it", we're just trying to find someone to give it to. Life is too short, and there's more organizing to be done, so just donate it, get the tax write off if you want, and move on.

3. **Pick a Single Point of Focus**. Don't try to organize your whole house at once: pick a single location. I like to start with the bathroom. It's easy for me to pick out what is going to be used and what isn't, and (for me) there usually isn't very much excess to get rid of except for wayward travel supplies and the like.

4. **If It's Overwhelming, Schedule It In – and Set a Timer**. If you have a few hours and a small amount of organizing, you can try to finish it all at once. Sometimes though, if it's a large amount of work, it can overwhelm us. We look at the scale of the task and think to our selves "I'll never be able to do that!", so we don't even start. Don't fall into that trap. As I talked about in my recent article about keeping your dreams alive, even spending just a few minutes a day makes a difference. Schedule a regular de-cluttering block of time, and then set a timer and perhaps de-clutter for 15 or 30 minutes. You'll be amazed how much you can clear in a short amount of time, and organizing every day will also help make it a habit.

5. **Get Boxes or Garbage Bags**. Don't just sort the piles into more piles. Physically take the clutter you are going to donate (or otherwise remove) and place it in garbage bags. I recommend starting with three bags: trash, donations, and "other room." Trash is items you don't need and can't be reused, donations are items that are in working order but that you no longer use. Sometimes I'll find something that's not really clutter, but it doesn't belong in the room it's in. If it is fragile you can immediately relocate it to another room, but in general I recommend not breaking your flow; take the excess items and place them in the **"other room"** bag to be sorted post organizing and de-cluttering.

6. **Designate an "Out of Place" Area.** If you can, designate an area in the room where you can put items you find in the room, that need to stay in the room to be organized. For example, you might be organizing your office and come across a stack of paperwork. You don't want that to derail you, so place that in a pile to get to later; hopefully once you've cleared some desk space so you CAN deal with it! I typically reserve a box for this. As I'm organizing, if I find something that I need to deal with, but is going to take a long time to organize (for relatively little space cleared) I just put it in my box and continue on in the section I was working on.

7. **Go In One Direction**. Some people may disagree, but I like to have a very thorough, systematic approach to organizing and de-cluttering. So for example, I'll start by the door and work all along one wall, and that may be all I do for the day. I'll completely organize

Everything over there, and if something doesn't belong there, I relocate it to either my "other room" trash bag, or I move it to my designated area in the room for items to organize.

8. **Finish Up – Clear The Trash and Donation Bags**. That's it , just repeat Steps 3-7 until your timer goes off. Then deal with the donation and trash bags, and if you want, deal with the items in the "other room" and "out of place" pile. Remember, those items were clutter to begin with , so having them in separate boxes and bags for a little while doesn't hurt.

9. **Once Cleared, Designate as DCZ: De-Clutterized Zones**. Once an area has been cleared, make sure you don't add clutter to it. For example, I might clear off a counter in the kitchen one day, and designate that as an area where no mess can be left. As I keep organizing and de-cluttering, this zone expands until the whole room is clear and organized.

Common Reasons We Hold On To Stuff

Let's talk about your "stuff".

"Stuff has gotten a lot cheaper, but our attitudes toward it haven't changed correspondingly. We overvalue stuff."
—Paul Graham

So while you're de-cluttering, how can you decide what stays or goes? Here's some advice on specific objections and reasons you may be holding onto clutter:

1. **I Might Need It.** I'll let you in on a secret – I've given away literally hundreds of items that I thought I might need someday. In over ten years of ruthlessly clearing out items, so far the only item I missed was a small toolbox, because I moved and needed a wrench to unscrew a light fixture. I've never missed any of the clothes that were taking up space in my closet, the random kitchen things I never used, or all those books I was holding onto to read "someday."

2. **It Has Sentimental Value.** This is the area I struggle with the most. I have a very difficult time getting rid of sentimental reminders. In the end, if I'm not displaying it, and I'm not using it – I give it away. Rather than keep lots of items, I try to display sentimental items for a year or (in cases of small items) even a few years. After that, I only hold onto a select few. People have suggested taking pictures and removing the item once it becomes clutter. This is difficult for me to do, but so far not only have I not missed the items – I rarely even look at the digital pictures of them.

3. **But They're Pictures – My Memories!** If you have many photos, consider archiving them digitally, and keeping only select ones in albums or on display. They're not doing anyone any good sitting upstairs in the attic or crammed in a corner, hidden away from people.

4. **I'm Going To Fix It**. Before we even talk about whether it's worth fixing something, consider this: ask yourself, if it was fixed, would I really need it? Very often the answer is no, something has been broken for months, and you haven't missed it. You've just been weighed down by the commitment you've made to yourself to fix it. Let go of the commitment, and let go of your broken items. If you insist you will fix it, give yourself a deadline. Write an exact date and time on a post it note and stick it to the item. Stick to your deadline, and get rid of the items if they aren't fixed by then.

5. **It Was a Present**. Sometimes we get gifts that don't have sentimental value, but we just feel guilty getting rid of. If you are holding onto something because someone gave it to you and you would feel guilty tossing it, realize that it's not the physical items you are holding on to, but rather the feelings and friendship. Once you accept that you can just get rid of it (donation or otherwise), I've never had a friend ask me where their gift went. If you have a hard time doing that, you could try and find a friend or family member who would enjoy and use the item, but I recommend really accepting that you don't need the physical gift and just letting it go. This lesson took me a long time to accept, but I have been much happier since.

6. **These Are Important Documents**. This is a really difficult one for me as well. I personally have tried to move all my important paperwork online, but there are some items that I keep physical backups of. My approach has been to designate a storage area in my bookshelf and purchase a number of 3 ring binders for some of these must-haves. However, I do regularly clear out other paperwork, invitations, Christmas cards, business cards, magazines, etc. Non "official documents" should be treated like any other clutter, no matter how small it is.

7. **It's not MY Clutter**. Got a messy roommate, significant other, etc? That's a tough situation , and is more in the realm of house politics than dealing with organizing items. The strategy that has always worked for me is I've had my own room in shared apartments, and the agreement has been, keep your mess in your room. Perhaps a similar agreement will work for you. Another way to compromise is pick a few activities that really bother you, for me, leaving dishes out and not taking out the trash are the worst offenders, so I insist on those while not picking fights with roommates over other less egregious offenses. I don't mind the newspapers, magazines and books left out.

8. **I'm Holding on to it For Someone**. The first step here is, stop doing that! Your home is not someone else's storage. As for items already in your home, just contact people and ask them to take the items. Often you'll find they'll tell you they no longer want it, or have even forgotten they left it in the first place. If they insist they can't take it, and you must store it for them; again, that's an issue that is more interpersonal relations than it is clutter. Maybe giving them a reasonable deadline by which to pick it up, or it goes to charity.

A Philosophical Discussion – Why Do You Have Clutter?

"In a sense, clutter is the end result of procrastination"
– Jeff Campbell

Managing Procrastination

Even when God helps you to find more time to give in all the different areas of our life, will you use that time wisely or will you procrastinate? If you've found yourself putting off important tasks over and over again, you're not alone. In fact, many people procrastinate to some degree – but some are so chronically affected by procrastination that it stops them fulfilling their potential and disrupts their careers. The key to controlling this destructive habit is to recognize when you start procrastinating, understand why it happens (even to the best of us), and take active steps to manage your time and outcomes better.

What is Procrastination? In a nutshell, you procrastinate when you put off things that you should be focusing on right now, usually in favor of doing something that is more enjoyable or that you're more comfortable doing. According to psychologist Professor Clarry Lay, a prominent writer on procrastination, procrastination occurs when there's "a temporal gap between intended behavior and enacted behavior." That is, procrastination is occurring when there's a significant time period between when people intend to do a job, and when they actually do it.

Follow these steps to deal with and control procrastination:

Step 1: Recognize That You're Procrastinating

If you're honest with yourself, you probably know when you're procrastinating. But to be sure, take this Are You a Procrastinator? self test. Here are some useful indicators that will help you know when you're procrastinating:

- Filling your day with low priority tasks from your To Do List.

- Reading e-mails several times without starting work on them or deciding what you're going to do with them.

- Sitting down to start a high-priority task, and almost immediately going off to make a cup of coffee.

- Leaving an item on your To Do list for a long time, even though you know it's important.

- Regularly saying "Yes" to unimportant tasks that others ask you to do, and filling your time with these instead of getting on with the important tasks already on your list.

- Waiting for the "right mood" or the "right time" to tackle the important task at hand.

Putting off an un-important task isn't necessarily procrastination: it may just be good prioritization! Putting off an important task for a short period because you're feeling particularly tired isn't necessarily procrastination either, so long as you don't delay starting the task for more than a day or so, and this is only an occasional event. If you have a genuine good reason for rescheduling something important, then you're not necessarily procrastinating. But if you're simply "making an excuse" because you really just don't want to do it, then you are.

In his 1986 article "At Last, My Research Article on Procrastination", published in the *Journal of Research on Personality,* Lay noted that procrastinatory behavior is independent of need for achievement, energy, or self-esteem. In other words, you may be a procrastinator even if you're confident in your own abilities, energetic, and enjoy achieving things.

Step 2: Work Out WHY You're Procrastinating

Why you procrastinate can depend on both you and the task. But it's important to understand which of the two is relevant in a given situation, so that you can select the best approach for overcoming your reluctance to get going. One reason for procrastination is that people find a particular job unpleasant, and try to avoid it because of that. Most jobs have unpleasant or boring aspects to them, and often the best way of dealing with these is to get them over and done with quickly, so that you can focus on the more enjoyable aspects of the job.

Another cause is that people are disorganized. Organized people manage to fend of the temptation to procrastinate, because they will have things like prioritized to-do lists and schedules which emphasize how important the piece work is, and identify precisely when it's due. They'll also have planned how long a task will take to do, and will have worked back from that point to identify when they need to get started in order to avoid it being late. Organized people are also better placed to avoid procrastination, because they know how to break the work down into manageable "next steps".

Even if you're organized, you can feel overwhelmed by the task. You may doubt that you have the skills or resources you think you need, so you seek comfort in doing tasks you know you're capable of completing. Unfortunately, the big task isn't going to go away – truly important tasks rarely do. You may also fear success as much as failure. For example, you may think that success will lead to you being swamped with more requests to do this type of task, or that you'll be pushed to take on things that you feel are beyond you. Surprisingly, perfectionists are often procrastinators, as they can tend to think "I don't have the right skills or resources to do this perfectly now, so I won't do it at all."

One final major cause of procrastination is having underdeveloped decision-making skills. If you simply can't decide what to do, you're likely to put off taking action in case you do the wrong thing.

Step 3: Adopt Anti-Procrastination Strategies

Procrastination is a habit, a deeply ingrained pattern of behavior. That means that you won't just break it overnight. Habits only stop being habits when you have persistently stopped practicing them, so use as many approaches as possible to maximize your chances of beating procrastination. Some tips will work better for some people than for others, and for some tasks than others. And, sometimes, you may simply need to try a fresh approach to beat the "procrastination peril"!

These general tips will help motivate you to get moving:

- Make up your own rewards. For example, promise yourself a piece of tasty flapjack at lunchtime if you've completed a certain task. And make sure you notice how good it feels to finish things!
- Ask someone else to check up on you. Peer pressure works! This is the principle behind slimming and other self-help groups, and it is widely recognized as a highly effective approach.
- Identify the unpleasant consequences of NOT doing the task.
- Work out the cost of your time to your employer. As your employers are paying you to do the things that they think are important, you're not delivering value for money if you're not doing those things. Shame yourself into getting going!
- Aim to "eat an elephant beetle" first thing, every day!

If you're procrastinating because you're disorganized, here's how to get organized!

- Keep a To-Do list so that you can't "conveniently" forget about unpleasant or overwhelming tasks.
- Use an Urgent/Important Matrix to help prioritize your to-do list so that you can't try to kid yourself that it would be acceptable to put off doing something on the grounds that it's unimportant, or that you have many urgent things which ought to be done first when, in reality, you're procrastinating.
- Become a master of scheduling and project planning, so that you know when to start those all-important projects.
- Set yourself time-bound goals: that way, you'll have no time for procrastination!
- Focus on one task at a time.

If you're putting off starting a project because you find it overwhelming, you need to take a different approach. Here are some tips:

- Break the project into a set of smaller, more manageable tasks. You may find it helpful to create an action plan.
- Start with some quick, small tasks if you can, even if these aren't the logical first actions. You'll feel that you're achieving things, and so perhaps the whole project won't be so overwhelming after all. If you're procrastinating because you find the task unpleasant:
- Many procrastinators overestimate the unpleasantness of a task. So give it a try! You may find that it's not as bad as you thought!
- Hold the unpleasant consequences of not doing the work at the front of your mind.
- Reward yourself for doing the task.

Finally, if you're procrastinating because you can't decide what action to take, and are putting off making a decision because you're nervous about making the wrong choice, see our decision-making section. This teaches a range of powerful and effective decision-making techniques.

Remember: the longer you can spend without procrastinating, the greater your chances of breaking this destructive habit for good! To have a good chance of conquering procrastination, you need to spot straight away that you're doing it. Then, you need to identify why you're procrastinating and taken appropriate steps to overcome the block. Part of the solution is to develop good time management, organizational and personal effectiveness habits, such as those described in Make Time for Success! This helps you establish the right priorities, and manage your time in such a way that you make the most of the opportunities open to you.

Conclusion

In conclusion, God's plan in your life is for you to have peace and spiritual fulfillment. I challenge you to strive to obtain the best that God has ordained for you and your family. If we choose not to pursue balance within our hectic schedules, it can produce a negative effect in many areas of our life. Desperate women must take desperate measures in prioritizing their individual life and coping with challenges strategically.

We have learned that you have to become desperate for balance in order to produce "change". God is looking to fulfill the desires of your heart; allow balance to be one of those desires. Now that you understand that God has an order that he expects for you follow, allow God to set your priorities in everything you do. Become the virtuous woman that Proverb 31 talks about. She is a perfect example of what you are capable of accomplishing when you have acquired balance and organization in your life. She is a very busy woman, but somehow she is fulfilled and her family is happy.

We have discussed the ministry of your family. You must continue to strive for a Godly home; accept nothing less. You must begin to take the steps toward spiritual housecleaning and begin to de-clutter your natural and spiritual house. Remember that it starts with you.

We have discussed the ministry of living single. There are many challenges that single parents face in today's society. You must stay in tune to strategic approaches on how to tackle the specific challenges of children who are left with only one parent. Balancing your home will be a key factor to becoming successful and accomplishing goals in a single parent household.

We have discussed the ministry of your marriage. Before we can approach the role of marriage we must first remember that we are individuals. We must also take into account that men and women have different ways of approaching and dealing with life. Now that we have established differences, we can begin to move forward on common ground. We have reviewed the different characteristics of a Godly marriage. You now know that a woman has the power to set the mood in her house; use the power for good and not to hurt your family.

We have discussed the ministry of your children. It is not a coincidence that you are the mother of your children. God has put you in the position of motherhood because He trusts that you will follow his plan in raising your children in the way they should go. As a mother and father you have been positioned for a mission. We have discussed the different ways to spend time with our children, even when you struggle with a busy schedule. Take the parenting skills you have learned and apply them to your household and watch your relationship with your children become healthier.

We have discussed your ministry within your church. We know that the body of Christ is made up of intricate parts. We must work in the areas of ministry that God has called us to work in order for the body to operate in accordance to the Word of God. You also must remind yourself that if you are in a church that has many different programs going on, you must be wise not to overextend yourself because your ministry goes beyond the four walls of the church. God is expecting for you to make time for your husband, children, and yourself; remember this is your ministry as well.

We have discussed the ministry of your job. Balancing your workload will be a key factor to your success at work. God is looking for you to be organized in all the areas of your life. Now that you have obtained some skill sets, you should be able to work with difficult people and be a shining light to all that know you; yes even at work. Daily devotion will get your day off to a wonderful start.

We have discussed the ministry of YOU. Taking care of YOU is extremely important because if you don't take care of yourself, how will you be able to help others in your life. We have discussed different ways to deal with stress, anxiety, and depression. Letting go of grudges will be vital to forgiveness and moving on in your life. When taking care of YOU, don't forget to eat healthy, exercise, and stay positive. God is expecting you to take care of your spiritual and natural body.

We also discussed the key to finding balance and that is "time management". Take the information you have learned and begin to create long term and short term goals. Manage your home and de-clutter your life. Stop procrastinating and begin to step towards your newly organized life of balance.

Spiritually Desperate Housewives understand that life is our ministry, and finding balance is our mission.

Bibliography

Spiritually Desperate Housewives

Alexander, Jack. "Single Parent Life Style". *Bizymoms*
http://www.bizymoms.com/parenting/single-parent-balance.html

Beek, Henry "Cleaning House". Christian Reformed Church. www.content.crnalorg
2010.

Borchard, Therese J. "Compulsive Hoarding and 6 Tips to Help". *Single-parenting Families.* 2012.
http://single-arenting.families.com/blog/balancing-life-as-a-single-parent/htm

Christian Counseling. "Choosing A. Counselor". CCEF Website. 2011. www.CCEF.org

Collins, Gary R. "Christian Counseling: A Comprehensive Guide". Nashville, Dallas, Mexico. City, Rio De Janeiro, Beijing. Thomas Nelson 2007. Third Edition.

"Desperate". American Heritage Dictionary. 3rd Edition. 1997. Print

Dietz, Renee. "Balancing Life as a Single Parent". *Single-Parenting Families.* 2012
http://single-parenting.families.com/blog/balancing-life-as-a-single-parent/htm

Fletcher, Dale. "5 Reasons Why God Wants Us Healthy, Well, and Fit". *Faith and Health. Connection.* May 12, 2009.
http://www.faithandhealthconnection.org/5-reasons-why-god-wants- us-healthy-well-and-fit

Grohol, John M. "Family Stress Affects Kids Physical Health". *Good Parent.*2007.
http://psychcentral.com/news/2007/family-stress-affects-kids-physical
health/669.html

King James Bible. Zondervan. Grand Rapids, Michigan: Zonderuan, 2000. Print.

Maxwell, Matthew. "Eating Disorders". Feb 2010.
http://www.namedinc.org/stress.asp

Middletown Bible Church. "The Virtuous Woman". 2008
http:llwww.middletownbiblechurch.org/homefam/prov31.htm

Mollusk (Shellfish – The Color Purple). *The International Standard Bible Encyclopedia*. Vol. IV, 1997. P.2509.

Peterson, Mike. "Commandments of Good Parenting". *Better Health*. 2011. http://www.webmd.com/parenting/features/10-commandments-good-parenting-page4

Pinckney, Coty. "What Does the Bible Say About Family Relationships?" *Community Bible* - Church. May 1993. http://tcpiii.tripod.com/familiy.htm

Savara, Sid. "The Definitive to Organizing Your Life of Clutter". Personal Development with. Sid Savara. 2011. http://sidsavara.com/personal-productivity/how-to-organize-your-life

Simpson, Edward. "Coping with Grief and Loss". Toledo, Ohio. Johnson Publication 2010.

Wilson, David. "Balancing Our Workload on Our Job". *Job.ac*. 2012 http://www.jobs.ac.uk/careers-advice/managing-your-career/1254/tips-for-time-management-and-balancing-a-busy-workload/

Wilson, Jared C. "10 Reasons to Under-program Your Church." The Gospel Coalition. Aug 12, 2011. http://thegospelcoalition.org/blogs/gospeldrivenchurch/2011/08/12/10/htm.

50754611R00106

Made in the USA
San Bernardino, CA
02 July 2017